D1325389

THE WORKS OF SHAKESPEARE

EDITED FOR THE SYNDICS OF THE CAMBRIDGE UNIVERSITY PRESS
BY
SIR ARTHUR QUILLER-COUCH
AND JOHN DOVER WILSON

ALL'S WELL THAT ENDS WELL

William Harvey

ALL'S WELL THAT ENDS WELL

CAMBRIDGE
AT THE UNIVERSITY PRESS
1955

PUBLISHED BY
THE SYNDICS OF THE CAMBRIDGE UNIVERSITY PRESS

London Office: Bentley House, N.W. 1
American Branch: New York

Agents for Canada, India, and Pakistan: Macmillan

First Edition 1929
Reprinted 1955

Places where editorial changes or additions introduce variants from the first edition are, where possible, marked in square brackets by the date [1952] when the changes were first made.

Printed in Great Britain at the University Press, Cambridge
(Brooke Crutchley, University Printer)

CONTENTS

THE FRONTISPIECE IS REPRODUCED, BY PERMISSION OF THE MASTER AND FELLOWS OF GONVILLE AND CAIUS COLLEGE, FROM THE PORTRAIT PRESENTED TO THE COLLEGE IN 1798 BY THE EARL OF LEICESTER, AFTERWARDS MARQUIS OF TOWNSHEND. IT SHOWS WILLIAM HARVEY, WHO WAS IN SHAKESPEARE'S DAY THE MOST DISTINGUISHED MEMBER OF THE CONGREGATED COLLEGE REFERRED TO AT ACT 2, SCENE 1, L. 117.

ALL'S WELL THAT ENDS WELL

I

In dealing with this play let us rid ourselves at the outset of speculation whether it be or no that lost one mentioned by Meres in *Palladis Tamia* (1598) under the name of *Love's Labour's Wonne*. Its plot would warrant the title; passages in it are plainly juvenile work and date back to a period before, if but a little before, 1598; so that Meres may have seen it, in its first shape, billed under the title he reports, as again that old title may possibly lurk in Helena's words in Act 5. 3. 313—

> Will you be mine, now you are doubly won?

upon which the curtain might well have closed.

On the other hand many other passages belong as convincingly to Shakespeare's later period, if not to his very last. The play as we have it in the First Folio—our only text and a vile one—has quite obviously been scratched over by a master's hand upon a poor original: and the improvements are numerous enough to have excused a new title. But it remains that on any evidence as yet discovered, *All's Well* can only be identified with *Love's Labour's Wonne* by guessing: and our text covers problems to a critical mind far deeper than any suggested by that puzzling entry of Meres'.

II

Let us first, however, and before attempting these, justify our assertion that *All's Well* is largely a palimpsest and overwritten upon juvenile work after a considerable interval of time. This, at any rate, any reader can easily ascertain for himself. Let him consider, and say if they be not juvenile, the following lines—Helena and the King consulting upon his malady—

King. Thou thought'st to help me, and such thanks I give
As one near death to those that wish him live:
But what at full I know, thou know'st no part,
I knowing all my peril, thou no art.
Helena. What I can do, can do no hurt to try,
Since you set up your rest 'gainst remedy:
He that of greatest works is finisher,
Oft does them by the weakest minister, etc.

That, if Shakespeare at all, is very juvenile Shakespeare; as raw at least as anything in *Love's Labour's Lost*: while —for another instance, Parolles' silly sonnet of betrayal—

Dian, the count's a fool, and full of gold;
When he swears oaths, bid him drop gold, and take it;
After he scores, he never pays the score:
Half won is match well made, match, and well make it...

is falser to key, stagier, less credible, than any of the pretty trifles in *Love's Labour's Lost*, wherein we find any poor sonnet to a mistress eyebrow suitable and therefore artistically relevant.

Against such stuff let anyone ponder the language of Act I, Scene 2, in which the French King, bowed by his malady, welcomes young Bertram to Court.

King. Youth, thou bear'st thy father's face.
Frank nature, rather curious than in haste,
Hath well composed thee: thy father's moral parts
Mayst thou inherit too! Welcome to Paris.
Bertram. My thanks and duty are your majesty's.
King. I would I had that corporal soundness now,
As when thy father and myself in friendship
First tried our soldiership! He did look far
Into the service of the time, and was
Discipled of the bravest: he lasted long,
But on us both did haggish age steal on,
And wore us out of act...It much repairs me
To talk of your good father...In his youth

He had the wit, which I can well observe
To-day in our young lords; but they may jest
Till their own scorn return to them unnoted
Ere they can hide their levity in honour:
So like a courtier, contempt nor bitterness
Were in his pride or sharpness; if they were,
His equal had awaked them, and his honour,
Clock to itself, knew the true minute when
Exception bid him speak, and at this time
His tongue obeyed his hand. Who were below him
He used as creatures of another place,
And bowed his eminent top to their low ranks,
Making them proud of his humility,
In their poor praise he humbled. Such a man
Might be a copy to these younger times;
Which, followed well, would demonstrate them now
But goers backward.
Bertram. His good remembrance, sir,
Lies richer in your thoughts than on his tomb;
So in approof lives not his epitaph
As in your royal speech.
King. Would I were with him! He would always say—
Methinks I hear him now; his plausive words
He scattered not in ears, but grafted them,
To grow there, and to bear—'Let me not live,'—
This his good melancholy oft began,
On the catastrophe and heel of pastime,
When it was out—'Let me not live,' quoth he,
'After my flame lacks oil, to be the snuff
Of younger spirits, whose apprehensive senses
All but new things disdain; whose judgements are
Mere fathers of their garments; whose constancies
Expire before their fashions'...This he wished:
I after him do after him wish too,
Since I nor wax nor honey can bring home,
I quickly were dissolvéd from my hive,
To give some labourers room.
Second Lord. You are loved, sir,
They that least lend it you shall lack you first.
King. I fill a place, I know't....

We cite this passage at length, and italicise its conclusion. We observe, of course, and to begin with, that its thought belongs to a mature man and its language conforms with maturity. Its very breaks and hesitancies befit the royal speaker bestowing large habitual politeness, but in sentences now trailing off into wistful remembrance, at times broken by the panting of physical disease. The words, with every break of rhythm, perfectly suit the speaker and the occasion.

But we are only at the beginning here. The passage bewrays not only mature thought admirably fitted upon its utterer: it bewrays, to anyone passably well acquainted with the order of the plays and Shakespeare's progress in the handling of his blank verse, a style immediately recognisable as that of his later (or latest) manner. It has at once the powerful compactedness most evident perhaps in *Antony and Cleopatra*. Consider the lines

His honour,
Clock to itself, knew the true minute when
Exception bid him speak, and at this time
His tongue obey'd his hand. Who were below him
He used as creatures of another place,
And bowed his eminent top to their low ranks,
Making them proud of his humility,
In their poor praise he humbled.

If this be close-packed, equally loosed for the occasion are the lines—

Would I were with him! He would always say—
Methinks I hear him now....

Let the subsequent lines be studied (or the preceding for that matter) and no one can miss either that breaking-up of the standard *caesura* by which the later Shakespeare made a blank verse of his own, completely malleable to its office, or that concomitant welding of it to realism by which he came to make the iambic line (noted by Aristotle as 'most conversational') adapt itself from stilted hendecasyllabics to anything from polite or easy-going converse to very highest passion, perfect vehicle of both. This easy realistic, yet poetical, invention of style was (we suggest) a legacy of Shakespeare's to English poets who chose to use it[1].

Several passages such as the above, in and out, belong quite obviously to the later and greater Shakespeare, while the mass of the writing would seem to belong to a Shakespeare at his most immature and most inept: and irritates the reader, jolted between two styles. He never knows for five minutes together what his author is about. Out of mere jog-trot he may find himself, at any moment, in face of some magnificent fence. By degrees he discovers, still to his discontentment, that the lines which actually advance the action are the poorest, whereas the finer passages occur in its nobler characters' discussions; and thereby is driven to conclude that this play is a bad one in handling, touched up or over-scored here and there by a masterly hand. Before we decide on this, let us simply note that the inequality of language keeps us constantly restive: and that when we come to any real crux in the action we are likely enough let down with fustian. For instance—and all Helena's fortune and life depend on it—when the King asks her how soon she can cure him, she promises forty-eight hours. (The original story gives her a more cautious eight days.) But how does she promise it?

The great'st grace lending grace,
Ere twice the horses of the sun shall bring
Their fiery torcher his diurnal ring,

[1] To Browning for example. See *The Ring and the Book*, *passim*, or compare with the King's speech above the opening gambit of *Filippo Baldinucci*—

'No, boy, we must not'—so began
My Uncle (he's with God long since)
A-petting me, the good old man!
'We must not'—and he seem'd to wince,
And lost that laugh whereto had grown
His chuckle at my piece of news,
How cleverly I aim'd my stone—
'I fear we must not pelt the Jews!'

Ere twice in murk and occidental damp
Moist Hesperus hath quenched her sleepy lamp;
Or four and twenty times the pilot's glass
Hath told the thievish minutes how they pass;
What is infirm from your sound parts shall fly,
Health shall live free, and sickness freely die!

—which is mere bombast, and out of place at that. The right Helena would have answered simply, 'Grant me two days, Sire.'

III

But this inconsequence in its diction does not begin, or scarcely begins, to account for our uneasiness. If we take the play apart from these curiosities, that uneasiness goes right down into its artistry; and yet further down into its ethics, in which critics have endlessly boggled.

For its artistry we have, as it happens, a simple, sufficient touchstone. The story of *All's Well* comes out of Boccaccio. It is the ninth story told on the third day of the *Decamerone*; and our play, using its main outline, retells it unmistakably, albeit with certain variations and additions well worth studying; so that, for once in a way, a detailed examination of one of Shakespeare's 'sources' definitely advances the critic in his business.

Moreover, we know the book in which Shakespeare found this story of Boccaccio's. He found it (as he found Bandello's tales of *Romeo and Juliet* and *The Merchant of Venice*) in a compendium of translated *contes* published by one William Paynter, from 1566 onward, under the title of *The Palace of Pleasure*. A First Tome of this, containing sixty stories (ours among them)[1] appeared in 1566; a Second Tome, containing thirty-four,

[1] For a trivial but significant piece of evidence that Shakespeare used Paynter's version—both he and Paynter call the folk of Siena 'the Senois' for Boccaccio's 'Sanesi.'

in 1568; to be quickly followed in 1569 with a reprint of the First Tome, with additional matter. Finally the whole work, raised to one hundred tales, came out in 1575 in a collected edition[1]. The precipitancy of these dates can only mean that Paynter's book achieved much of the popularity it deserved: but the dates themselves, starting in 1566, give us, of course, no clue to the age of *All's Well* in any version. In 1566 Shakespeare was two years old.

IV

But almost undoubtedly when he grew up and the occasion came, he 'lifted' this story of Boccaccio's out of William Paynter—who now becomes the more useful to us since he aimed to be a 'faithful or literal translator.' Wherefore, withholding excuse for the tax of time it now claims out of our argument, we give here the Story of Giletta in full, as Paynter took it from the *Decamerone* and gave it in his own words and spelling.—

Giletta a phisician's doughter of Narbon, healed the Frenche Kyng of a fistula, for reward whereof she demaunded Beltramo Counte of Rossiglione to husbande. The Counte beying maried againste his will, for despite fled to Florence and loved an other. Giletta his wife, by pollicie founde meanes to lye with her husbande, in place of his lover, and was begotten with child of two soonnes: which knowen to her husbande, he received her againe, and afterwardes he lived in greate honor and felicitie.

In Fraunce there was a gentleman called Isnardo, the Counte of Rossiglione, who bicause he was sickly and diseased, kepte alwaies in his house a phisicion, named

[1] *The Palace of Pleasure* was carefully reprinted in a limited edition by Joseph Hazlewood (3 vols.) in 1813; again by Joseph Jacobs (3 vols.) in 1890. Mr Peter Haworth has lately published a selection of ten of the most significant (with the spelling modernised) in *An Elizabethan Story-Book*, Longmans, 1925.

maister Gerardo of Narbona. This counte had one onely sonne called Beltramo, a verie yonge childe, pleasaunt and faire. With whom there was nourished and broughte up, many other children of his age: emonges whom one of the doughters of the said phisicion, named Giletta, who ferventlie fell in love with Beltramo, more then was meete for a maiden of her age. This Beltramo, when his father was dedde, and left under the roial custodie of the Kyng, was sente to Paris, for whose departure the maiden was very pensive. A little while after, her father beyng likewise dedde, she was desirous to goe to Paris, onely to see the younge counte, if for that purpose she could gette any good occasion. But beyng diligently looked unto by her kinsfolke (bicause she was riche and fatherless) she could see no conviente waie for her intended journey: and being now mariageable, the love she bare to the counte was never out of her remembraunce, and she refused many husbandes with whom her kinsfolke would have placed her, without making them privie to the occasion of her refusall. Now it chaunced that she burned more in love with Beltramo than ever she did before, bicause she heard tell that hee was growen to the state of a goodly yonge gentlemanne. She heard by report, that the Frenche Kyng had a swellyng upon his breast, whiche by reason of ill cure was growen to a fistula, and did putte him to merveilous pain and grief, and that there was no phisicion to be founde (although many were proved) that could heale it, but rather did impaire the grief and made it worsse and worsse. Wherfore the Kyng, like one that was in dispaire, would take no more counsaill or helpe. Whereof the yonge maiden was wonderfull glad, and thought to have by this meanes, not onelie a lawfull occasion to goe to Paris, but if the disease were suche (as she supposed) easely to bryng to passe that she might have the Counte Beltramo to her husbande. Whereupon with such knowledge as she had learned at her fathers handes before time, shee made a pouder of certain herbes, which she thought meete for that disease, and rode to Paris. And the first thing she went about when she cam thither was to see the Counte Beltramo. And then she repaired to the Kyng, praying his grace to vouchsafe to shewe her his disease. The Kyng perceivyng her to be a faire yonge maiden and a comelie, would not hide it, but opened the same unto her. So soone as she sawe it, shee putte hym in comforte, that she was able to heale hym, saiyng: 'Sire, if it shall please your grace, I trust in God without any paine or grief unto your highness, within eighte daies I will make you whole of this disease.' The Kyng hearyng her saie so, began to mocke her, saiyng: 'How is it possible for thee, beyng a yong woman, to doe that which the best renouned phisicions in the worlde can not?' He thanked her for her good will, and made her a directe answere, that he was determined no more to followe the counsaile of any phisicion. Whereunto the maiden answered: 'Sire, you dispise my knowledge bicause I am yonge and a woman, but I assure you that I doe not minister phisicke by profession, but by the aide and helpe of God: and with the cunnyng of maister Gerardo of Narbona, who was my father, and a phisicion of greate fame so longe as he lived.' The Kyng hearyng those wordes, saied to hymself: 'This woman, peradventure, is sent unto me of God, and therefore why should I disdain to prove her cunnyng? sithens she promiseth to heale me within a little space, without any offence or grief unto me.' And beyng determined to prove her, he said: 'Damosell, if thou doest not heale me, but make me to breake my determinaction, what wilt thou shall folowe thereof.' 'Sire,' saied the maiden: 'Let me be kept in what guarde and kepyng you list: and if I dooe not heale you within these eight daies, let me bee burnte: but if I doe heale your grace what recompence shall I have then?' To whom the Kyng answered: 'Bicause thou art a maiden and unmarried, if thou heale me accordyng to thy promise, I wil bestowe thee upon some gentleman, that shalbe of right good worship and estimaction.' To whom she answered: 'Sire, I am verie well content that you bestowe me in mariage: but I will have suche a husbande as I my self shall demaunde, without presumption to any of your children or other of your bloudde.' Which requeste the Kyng incontinently graunted. The yong maiden began to minister her phisicke, and in shorte space before her appoincted tyme, she had throughly cured the Kyng. And when the Kyng perceived himself whole, said unto her: 'Thou hast well deserved a husbande (Giletta) even suche a one as thy selfe shalt chose.' 'I have then my lorde (quod she) deserved the Countie Beltramo of Rossiglione, whom

I have loved from my youthe.' The Kyng was very lothe to graunte hym unto her: but bicause he had made a promis which he was lothe to breake, he caused hym to be called forthe, and saied unto hym: 'Sir counte, bicause you are a gentleman of greate honour, our pleasure is, that you retourne home to your owne house, to order your estate according to your degree: and that you take with you a damosell which I have appoincted to be your wife.' To whom the counte gave his humble thankes, and demaunded what she was? 'It is she (quoth the Kyng) that with her medicines hath healed me.' The counte knewe her well, and had alreadie seen her, although she was faire, yet knowing her not to be of a stocke convenable to his nobilitie, disdainfullie said unto the King, 'Will you then (sir) give me a phisicion to wife? It is not the pleasure of God that ever I should in that wise bestowe my self.' To whom the Kyng said: 'Wilt thou then, that we should breake our faithe, which we to recover healthe have given to the damosell, who for a rewarde thereof asked thee to husband?' 'Sire (quoth Beltramo) you maie take from me al that I have, and give my persone to whom you please, bicause I am your subject: but I assure you I shall never be contented with that mariage.' 'Well you shall have her, (saied the Kyng) for the maiden is faire and wise, and loveth you moste intirely: thinkyng verelie you shall leade a more joyfull life with her, then with a ladie of a greater house.' The counte therewithal helde his peace, and the King made great preparacion for the mariage. And when the appoincted daie was come, the counte in the presence of the Kyng (although it were against his will) maried the maiden, who loved hym better than her owne self. Whiche dooen, the counte determinyng before what he would doe, praied licence to retourne to his countrie to consummat the mariage. And when he was on horsebacke he went not thither, but tooke his journey into Thuscane, where understandyng that the Florentines and Senois were at warres, he determined to take the Florentines parte, and was willinglie received and honourablie interteigned, and made capitaine of a certaine nomber of men, continuyng in their service a longe tyme. The newe maried gentlewoman, scarce contented with that, and hopyng by her well doyng to cause hym to retourne into his countrie, went to Rossiglione, where she was received of all his subjectes for their ladie. And perceivyng that through the countes absence all thinges were spoiled and out of order, she like a sage lady, with greate diligence and care, disposed all thynges in order againe; whereof the subjectes rejoysed verie much, bearyng to her their hartie love and affection, greatlie blamyng the counte bicause he could not content himself with her. This notable gentlewoman having restored all the countrie againe, sent worde thereof to the counte her husbande, by two knightes of the countrie, whiche she sent to signifie unto hym, that if it were for her sake that he had abandoned his countrie, he should sende her worde thereof, and she to doe hym pleasure, would depart thence. To whom he chorlishlie saied: 'Lette her doe what she list: for I doe purpose to dwell with her, when she shall have this ryng (meanyng a ryng which he wore) upon her finger, and a soone in her armes begotten by me.' He greatly loved that ryng, and kepte it verie carefullie, and never tooke it of from his finger, for a certaine vertue that he knewe it had. The knightes hearyng the harde condicion of twoo thinges impossible: and seying that by them he could not be removed from his determinacion, thei retourned againe to the ladie, tellinge her his answere: who, verie sorrowfull, after she had a good while bethought herself, purposed to finde meanes to attaine to those twoo thynges, to the intente that thereby she might recover her husbande. And havyng advised with her self what to doe, she assembled the noblest and chiefest of her countrie, declaring unto them in lamentable wise what shee had alredie dooen, to winne the love of the counte, shewyng them also what followed thereof. And in the ende saied unto them, that she was lothe the counte for her sake should dwell in perpetuall exile: therefore she determined to spende the rest of her tyme in pilgrimages and devocion, for preservacion of her soule, praiyng them to take the charge and governmente of the countrie, and that they would lette the counte understande, that she had forsaken his house, and was removed farre from thence: with purpose never to retourne to Rossiglione againe. Many teares were shedde by the people, as she was speakyng these wordes, and divers supplications were made unto him to alter his opinion, but al in vaine. Wherefore commending them all unto God, she tooke her waie with her maide, and one of her kinsmen, in the habite of a pilgrime, well furnished with silver and precious jewelles: tellyng no man whither shee wente, and never rested till she came to Florence: where arrivyng by fortune at a poor widowes house, she contented her self with the state of a poore pilgrime, desirous to here newes of her lorde, whom by fortune she sawe the next daie passing by the house (where she lay) on horsebacke with his companie. And although she knewe him well enough, yet she demaunded of the good wife of the house what he was: who answered that he was a straunge gentleman, called the counte Beltramo of Rossiglione, a curteous knighte, and wel beloved in the citie, and that he was mervellously in love with a neighbor of hers, that was a gentlewoman, verie poore and of small substaunce, neverthelesse of right honest life and report, and by reason of her povertie was yet unmarried, and dwelte with her mother, that was a wise and honest ladie. The countess well notyng these wordes, and by litle and litle debatyng every particular point thereof, comprehendyng the effecte of those newes, concluded what to doe, and when she had well understanded whiche was the house, and the name of the ladie, and of her daughter that was beloved of the counte: upon a daie repaired to the house secretlie in the habite of a pilgrime, where finding the mother and doughter in poore estate emonges their familie, after she hadde saluted them, tolde the mother that she had to saie unto her. The gentlewoman risyng up, curteouslie interteigned her, and beying entred alone into a chamber, thei sette doune, and the countesse began to saie unto her in thise wise. 'Madame we thinke that ye be one upon whom fortune doeth frowne, so well as upon me: but if you please, you maie bothe comfort me and your self.' The ladie answered, 'That there was nothyng in the worlde whereof she was more desirous then of honest comforte.' The countesse procedyng in her talke, saied unto her: 'I have nede now of your fidelitie and trust, whereupon if I doe staie, and you deceive mee, you shall bothe undoe me and your self.' 'Tel me then what it is hardelie (saied the gentlewoman:) if it be your pleasure: for you shall never bee deceived of me.' Then the countesse begaune to recite her whole estate of love: tellyng her what she was, and what had chaunced to that present daie, in such perfite order that the gentlewoman belevyng her woordes, bicause she had partlie heard report thereof before, begaune to have compassion upon her, and after that the countesse had rehearsed all the whole circumstance, she continued her purpose, saying: 'Now you have heard emonges other my troubles, what twoo thynges thei bee, whiche behoveth me to have, if I do recover my husbande, which I knowe none can helpe me to obtain, but onely you, if it bee true that I heare, which is, that the counte my husbande, is farre in love with your doughter.' To whom the gentlewoman saied: 'Madame, if the counte love my doughter, I knowe not, albeit the likelihoode is greate: but what am I able to doe, in that which you desire?' 'Madame,' answered the countesse, 'I will tell you: but first I will declare what I mean to doe for you, if my determinacion be brought to effect: I see your faier doughter of good age, redie to marie, but as I understand the cause why she is unmarried, is the lacke of substance to bestowe upon her. Wherfore I purpose, for recompense of the pleasure, which you shall doe for me, to give so much redie money to marie her honorably, as you shall thinke sufficient.' The countesse' offer was very well liked of the ladie, bicause she was but poore: yet having a noble hart she said unto her, 'Madame, tell me wherein I maie do you service: and if it be a thing honest, I will gladlie performe it, and the same being brought to passe, do as it shal please you.' Then saied the countesse: 'I thinke it requisite, that by some one whom you trust, that you give knowledge to the counte my husbande, that your doughter is, and shalbe at his commaundment: and to the intent she maie bee well assured that he loveth her in deede above any other, that she praieth him to sende her a ring that he weareth upon his finger, whiche ring she heard tell he loved verie derely: and when he sendeth the ryng, you shall give it unto me, and afterwardes sende hym woorde, that your doughter is redie to accomplishe his pleasure, and then you shall cause him secretly to come hither, and place me by hym (in steede of your doughter) peradventure God will give me the grace, that I maie bee with childe, and so havyng this ryng on my finger, and the childe in myne armes begotten by him, I shall recover him, and by your meanes continue with hym, as a wife ought to doe with her husbande.' This thing seemed difficulte unto the gentlewoman: fearyng that there would followe reproche unto her doughter. Notwithstandyng, consideryng what an honest parte it were, to be a meane that the good ladie should recover her husband, and that she should doe it for a good purpose, havyng affiaunce in her honest affection, not onely promised the countesse to bryng this to passe, but in fewe daies with greate subtiltie, folowyng the order wherein she was instructed, she had gotten the ryng, although it was with the countes ill will, and toke order that the countesse in stede of her doughter did lye with hym. And at the first meetyng, so affectuously desired by the counte: God so disposed the matter that the countesse was begotten with child, of twoo goodly soones, and her delivery chaunced at the due time. Whereupon the gentlewoman, not onely contented the countesse at that tyme with the companie of her husbande, but at many other tymes so secretly that it was never knowen: the counte not thinkyng that he had lien with his wife, but with her whom he loved. To whom at his uprising in the mornyng, he used many curteous and amiable woories, and gave divers faire and precious jewelles, whiche the countesse kepte most carefullie: and when shee perceived herself with childe, she determined no more to trouble the gentlewoman, but saied unto her, 'Madame, thankes be to God and you, I have the thyng that I desire, and even so it is tyme to recompence your desert, that afterwardes I maie departe.' The gentlewoman saied unto her, that if she had doen any pleasure agreable to her mind, she was right glad thereof whiche she did, not for hope of rewarde, but because it apperteined to her by well doyng so to doe. Whereunto the countesse saied: 'Your saiyng pleaseth me well, and likewise for my parte, I dooe not purpose to give unto you the thing you shall demaunde of me in rewarde, but for consideraction of your well doyng, which duetie forceth me to so dooe.' The gentlewoman then constrainged with necessitie, demaunded of her with greate bashfulnesse, an hundred poundes to marie her doughter. The countesse perceiving the shamefastnesse of the gentlewoman, and hearyng her curteous demaunde, gave her five hundred poundes, and so many faire and costly jewels whiche almoste amounted to like valer. For whiche the gentlewoman more than contented, gave most hartie thankes to the countesse, who departed from the gentlewoman and retourned to her lodging. The gentlewoman to take occasion from the counte of any farther repaire, or sendyng to her house, tooke her doughter with her, and went into the countrie to her frendes. The counte Beltramo, within fewe daies after, beyng revoked home to his owne house by his subjectes (hearyng that the countesse was departed from thence) retourned. The countesse knowynge that her husband was gone from Florence and returned into his countrie, was verie glad and contented, and she continewed in Florence till the tyme of her child-bedde was come, and was brought a bedde of twoo soones, which were verie like unto their father, and caused them carefullie to be noursed and brought up, and when she sawe tyme, she toke her journey (unknowen to any manne) and arrived at Montpellier, and restyng her self there for certaine daies, hearyng newes of the counte, and where he was, and that upon the daie of All Sainctes, he purposed to make a great feast and assemblie of ladies and knightes, in her pilgrimes weeds she wente thither. And knowyng that thei were all assembled, at the palace of the counte, redie to sitte doune at the table, she passed through the people without change of apparell, with her twoo soones in her armes: and when she was come up into the hall, even to the place where the counte was, fallyng dounc prostrate at his feete, wepyng, saied unto him: 'My lorde, I am thy poor infortunate wife, who to the intent thou mightest returne, and dwel in thine owne house, have been a great while beggyng about the worlde. Therefore I now beseche thee, for the honour of God, that thou wilt observe the condicions, whiche the twoo knightes (that I sent unto thee) did commaunde me to doe: for beholde, here in myne armes, not onelie one sonne begotten by thee, but twaine and likewise thy rynge. It is now tyme then (if thou kepe promis) that I should be received as thy wife.' The counte hearyng this, was greatly astonned, and knewe the rynge and the children also, thei were so like hym. 'But tell me (quod he) how is this come to passe?' The countesse to the great admiracion of the counte, and of all those that were in presence, rehearsed unto them in order all that, whiche had been doen, and the whole discourse thereof. For whiche cause the counte knowyng the thynges she had spoken to be true (and perceivyng her constaunt minde and good witte, and the twoo faier yonge boies to kepe his promise made, and to please his subjectes, and the ladies that made sute unto him, to accept her from that time forthe as his lawful wife, and to honour her) abjected his obstinate rigour: causyng her to rise up, and imbraced and kissed her, acknowledgyng her againe for his lawful wife. And after he had apparelled her according to her estate, to the greate pleasure and contentacion of those that were there, and of all his other frendes not onelie that daie, but many others, he kepte great chere, and from that tyme forthe, he loved and honoured her, as his dere spouse and wife.

V

'It was from this uncouth version of the story that Shakespeare drew inspiration for Helena...'

Why will commentators and editors continue to talk like that?

Boccaccio was never uncouth in his life. One might as intelligently call Botticelli uncouth. He can, if one will, be licentious, with the proper licence of his age; or apparently heartless to our thinking, being unsentimental; or again he may seem to us somewhat primitively wooden in the telling of a tale, cutting it so closely down to its bare anatomy that it reads like a *précis*. But the anatomy is always there.

Hazlitt, indeed, who holds that Shakespeare 'has dramatised the original novel with great skill and comic spirit, and has preserved all the beauty of character and sentiment,' is forced to add, 'without *improving upon* it, which was impossible.' (The italics are his.) Moreover, after saying what he can for *All's Well*—and it is little enough—he goes on to devote about one-half of his critique to a lively and sensible correction of those who accept Boccaccio as a mere narrator of lascivious tales or idle jests.

> There is indeed in Boccaccio's serious pieces a truth, a pathos, and an exquisite refinement of sentiment, which is hardly to be met with in any other prose writer whatever. Justice has not been done him by the world....But the truth

is that he has carried sentiment of every kind to its very highest purity and perfection. By sentiment we would here understand the habitual workings of some one powerful feeling, where the heart reposes almost entirely upon itself, without the violent excitement of opposing duties or untoward circumstances.

Now Shakespeare can be, and quite often is, uncouth. In our examination of his Comedies, we have been forced to recognise this again and again. It would be hard indeed to find in serious literature uncouthness more devoid of pith, point, or any conceivable human interest, than the base coinage Speed is made to utter in *The Two Gentlemen of Verona* or Grumio in *The Shrew*. We yawn while the greatest of geniuses insults our interest with the bawdy back-chat of serving-men to the interruption of the drama; even as we yawn over the Clown and Parolles. We may, if we are foolish enough, talk of Shakespeare's superabundant, effervescing vitality, and all that sort of thing. It remains that these are faults of uncouthness; that Shakespeare was addicted to them; and (historically) that this immoderacy—this uncouthness—(though we may think it but a defect of his wealth) has kept the best French critics—from Voltaire down—so curiously attracted and repelled by him as they have been. What, for example, can any critic trained to know instinctively what language fits the occasion, make of Helena's rant—

> Ere twice the horses of the sun shall bring
> Their fiery torcher his diurnal ring...?

As Dryden says,

> 'Tis neither height of thought that is discommended, nor pathetic vehemence, nor any nobleness of expression *in its proper place*; but 'tis a false measure of all these.

Most fortunately we have here in apposition two pieces of literature—an Italian *novella* and an English play based on it—on which we can use definite criticism, test for test.

VI

To begin with, then, Boccaccio's story is straighter and more dignified than the plot of *All's Well*: straighter because it keeps to its theme, without pushing in the business of Parolles, Lafeu and the clowning of the Clown; more dignified in that it conducts Helena (as for convenience we shall call her, sinking 'Giletta') to her determined purpose, yet consistently with the behaviour of a great lady. Rejected by her husband, who deserts his estates, she goes home to them—as she as his Countess has a right to do—finds them in disrepair, restores them to order while earning the love of his liegemen. This repair of his negligence conscientiously fulfilled, she sends two knights to her lord with a message that if her hateful presence alone forbids his return, she will liefly depart into exile and make room for him. He sends back a churlish answer, proposing conditions he deems impossible; whereupon, to the unfeigned grief of her people, she takes pilgrim's scrip and departs. Up to this point, reserving for the moment the intrigue of her final success, we ask, What behaviour could be nobler than Helena's?

VII

All this, or almost all, Shakespeare ignores or slurs over in hopeless skrimble-skramble.

Worse than this, he obtrudes, upon a story in itself serious and strong, the inept business of Parolles.

We conceive Parolles to be on the whole, with all his concern in this play, about the inanest of all Shakespeare's inventions. Likely enough our author 'wrote in' this stuff for some popular low-comedian of the theatre. Likely enough it made in its time the 'hit' of the play. In the famous copy of the Second Folio owned by Charles I and preserved in Windsor Castle the play is annotated 'Monsieur Parolles,' apparently in Charles's own hand.

Popularity of this sort the play may easily have achieved in its day. But examining it now we can as easily note how compactly the whole Parolles business can be put into square brackets, so to speak, and cut out of the story, like a wen, without the smallest detriment to the remaining tissue. Apart from the business of the drum and his exposure as a poltroon, all Parolles does is to engage Helena early in chat which he intends to be bawdy. But such chat is more than offensive; it is pointless lacking a listener; and as we wish Helena to be, and as Boccaccio conceives Helena, she would have dismissed Parolles by a turn of the back. Shakespeare degrades her for us by allowing her to remain in the room with this impertinent.

Out with Parolles might well go Lafeu, who surely has no business in the story, save (1) as usher, and (2) to tell Parolles what we already think of him. His proffer to console the supposedly widowed Bertram with the hand of his daughter (who does not appear among the *dramatis personae*, but is kept 'off' yet willing to be marched forward) may surely challenge the crown for fatuity among all Shakespeare's last-Acts devices.

The Clown Lavache again is, for furtherance of the action, nothing to any purpose. Shakespeare could do more than any of his contemporaries could do with Clowns—Touchstone, Feste, Lear's Fool—as satiric commentators on life and correctors, useful as a typical Greek Chorus, of human exorbitance, of the 'swelled head.' But Lavache in this play is a poor thin fellow, and we find ourselves throughout impatiently echoing his mistress's first enquiry, 'What does this knave here?' His business, if he had any, was to provide a glancing satire upon human conduct and its motives: but actually he utters few sentences worth attention. Our trouble, in short, with Lavache is that, to our knowledge, Shakespeare could have made him ten times a better Clown than he is.

There remain, up to Helena's arrival at Florence, but three characters that engage our sympathy and respect: Helena herself, the King and the Countess—a dear old creature for whom Shakespeare's invention has its due credit in general praise.

VIII

Bertram does not, in these days, engage our respect; but if we remind ourselves that other times have other manners, with other notions of birth and rank, and of their natural barriers, we think he deserves some sympathy; more, at least, than he gets in general from the critics, who, uneasily aware that something goes wrong in the latter half of the play, incline to blame it upon the behaviour of this hard boy. No doubt his hardness paves the stony way of Helena's penance, as only by overcoming *that* can she win. *He* is her prize, steadily pursued, if won by a trick in the end. She will merit him through sheer persistence of love: and the language in which she avows that love persuades us that, although Bertram repel us by his way of repelling it, he is somehow worthy of it, though Shakespeare (and this is one of the faults of the play) just misses to indicate how. It is possible, however, that he left it to be conveyed by some actor on whose capacity he could count.

Let us be just to Bertram. Here is a high-bred, brave and spirited lad: brought up among solicitous women without fatherly counsel or correction: 'spoilt' therefore as such lads are wont to be—and, if one may make a guess, Helena herself has had her share in spoiling him; selfish therefore a little beyond the ordinary selfishness of youth; contemptuous and callous towards his inferiors: lustful too, with the will to have his way. So far he is quite well drawn, and of a piece with more than one sparkful young 'hero' of Shakespeare's invention—with Bassanio, for instance, or the earlier Romeo. We may not admire this handsome young non-intellectual type: but it was one that Shakespeare knew; and we can gather from his writings (supported by all the little we know of his private life) that it was a type he admired, aspired towards, was possibly indebted to. Make what we will of it, all the evidence goes to show that in mundane affairs our peerless poet was intent (small blame for it) on 'bettering himself.' Admitted friend of young Southampton—on whatever terms—and acquainted with Southampton's associates, he knew the careless arrogance of these young nobles towards their social inferiors: and although in this and other plays he preaches *merit* against rank—maybe in self-defence, conscious of his own towering genius—he understood that arrogance, possibly admired it. At any rate in play after play he passes it down to the Mob in largess upon its stink of garlic and sweaty nightcaps.

But putting aside this personal curiosity about Shakespeare—which keeps irritating us the while we are ashamed of it—and just taking Bertram as he might be in a story written by anybody, one has to admit that he has something to say for himself against the moralisers. He is young, proud, brave, lusty, spoilt, used to think of women as amorous game. He longs to prove himself in arms as one worthy of his lineage. This opportunity arrives at the edge of proof when he is commanded to renounce it and to marry a maiden of lowlier birth—long acquaintance with whom has kindled no love—just because she has cured a royal fistula in which, as he had no responsibility for it, he took no more than a loyal concern. His refusal and the terms of his subsequent acceptance seem harsh to us because Helena has already engaged our sympathy and our wishes for her. But putting ourselves in his place, understanding a boy nowise in love, itching for the wars, inhibited by all custom of deference to a royal wish, may we not grant that he behaves with spirit up to a point? There is nothing in him, until we come to the final scene, that we cannot find it in our hearts to forgive, if only he will give us the right excuse, as Beltramo of Rossiglione does in Boccaccio's tale, 'abjecting his obstinate rigour.' For, consciously or not, we have felt Helena's love pleading his cause with us all the while. The follies of youth—'lusty juventus'—come of nature and mettle; and arrogance of birth may be a fault well on this side of sin. There *must* be some attractiveness in Bertram to justify such devotion, and this will surely reveal itself, to satisfy us or nearly, before the curtain falls. But the final scene destroys our hope. He has consorted too much with Parolles, and evil communications corrupt good manners. Confronted with Diana's letter, he quails so that old Lafeu, his prospective father-in-law (throughout nothing if not shrewd), promptly renounces him—'I will buy me a son-in-law in a fair and toll for this: I'll none of him.' Confronted with Diana, he forgets all obligation of honour and seeks to protect himself by lying against her as basely as ever did any farm lout in a bastardy case.—

> My lord, this is a fond and desp'rate creature,
> Whom sometime I have laughed with...
> She's impudent, my lord,
> And was a common gamester to the camp—

our only condonation for such business being that the original Beltramo was no such fellow, and this Bertram is just such a stage puppet as Shakespeare inartistically makes him.

IX

Still, the real moral difficulty of this play (which so vexes critics that one of the sanest has to confess, 'There are other works of Shakespeare which are more painful; there are none less pleasing, none on which one cares less to dwell') does not reside in the character of Bertram; and much less, of course, is it chargeable upon Helena.

Remembering Imogen, we hold Coleridge's verdict on Helena as Shakespeare's 'loveliest creation' to be more than exorbitant. Let us recall a cry or two of Imogen's—of that divinest wife's innocent heart.—

> O! for a horse with wings. Hear'st thou Pisanio?
> He is at Milford Haven; read and tell me...
> how far it is
> To this same blessed Milford...

and anon—

> False to his bed! What is it to be false?
> To lie and watch there and to think on him?
> To weep 'twixt clock and clock? if sleep change nature
> To break it with a fearful dream of him,
> And cry myself awake? That's false to's bed, is it?

Helena, not yet a wife in deed, commands not these high passionate tones. Her tracking-down of her loved one over rough ways is as old in its basic theme as the tale of Psyche: in medieval legend it takes many forms of patient womanly patience in pursuit, acknowledged pure and good and therefore, by all consent, admirable. It is the note of *Griselda*; of that tale of the Saracen woman who found her way into the streets of London, knowing no English word but 'Becket.' It is the note sounded in *The Nut-Browne Mayd* and other old balladry.—

> Though it be sung of old and young
> That I should be to blame,

Theirs be the charge that speak so large
In hurting of my name.
For I will prove that faithful love
It is devoid of shame:
In your distress and heaviness
To part with you the same:
And sure all they that do not so
True lovers are they none:
For in my mind of all mankind
I love but you alone.

Add upon this the old song:

Over the mountains
And over the waves,
Under the fountains
And under the graves:
Under floods that are deepest
Which Neptune obey,
Over rocks that are steepest,
Love will find out the way.

With Helena then, as a true medieval woman—with her love, her suit, her desire to have children begotten on her by the man she adores—we can have no quarrel whatever. That which offends a modern mind is not her manner of winning his hand, but her artifice in winning his bed. And this artifice—repeated in or from *Measure for Measure*—is to us, in this age, a blot upon Shakespeare and upon both of these plays.

If we return to medievalism—to the tale of Iseult, for example, or to some early ballads—the business of a substituted bed-fellow for a bride scarcely shocks us at all. Why then should it so much offend—as surely it does—when contrived in the one play by Isabella, in the other by Helena? It offends more in Isabella (we think) because she has been carefully presented to us beforehand as an angel of purity, and squeamish at that. It offends with us, if less, in Helena because in the last Act the substituted Diana forgets the simple dignity of the part she played in Boccaccio's story, and turns to be a clamant young woman shouting alternatively her wifehood and her maidenhood, until the King very excusably commands,

> Take her away: I do not like her now.

And yet this curiously over-written play has a trick of suggesting afterthoughts here and there: one of which is that Helena cannot quite be explained by medieval tradition, to be condoned upon it. On this afterthought, the general unpleasantness of the plot helping, we detect in her a strain of the modern young woman familiar to us in modern dramas and novels; a heroine of the pushing, calculating sort, that knows its own mind and will get its own way to its own ends without inconvenient scruple—and if affection help advancement, so much the better! Be it observed that all Shakespeare's heroines, save Helena, have royal or noble blood; that she alone belongs to what we call the upper-middle class; that the quarry on which Venus so ruthlessly attaches herself is a prey with two heads. She is perhaps too 'efficient' to engage our complete sympathy.

Upon this we incline to revise our comparison with Isabella; who, after all, consented to the bed-fellow-trick to save a brother's life, whereas Helena devises it for her own present satisfaction and ultimate triumph. But we are all prone, accepting Shakespeare as 'for all time,' to read too much of the modern into him backwards: and these afterthoughts may be merely fanciful, nastily suggested by a rather nasty play.

X

The whole of the concluding Scene is clearly bad playwright's work, being at once spun-out and scamped. The Folio text would even seem, here and there, to be attributing its words to the wrong speakers[1]. The

[1] See Notes.

eleventh-hour suggestion of plighting Bertram to Lafeu's daughter (who does not so much as appear in the story or is even mentioned, until her eligibility for this honour 'crops up' as it were) gives the old mocking lord indeed a chance for his scornful rounding upon Bertram, and (let us admit) for his admirable lines on Helena, supposed dead:

> Whose beauty did astonish the survey
> Of richest eyes, whose words all ears took captive,
> Whose dear perfection hearts that scorned to serve
> Humbly called mistress.

But his Polonius-like alacrity in jumping at the King's suggestion of bridal between the (supposed) widower Bertram and his daughter implicitly leaves him about as shrewdly exposed as the more elaborately exposed Polonius. In short this final Scene, carefully considered, is found to be a hugger-mugger. Here and there some fine lines have been written in, and show as inappropriately as cloth-of-gold in a quilt of cheap patchwork not well stitched. But the whole action is of the stage, not of life: unconscionably dragged out to admit of flashy and false 'effects,' and closing on possibly the *bête*-est lines of recognition ever penned by dramatist:

> If she, my liege, can make me know this clearly,
> I'll love her dearly, ever, ever dearly.

—but if she cannot (one supposes) he'll love not nearly, nearly, half so dearly.

It was such a besetting sin with the Elizabethan dramatists to prolong their last Acts with a series of dénouements, and, having everything in a tangle, to huddle it all up in a few lines, that one must suppose their audiences to have liked that sort of thing, and may even suspect the authors to have vied in such *tours de force*. *Cymbeline*, perhaps, provides us with the *non plus ultra* of this skill.—

Until the very last scene the remarkably involved story tangles itself in a way which is utterly bewildering. At any given point, overwhelmed with a mass of facts presented pell-mell, you are apt to find that you have forgotten something important. Coming after such confusion, the last scene in *Cymbeline* is among the most notable bits of dramatic construction anywhere. The more one studies it, the more one is astonished at the ingenuity with which denoument follows denoument[1].

The late Professor Barrett Wendell, examining the 485 lines of that last scene of *Cymbeline*, has counted for us no less than twenty-four distinct 'recognitions,' or stage situations, each evolved from that immediately preceding! But it is a general characteristic of the Elizabethan Theatre to huddle its endings: in tragedy with swift stabbings or poisonings, to let the curtain fall upon a stage piled with corpses; in comedy—or in plays so labelled because they end happily—to display the virtuosity of the business in needless explications of complications, and at last to snap all down upon sudden repentances, changes of heart, reconciliations—with, maybe, a dance.

XI

Our argument then comes to this: that, as different generations of men differ in their accepted codes and standards of moral judgment and their valuations of sin or virtue: so a playwright of Shakespeare's time would almost, being of that age, as necessarily *sophisticate* a tale of Boccaccio's as did Tennyson the *Mort D'Arthur* or Browning the little volume on which he built *The Ring and the Book*, or as must any writer of our generation who recasts the story of Faustus in tale or drama. This is not to deny that the old stark stories are perennial

[1] Barrett Wendell, *William Shakespeare, A Study in Elizabethan Literature*, 1894.

among men and unquenchable: but merely to urge that an author who takes over his subject from its memorable report in a past age runs grave risk. He may not understand that age morally: not understanding it so, he cannot treat it with artistic exactitude any more than Rubens for instance could use the ways and means of appeal that Giotto used. He may, as Shakespeare often did, of his genius, 'make all things new.' But in the Elizabethan riot of floreating upon old grave things in the anti-classical, and equally anti-ecclesiastical, fashion of treating man as the measure of the universe, even Shakespeare was bound to go wrong now and then; and the farther he went, the more immitigably.

XII

But our criticism cannot end here. In two plays of his, *All's Well* and *Measure for Measure*, Shakespeare uses the same trick of the substituted bed-fellow: for both he goes to Italian originals; in both he protracts his last Act and then unseemlily patches its close. Both leave us, on general admission, with something of a nasty taste in the mouth. But with how wide a difference of visual apprehension, of mental comprehension! The Vienna of *Measure for Measure*, be it true Vienna or a Vienna imagined out of London lanes, prisons and brothels, is a *place*; with an atmosphere of its own and a populace ringed around and separated by walls from the romantic beauty (equally real to us in a recall of mood), ringed around by the moat of Mariana's grange. The obscenities of the one, the luted sadness of the other, belong each to each and sensibly inhabit there.

But *All's Well* has no atmosphere save that of the stage; as the most of its *dramatis personae* have none but a stage existence. It is a thing 'of the boards.' The truest of plays may happen anywhere—in fairyland for instance—and be the more universal for it. But no true drama can belong to the 'boards.' What reader or playgoer can carry away any belief in any of its characters but Helena, the King, and the charming old Countess—Shakespeare's *punctum indifferens* for this distorted story?

In fine we hold this play to be one of Shakespeare's worst: in the beginning travestied upon a fine prose-story, subsequently farced with insertions of many noble lines: and that the uneasiness which so many critics feel over its morality has already done as much credit to their hearts as the discovery and plain admission of its aesthetic obliquities will do to their heads. When it comes to be realised that this giant of a Shakespeare, tamed to the theatre, could make his own mistakes and afterwards have them exaggerated in play-copies which he was unable to correct, being dead, then all may be well that ends well.

[1929] Q.

TO THE READER

The following is a brief description of the punctuation and other typographical devices employed in the text, which have been more fully explained in the *Note on Punctuation* and the *Textual Introduction* to be found in *The Tempest* volume:

An obelisk (†) implies corruption or emendation, and suggests a reference to the Notes.

A single bracket at the beginning of a speech signifies an 'aside.'

Four dots represent a *full-stop* in the original, except when it occurs at the end of a speech, and they mark a long pause. Original *colons* or *semicolons*, which denote a somewhat shorter pause, are retained, or represented as three dots when they appear to possess special dramatic significance. Similarly, significant *commas* have been given as dashes.

Round brackets are taken from the original, and mark a significant change of voice; when the original brackets seem to imply little more than the drop in tone accompanying parenthesis, they are conveyed by commas or dashes.

In plays for which both Folio and Quarto texts exist, passages taken from the text not selected as the basis for the present edition will be enclosed within square brackets. Lines which Shakespeare apparently intended to cancel, have been marked off by frame-brackets.

Single inverted commas (' ') are editorial; double ones (" ") derive from the original, where they are used to draw attention to maxims, quotations, etc.

The reference number for the first line is given at the head of each page. Numerals in square brackets are placed at the beginning of the traditional acts and scenes.

ALL'S WELL THAT ENDS WELL

The scene: Rousillon, Paris, Florence, Marseilles

CHARACTERS IN THE PLAY

KING OF FRANCE

DUKE OF FLORENCE

BERTRAM, *the young Count of Rousillon*

LAFEU, *an old lord*

PAROLLES, *a follower of Bertram*

RINALDO, *Steward to the Countess of Rousillon*

LAVACHE, *Clown to the Countess*

Two French gentlemen at Court named DUMAIN, *later captains in the Florentine army*

A soldier, pretending to be an interpreter

A gentleman, astringer to the French king

A Page

COUNTESS OF ROUSILLON, *mother to Bertram*

HELENA, *a waiting-gentlewoman to the Countess*

A Widow of Florence

DIANA, *daughter to the widow*

MARIANA, *neighbour to the widow*

Lords, officers, soldiers, &c., French and Florentine

ALL'S WELL THAT ENDS WELL

[1. 1.] *A room in the palace of Rousillon*

Enter BERTRAM *the young Count of Rousillon, his mother the* COUNTESS, HELENA, *and Lord* LAFEU, *'all in black'*

Countess. In delivering my son from me I bury a second husband.

Bertram. And I in going, madam, weep o'er my father's death anew: but I must attend his majesty's command, to whom I am now in ward, evermore in subjection.

Lafeu. You shall find of the king a husband, madam—you, sir, a father. He that so generally is at all times good, must of necessity hold his virtue to you, whose worthiness would stir it up where it wanted rather than lack it where there is such abundance. 10

Countess. What hope is there of his majesty's amendment?

Lafeu. He hath abandoned his physicians, madam, under whose practices he hath persecuted time with hope, and finds no other advantage in the process but only the losing of hope by time.

Countess. This young gentlewoman had a father—O, that 'had,' how sad a passage 'tis—whose skill was almost as great as his honesty; had it stretched so far, 20 would have made nature immortal, and death should have play for lack of work. Would, for the king's sake, he were living. I think it would be the death of the king's disease.

Lafeu. How called you the man you speak of, madam?

Countess. He was famous, sir, in his profession, and it was his great right to be so: Gerard de Narbon.

Lafeu. He was excellent, indeed, madam. The king
30 very lately spoke of him admiringly and mourningly: he was skilful enough to have lived still, if knowledge could be set up against mortality.

Bertram. What is it, my good lord, the king languishes of?

Lafeu. A fistula, my lord.

Bertram. I heard not of it before.

Lafeu. I would it were not notorious....Was this gentlewoman the daughter of Gerard de Narbon?

Countess. His sole child, my lord, and bequeathed to
40 my overlooking. I have those hopes of her good that her education promises: her dispositions she inherits, which make fair gifts fairer; for where an unclean mind carries virtuous qualities, there commendations go with pity, they are virtues and traitors too; in her they are the better for their simpleness; she derives her honesty and achieves her goodness.

Lafeu. Your commendations, madam, get from her tears.

Countess. 'Tis the best brine a maiden can season her
50 praise in. The remembrance of her father never approaches her heart but the tyranny of her sorrows takes all livelihood from her cheek....No more of this, Helena, go to, no more, lest it be rather thought you affect a sorrow than to have—

Helena. I do affect a sorrow indeed, but I have it too.

Lafeu. †How understand we that? Moderate lamentation is the right of the dead, excessive grief the enemy to the living.

Countess. If the living be enemy to the grief, the excess makes it soon mortal. 60

Bertram. Madam, I desire your holy wishes.

Countess. Be thou blest, Bertram, and succeed thy father
In manners as in shape: thy blood and virtue
Contend for empire in thee, and thy goodness
Share with thy birthright. Love all, trust a few,
Do wrong to none: be able for thine enemy
Rather in power than use; and keep thy friend
Under thy own life's key: be checked for silence,
But never taxed for speech....What heaven more will,
That thee may furnish, and my prayers pluck down, 70
Fall on thy head....[*she kisses him*] Farewell, my lord.

[*she turns to go, passing Lafeu on the way*

'Tis an unseasoned courtier. Good my lord,
Advise him.

Lafeu. He cannot want the best
†That shall attend his lord.

Countess. Heaven bless him! Farewell, Bertram.

[*she departs*

Bertram. The best wishes that can be forged in your thoughts be servants to you! [*to Helena*] Be comfortable to my mother, your mistress, and make much of her.

Lafeu. Farewell, pretty lady, you must hold the credit of your father. 80

[*Bertram and Lafeu go out by another door*

Helena. O, were that all! I think not on my father,
And these great tears grace his remembrance more
Than those I shed for him. What was he like?
I have forgot him: my imagination
Carries no favour in't but Bertram's....
I am undone, there is no living, none,
If Bertram be away....'Twere all one

That I should love a bright particular star,
And think to wed it, he is so above me:
90 In his bright radiance and collateral light
Must I be comforted, not in his sphere....
Th'ambition in my love thus plagues itself:
The hind that would be mated by the lion
Must die for love. 'Twas pretty, though a plague,
To see him every hour, to sit and draw
His archéd brows, his hawking eye, his curls,
In our heart's table; heart too capable
Of every line and trick of his sweet favour....
But now he's gone, and my idolatrous fancy
100 Must sanctify his relics. Who comes here?

PAROLLES enters

One that goes with him: I love him for his sake,
And yet I know him a notorious liar,
Think him a great way fool, solely a coward.
Yet these fixed evils sit so fit in him,
That they take place, when virtue's steely bones
Look bleak i'th' cold wind: withal, full oft we see
Cold wisdom waiting on superfluous folly.

Parolles. Save you, fair queen.

Helena. And you, monarch.

110 *Parolles.* No.

Helena. And no.

Parolles. Are you meditating on virginity?

Helena. Ay...You have some stain of soldier in you; let me ask you a question. Man is enemy to virginity, how may we barricado it against him?

Parolles. Keep him out.

Helena. But he assails, and our virginity, though valiant in the defence, yet is weak: unfold to us some warlike resistance.

Parolles. There is none: man, setting down before 120
you, will undermine you and blow you up.

Helena. Bless our poor virginity from underminers
and blowers up! Is there no military policy, how
virgins might blow up men?

Parolles. Virginity being blown down, man will
quicklier be blown up: marry, in blowing him down
again, with the breach yourselves made, you lose your
city. It is not politic in the commonwealth of nature to
preserve virginity. Loss of virginity is rational increase,
and there was never virgin got till virginity was first lost. 130
That you were made of is mettle to make virgins.
Virginity by being once lost may be ten times found:
by being ever kept, it is ever lost: 'tis too cold a companion: away with't!

Helena. I will stand for't a little, though therefore
I die a virgin.

Parolles. There's little can be said in't—'tis against the
rule of nature. To speak on the part of virginity, is to
accuse your mothers; which is most infallible disobedience. He that hangs himself is a virgin: virginity 140
murders itself, and should be buried in highways out
of all sanctified limit, as a desperate offendress against
nature. Virginity breeds mites—much like a cheese—
consumes itself to the very paring, and so dies with
feeding his own stomach. Besides, virginity is peevish,
proud, idle, made of self-love, which is the most inhibited sin in the canon. Keep it not—you cannot choose
but lose by't. Out with't: within ten year it will make
itself ten, which is a goodly increase—and the principal
itself not much the worse. Away with't. 150

Helena. How might one do, sir, to lose it to her own
liking?

Parolles. Let me see. Marry, ill, to like him that ne'er

it likes. 'Tis a commodity will lose the gloss with lying; the longer kept, the less worth: off with't while 'tis vendible; answer the time of request. Virginity, like an old courtier, wears her cap out of fashion, richly suited, but unsuitable, just like the brooch and the tooth-pick, which wear not now...Your date is better in your
160 pie and your porridge than in your cheek: and your virginity, your old virginity, is like one of our French withered pears, it looks ill, it eats drily, marry 'tis a withered pear; it was formerly better, marry yet 'tis a withered pear: will you any thing with it?

Helena. †Not my virginity yet...
There shall your master have a thousand loves,
A mother, and a mistress, and a friend,
A phœnix, captain, and an enemy,
A guide, a goddess, and a sovereign,
170 A counsellor, a traitress, and a dear;
His humble ambition, proud humility:
His jarring concord, and his discord dulcet:
His faith, his sweet disaster; with a world
Of pretty, fond, adoptious christendoms,
That blinking Cupid gossips. Now shall he...
I know not what he shall. God send him well!
The court's a learning place, and he is one—

Parolles. What one, i' faith?

Helena. That I wish well. 'Tis pity—

180 *Parolles.* What's pity?

Helena. That wishing well had not a body in't,
Which might be felt, that we, the poorer born,
Whose baser stars do shut us up in wishes,
Might with effects of them follow our friends,
And show what we alone must think, which never
Returns us thanks.

A page enters

Page. Monsieur Parolles, my lord calls for you.

[*he goes*

Parolles. Little Helen, farewell. If I can remember thee, I will think of thee at court.

Helena. Monsieur Parolles, you were born under a charitable star. 190

Parolles. Under Mars, I.

Helena. I especially think, under Mars.

Parolles. Why under Mars?

Helena. The wars have so kept you under, that you must needs be born under Mars.

Parolles. When he was predominant.

Helena. When he was retrograde, I think, rather.

Parolles. Why think you so?

Helena. You go so much backward when you fight. 200

Parolles. That's for advantage.

Helena. So is running away, when fear proposes the safety: but the composition that your valour and fear makes in you is a virtue of a good wing, and I like the wear well.

Parolles. I am so full of businesses, I cannot answer thee acutely: I will return perfect courtier, in the which my instruction shall serve to naturalize thee, so thou wilt be capable of a courtier's counsel, and understand what advice shall thrust upon thee—else thou diest in thine 210 unthankfulness, and thine ignorance makes thee away. Farewell: when thou hast leisure, say thy prayers; when thou hast †money, remember thy friends: get thee a good husband, and use him as he uses thee: so farewell.

[*he goes*

Helena. Our remedies oft in ourselves do lie,
Which we ascribe to heaven: the fated sky

Gives us free scope; only doth backward pull
Our slow designs when we ourselves are dull.
What power is it which mounts my love so high?
220 That makes me see, and cannot feed mine eye?
The mightiest space in fortune nature brings
To join like likes, and kiss like native things.
Impossible be strange attempts to those
That weigh their pains in sense, and do suppose
What hath been cannot be: who ever strove
To show her merit that did miss her love?
The king's disease—my project may deceive me,
But my intents are fixed, and will not leave me.
[*she goes*

[1.2.] *A room in the King's palace at Paris*

A flourish of cornets: the KING OF FRANCE *enters supported by attendants, lords and councillors following; he sits in the chair of state and letters are placed before him*

King. The Florentines and Senoys are by th'ears,
Have fought with equal fortune, and continue
A braving war.
1 *Lord.* So 'tis reported, sir.
King. Nay, 'tis most credible. We here receive it
A certainty, vouched from our cousin Austria,
With caution, that the Florentine will move us
For speedy aid; wherein our dearest friend
Prejudicates the business, and would seem
To have us make denial.
1 *Lord.* His love and wisdom,
10 Approved so to your majesty, may plead
For amplest credence.
King. He hath armed our answer,
And Florence is denied before he comes:
Yet, for our gentlemen that mean to see

The Tuscan service, freely have they leave
To stand on either part.
2 *Lord.* It well may serve
A nursery to our gentry, who are sick
For breathing and exploit.

BERTRAM, LAFEU, and PAROLLES enter the chamber

King. What's he comes here?
1 *Lord.* It is the Count Rousillon, my good lord,
Young Bertram.
King. Youth, thou bear'st thy father's face.
Frank nature, rather curious than in haste, 20
Hath well composed thee: thy father's moral parts
Mayst thou inherit too! Welcome to Paris.
Bertram. My thanks and duty are your majesty's.
King. I would I had that corporal soundness now,
As when thy father and myself in friendship
First tried our soldiership! He did look far
Into the service of the time, and was
Discipled of the bravest: he lasted long,
But on us both did haggish age steal on,
And wore us out of act...It much repairs me 30
To talk of your good father...In his youth
He had the wit, which I can well observe
To-day in our young lords; but they may jest
Till their own scorn return to them unnoted
Ere they can hide their levity in honour:
So like a courtier, contempt nor bitterness
Were in his pride or sharpness; if they were,
His equal had awaked them, and his honour,
Clock to itself, knew the true minute when
Exception bid him speak, and at this time 40
His tongue obeyed his hand. Who were below him
He used as creatures of another place,

And bowed his eminent top to their low ranks,
Making them proud of his humility,
†In their poor praise he humble...Such a man
Might be a copy to these younger times;
Which, followed well, would demonstrate them now
But goers backward.

Bertram. His good remembrance, sir,
Lies richer in your thoughts than on his tomb;
50 So in approof lives not his epitaph
As in your royal speech.

King. Would I were with him! He would always say—
Methinks I hear him now; his plausive words
He scattered not in ears, but grafted them,
To grow there, and to bear—'Let me not live,'—
Thus his good melancholy oft began,
On the catastrophe and heel of pastime,
When it was out—'Let me not live,' quoth he,
'After my flame lacks oil, to be the snuff
60 Of younger spirits, whose apprehensive senses
All but new things disdain; whose judgements are
Mere fathers of their garments; whose constancies
Expire before their fashions'...This he wished:
I after him do after him wish too,
Since I nor wax nor honey can bring home,
I quickly were dissolvéd from my hive,
To give some labourers room.

2 Lord. You are loved, sir,
They that least lend it you shall lack you first.

King. I fill a place, I know't....How long is't, count,
70 Since the physician at your father's died?
He was much famed.

Bertram. Some six months since, my lord.

King. If he were living, I would try him yet.

Lend me an arm...the rest have worn me out
With several applications: nature and sickness
Debate it at their leisure. Welcome, count,
My son's no dearer.

Bertram. Thank your majesty.

The King departs with a flourish of trumpets; the court follows

[1. 3.] *A room in the palace of Rousillon*

The COUNTESS *enters with* RINALDO *her Steward;* LAVACHE *the Clown follows behind*

Countess. I will now hear. What say you of this gentlewoman?

Steward [*observes the Clown*]. Madam, the care I have had to even your content, I wish might be found in the calendar of my past endeavours, for then we wound our modesty, and make foul the clearness of our deservings, when of ourselves we publish them.

Countess [*understands*]. What does this knave here? Get you gone, sirrah: the complaints I have heard of you I do not all believe: 'tis my slowness that I do not: 10
for I know you lack not folly to commit them, and have ability enough to make such knaveries yours.

Clown. 'Tis not unknown to you, madam, I am a poor fellow.

Countess. Well, sir.

Clown. No, madam, 'tis not so well that I am poor, though many of the rich are damned, but, if I may have your ladyship's good will to go to the world, Isbel the woman and I will do as we may.

Countess. Wilt thou needs be a beggar? 20

Clown. I do beg your good will in this case.

Countess. In what case?

Clown. In Isbel's case and mine own...Service is no heritage, and I think I shall never have the blessing of God till I have issue o' my body: for they say barnes are blessings.

Countess. Tell me thy reason why thou wilt marry.

Clown. My poor body, madam, requires it. I am driven on by the flesh, and he must needs go that the devil drives.

30 *Countess.* Is this all your worship's reason?

Clown. Faith, madam, I have other holy reasons, such as they are.

Countess. May the world know them?

Clown. I have been, madam, a wicked creature, as you and all flesh and blood are, and indeed I do marry that I may repent.

Countess. Thy marriage, sooner than thy wickedness.

Clown. I am out o' friends, madam, and I hope to have friends for my wife's sake.

40 *Countess.* Such friends are thine enemies, knave.

Clown. Y'are shallow, madam, in great friends, for the knaves come to do that for me, which I am aweary of...He that ears my land spares my team, and gives me leave to in the crop: if I be his cuckold, he's my drudge; he that comforts my wife is the cherisher of my flesh and blood; he that cherishes my flesh and blood loves my flesh and blood; he that loves my flesh and blood is my friend: ergo, he that kisses my wife is my friend...If men could be contented to be what they
50 are, there were no fear in marriage; for young Chairbonne the puritan and old Poisson the papist, howsome'er their hearts are severed in religion, their heads are both one—they may jowl horns together like any deer i'th' herd.

Countess. Wilt thou ever be a foul-mouthed and calumnious knave?

Clown. A prophet I, madam, and I speak the truth the next way—

For I the ballad will repeat,
    Which men full true shall find, 60
Your marriage comes by destiny,
    Your cuckoo sings by kind.

Countess. Get you gone, sir. I'll talk with you more anon.

Steward. May it please you, madam, that he bid Helen come to you. Of her I am to speak.

Countess. Sirrah, tell my gentlewoman I would speak with her—Helen I mean.

Clown [*sings*]. Was this fair face the cause, quoth she,
    Why the Grecians sackéd Troy? 70
Fond done, done fond,
    Was this King Priam's joy?
With that she sighéd as she stood,
With that she sighéd as she stood,
    And gave this sentence then—
Among nine bad if one be good,
Among nine bad if one be good,
    There's yet one good in ten.

Countess. What, one good in ten? you corrupt the song, sirrah. 80

Clown. One good woman in ten, madam, which is a purifying o'th' song: would God would serve the world so all the year! we'd find no fault with the tithe-woman, if I were the parson. One in ten, quoth a'! an we might have a good woman born but or every blazing star, or at an earthquake, 'twould mend the lottery well —a man may draw his heart out, ere a' pluck one.

Countess. You'll be gone, sir knave, and do as I command you!

Clown. That man should be at woman's command, 90

and yet no hurt done! Though honesty be no puritan, yet it will do no hurt; it will wear the surplice of humility over the black gown of a big heart....[*the Countess stamps her foot*] I am going, forsooth. The business is for Helen to come hither. [*he goes*

Countess. Well, now.

Steward. I know, madam, you love your gentlewoman entirely.

Countess. Faith, I do: her father bequeathed her to
100 me, and she herself, without other advantage, may lawfully make title to as much love as she finds. There is more owing her than is paid, and more shall be paid her than she'll demand.

Steward. Madam, I was very late more near her than I think she wished me. Alone she was, and did communicate to herself her own words to her own ears. She thought, I dare vow for her, they touched not any stranger sense. Her matter was, she loved your son: Fortune, she said, was no goddess, that had put such
110 difference betwixt their two estates; Love no god, that would not extend his might, only where qualities were level; †Diana no queen of virgins, that would suffer her poor knight surprised, without rescue in the first assault, or ransom afterward...This she delivered in the most bitter touch of sorrow that e'er I heard virgin exclaim in, which I held my duty speedily to acquaint you withal, sithence in the loss that may happen it concerns you something to know it.

Countess. You have discharged this honestly, keep
120 it to yourself. Many likelihoods informed me of this before, which hung so tott'ring in the balance, that I could neither believe nor misdoubt...Pray you, leave me. Stall this in your bosom, and I thank you for your honest care: I will speak with you further anon. [*he goes*

HELENA enters by another door and stands
awaiting her mistress's will

[*aside*] Even so it was with me, when I was young...
 If ever we are nature's, these are ours. This thorn
Doth to our rose of youth rightly belong.
 Our blood to us, this to our blood is born.
It is the show and seal of nature's truth,
Where love's strong passion is impressed in youth. 130
By our remembrances of days foregone,
Such were our faults, or then we thought them none.
[*she beckons Helena to draw near*
Her eye is sick on't—I observe her now.
 Helena. What is your pleasure, madam?
 Countess. You know, Helen,
I am a mother to you.
 Helena. Mine honourable mistress.
 Countess. Nay, a mother.
Why not a mother? When I said 'a mother'
Methought you saw a serpent. What's in 'mother,'
That you start at it? I say, I am your mother,
And put you in the catalogue of those 140
That were enwombéd mine. 'Tis often seen
Adoption strives with nature, and choice breeds
A native slip to us from foreign seeds:
You ne'er oppressed me with a mother's groan,
Yet I express to you a mother's care—
God's mercy, maiden! does it curd thy blood
To say I am thy mother? What's the matter,
That this distempered messenger of wet,
The many-coloured Iris, rounds thine eye?
Why? that you are my daughter?
 Helena. That I am not. 150
 Countess. I say, I am your mother.

Helena. Pardon, madam;
The Count Rousillon cannot be my brother:
I am from humble, he from honoured name;
No note upon my parents, his all noble.
My master, my dear lord he is, and I
His servant live, and will his vassal die:
He must not be my brother.
Countess. Nor I your mother?
Helena. You are my mother, madam. Would you were—
So that my lord, your son, were not my brother—
160 Indeed my mother! or were you both our mothers.
†I care no more for't than I do for heaven,
So I were not his sister. Can't no other,
But I your daughter, he must be my brother?
Countess. Yes, Helen, you might be my daughter-in-law—
God shield you mean it not, 'daughter' and 'mother'
So strive upon your pulse! What, pale again?
My fear hath catched your fondness! Now I see
The mystery of your loneliness, and find
Your salt tears' head. Now to all sense 'tis gross...
170 You love my son! invention is ashamed,
Against the proclamation of thy passion,
To say thou dost not: therefore tell me true—
But tell me then, 'tis so—for look, thy cheeks
Confess it, th'one to th'other, and thine eyes
See it so grossly shown in thy behaviours,
That in their kind they speak it—only sin
And hellish obstinacy tie thy tongue,
That truth should be suspected. Speak, is't so?
If it be so, you have wound a goodly clew;
180 If it be not, forswear't: howe'er, I charge thee,
As heaven shall work in me for thine avail,

To tell me truly.
Helena [*kneels*]. Good madam, pardon me!
Countess. Do you love my son?
Helena. Your pardon, noble mistress!
Countess. Love you my son?
Helena. Do not you love him, madam?
Countess. Go not about; my love hath in't a bond
Whereof the world takes note: come, come, disclose
The state of your affection, for your passions
Have to the full appeached.
Helena. Then, I confess,
Here on my knee, before high heaven and you,
That before you, and next unto high heaven, 190
I love your son...
My friends were poor but honest, so's my love:
Be not offended, for it hurts not him
That he is loved of me: I follow him not
By any token of presumptuous suit,
Nor would I have him till I do deserve him,
Yet never know how that desert should be...
I know I love in vain, strive against hope;
Yet, in this captious and inteemable sieve,
I still pour in the waters of my love, 200
And lack not to lose still: thus, Indian-like,
Religious in mine error, I adore
The sun, that looks upon his worshipper,
But knows of him no more....My dearest madam,
Let not your hate encounter with my love
For loving where you do: but if yourself,
Whose agéd honour cites a virtuous youth,
Did ever in so true a flame of liking
†Love chastely, and wish dearly that your Dian
Was both herself and Love, O, then give pity 210
To her, whose state is such, that cannot choose

But lend and give where she is sure to lose;
That seeks not to find that her search implies,
But, riddle-like, lives sweetly where she dies.
Countess. Had you not lately an intent, speak truly,
To go to Paris?
Helena. Madam, I had.
Countess. Wherefore? tell true.
Helena. I will tell truth, by grace itself, I swear...
You know my father left me some prescriptions
Of rare and proved effects, such as his reading
220 And manifest experience had collected
For general sovereignty; and that he willed me
In heedfull'st reservation to bestow them,
†As notes, whose faculties inclusive were,
More than they were in note: amongst the rest,
There is a remedy, approved, set down,
To cure the desperate languishings whereof
The king is rendered lost.
Countess. This was your motive
For Paris, was it? speak.
Helena. My lord your son made me to think of this;
230 Else Paris, and the medicine, and the king,
Had from the conversation of my thoughts
Haply been absent then.
Countess. But think you, Helen,
If you should tender your supposéd aid,
He would receive it? He and his physicians
Are of a mind—he, that they cannot help him;
They, that they cannot help. How shall they credit
A poor unlearnéd virgin, when the schools,
Embowelled of their doctrine, have left off
The danger to itself?
Helena. †There's something hints,
240 More than my father's skill, which was the great'st

Of his profession, that his good receipt
Shall for my legacy be sanctified
By th' luckiest stars in heaven, and would
your honour
But give me leave to try success, I'd venture
The well-lost life of mine on his grace's cure
By such a day and hour.

Countess. Dost thou believe't?

Helena. Ay, madam, knowingly.

Countess. Why, Helen, thou shalt have my leave
and love,
Means and attendants, and my loving greetings
To those of mine in court. I'll stay at home 250
And pray God's blessing into thy attempt:
Be gone to-morrow, and be sure of this,
What I can help thee to, thou shalt not miss. [*they go*

[2. 1.] *A room in the King's palace at Paris; at the back a closet with a couch*

A flourish of cornets. 'Enter the KING' *borne by attendants in his chair 'with divers young lords taking leave for the Florentine war'; among them* BERTRAM *and* PAROLLES

King. Farewell, young lords! these warlike principles
Do not throw from you—and you, my lords farewell!
Share the advice betwixt you. If both gain all,
The gift doth stretch itself as 'tis received,
And is enough for both.

1 Lord. 'Tis our hope, sir,
After, well-entered soldiers to return
And find your grace in health.

King. No, no, it cannot be; and yet my heart
Will not confess he owes the malady

10 That doth my life besiege...Farewell, young lords!
Whether I live or die, be you the sons
Of worthy Frenchmen: let higher Italy
(Those bated that inherit but the fall
Of the last monarchy) see that you come
Not to woo honour, but to wed it. When
The bravest questant shrinks, find what you seek,
That fame may cry you loud...I say, farewell.

2 *Lord.* Health, at your bidding, serve your majesty!

King. Those girls of Italy, take heed of them.
20 They say, our French lack language to deny,
If they demand: beware of being captives,
Before you serve.

Both. Our hearts receive your warnings.

King. Farewell. [*to attendants*] Come hither to me.
[*he swoons and is carried to the couch, before which curtains are drawn*

1 *Lord.* O my sweet lord, that you will stay behind us!

Parolles. 'Tis not his fault, the spark.

2 *Lord.* O, 'tis brave wars!

(*Parolles* [*shudders*]. Most admirable! I have seen those wars.

Bertram. I am commanded here, and kept a coil with
'Too young,' and 'the next year,' and ''tis too early.'

Parolles. An thy mind stand to't, boy, steal away bravely.

30 *Bertram.* I shall stay here the forehorse to a smock,
Creaking my shoes on the plain masonry,
Till honour be bought up, and no sword worn
But one to dance with! By heaven, I'll steal away.

1 *Lord.* There's honour in the theft.

Parolles. Commit it, count.

2 *Lord.* I am your accessary, and so farewell.

Bertram. I grow to you, and our parting is a tortured body.

1 *Lord.* Farewell, captain.

2 *Lord.* Sweet Monsieur Parolles!

Parolles. Noble heroes, my sword and yours are kin. 40
Good sparks and lustrous, a word, good metals: you shall find in the regiment of the Spinii one Captain Spurio, with his cicatrice, an emblem of war, here on his sinister cheek; it was this very sword entrenched it: say to him, I live, and observe his reports for me.

1 *Lord.* We shall, noble captain.

Parolles. Mars dote on you for his novices! [*the lords go*] What will ye do?

At this, the curtains are drawn aside, discovering the King in his chair; attendants bear him forward

Bertram [*finger on lip*]. Stay: the king!

Parolles [*hurries him away*]. Use a more spacious 50
ceremony to the noble lords, you have restrained yourself within the list of too cold an adieu: be more expressive to them; for they wear themselves in the cap of the time, there do muster true gait, eat, speak, and move under the influence of the most received star, and though the devil lead the measure, such are to be followed; after them, and take a more dilated farewell.

Bertram. And I will do so.

Parolles. Worthy fellows; and like to prove most sinewy sword-men. [*Bertram and Parolles go off* 60

The attendants set down the chair; LAFEU *enters*

Lafeu [*kneels*]. Pardon, my lord, for me and for my tidings.

King. I'll fee thee to stand up.

Lafeu [*rises*]. Then here's a man stands that has brought his pardon.
I would you had kneeled, my lord, to ask me mercy,
And that at my bidding you could so stand up.

King. I would I had, so I had broke thy pate
And asked thee mercy for't.

Lafeu. Good faith, across!
But, my good lord, 'tis thus—will you be cured
Of your infirmity?

King. No.

Lafeu. O, will you eat
70 No grapes, my royal fox? yes, but you will
My noble grapes, an if my royal fox
Could reach them: I have seen a medicine
That's able to breathe life into a stone,
Quicken a rock, and make you dance canary
With spritely fire and motion, whose simple touch
Is powerful to araise King Pepin, nay,
To give great Charlemain a pen in's hand,
And write to her a love-line.

King. What 'her' is this?

Lafeu. Why, Doctor She: my lord, there's one arrived,
80 If you will see her: now, by my faith and honour,
If seriously I may convey my thoughts
In this my light deliverance, I have spoke
With one that, in her sex, her years, profession,
Wisdom and constancy, hath amazed me more
Than I dare blame my weakness: will you see her,
For that is her demand, and know her business?
That done, laugh well at me.

King. Now, good Lafeu,
Bring in the admiration, that we with thee
May spend our wonder too, or take off thine
By wond'ring how thou took'st it.

Lafeu. Nay, I'll fit you, 90
And not be all day neither. [*Lafeu hurries out*
King. Thus he his special nothing ever prologues.

LAFEU returns, holding open the door for one to follow him

Lafeu. Nay, come your ways.

HELENA timidly enters

King. This haste hath wings indeed.
Lafeu. Nay, come your ways!
This is his majesty, say your mind to him.
A traitor you do look like, but such traitors
His majesty seldom fears. I am Cressid's uncle,
That dare leave two together. Fare you well. [*he goes*
King. Now, fair one, does your business follow us?
Helena. Ay, my good lord. 100
Gerard de Narbon was my father;
In what he did profess, well-found.
King. I knew him.
Helena. The rather will I spare my praises towards him—
Knowing him is enough...On's bed of death
Many receipts he gave me, chiefly one,
Which as the dearest issue of his practice
And of his old experience th'only darling,
He bad me store up, as a triple eye,
Safer than mine own two, more dear; I have so:
And, hearing your high majesty is touched 110
With that malignant cause wherein the honour
Of my dear father's gift stands chief in power,
I come to tender it, and my appliance,
With all bound humbleness.
King. We thank you, maiden,
But may not be so credulous of cure,

When our most learnéd doctors leave us, and
The congregated College have concluded
That labouring art can never ransom nature
From her inaidible estate: I say we must not
120 So stain our judgement, or corrupt our hope,
To prostitute our past-cure malady
To empirics, or to dissever so
Our great self and our credit, to esteem
A senseless help, when help past sense we deem.
Helena. My duty then shall pay me for my pains:
I will no more enforce mine office on you;
Humbly entreating from your royal thoughts
A modest one, to bear me back again.
King. I cannot give thee less, to be called grateful...
130 Thou thought'st to help me, and such thanks I give
As one near death to those that wish him live:
But what at full I know, thou know'st no part,
I knowing all my peril, thou no art.
Helena. What I can do can do no hurt to try,
Since you set up your rest 'gainst remedy:
He that of greatest works is finisher,
Oft does them by the weakest minister:
So holy writ in babes hath judgement shown,
When judges have been babes; great floods have flown
140 From simple sources; and great seas have dried
When miracles have by the great'st been denied.
Oft expectation fails, and most oft there
Where most it promises; and oft it hits,
Where hope is coldest, and despair most fits.
King. I must not hear thee, fare thee well,
kind maid.
Thy pains not used must by thyself be paid.
Proffers not took reap thanks for their reward.
Helena. Inspiréd merit so by breath is barred.

It is not so with Him that all things knows,
As 'tis with us that square our guess by shows: 150
But most it is presumption in us, when
The help of heaven we count the act of men.
Dear sir, to my endeavours give consent,
Of heaven, not me, make an experiment.
I am not an impostor, that proclaim
Myself against the level of mine aim,
But know I think, and think I know most sure,
My art is not past power, nor you past cure.

King. Art thou so confident? Within what space
Hop'st thou my cure?

Helena. The great'st grace lending grace, 160
Ere twice the horses of the sun shall bring
Their fiery torcher his diurnal ring,
Ere twice in murk and occidental damp
Moist Hesperus hath quenched her sleepy lamp;
Or four and twenty times the pilot's glass
Hath told the thievish minutes how they pass;
What is infirm from your sound parts shall fly,
Health shall live free, and sickness freely die.

King. Upon thy certainty and confidence,
What dar'st thou venture?

Helena. Tax of impudence, 170
A strumpet's boldness, a divulgéd shame,
Traduced by odious ballads; my maiden's name
Seared; otherwise—ne worse of worst—extended
With vilest torture let my life be ended.

King. Methinks in thee some blesséd spirit doth speak
His powerful sound within an organ weak:
And what impossibility would slay
In common sense, sense saves another way...
Thy life is dear, for all that life can rate
Worth name of life in thee hath estimate; 180

†Youth, beauty, wisdom, courage, all
That happiness and prime can happy call:
Thou this to hazard needs must intimate
Skill infinite or monstrous desperate.
Sweet practiser, thy physic I will try,
That ministers thine own death if I die.

Helena. If I break time, or flinch in property
Of what I spoke, unpitied let me die,
And well deserved: not helping, death's my fee,
190 But if I help what do you promise me?

King. Make thy demand.

Helena. But will you make it even?

King. Ay, by my sceptre and my hopes of heaven.

Helena. Then shalt thou give me with thy kingly hand
What husband in thy power I will command:
Exempted be from me the arrogance
To choose from forth the royal blood of France,
My low and humble name to propagate
With any branch or image of thy state:
But such a one, thy vassal, whom I know
200 Is free for me to ask, thee to bestow.

King. Here is my hand—the premises observed,
Thy will by my performance shall be served:
So make the choice of thy own time, for I,
Thy resolved patient, on thee still rely...
More should I question thee, and more I must,
Though more to know could not be more to trust;
From whence thou cam'st, how tended on—but rest
Unquestioned welcome, and undoubted blest.
Give me some help here, ho! If thou proceed
210 As high as word, my deed shall match thy deed.

A flourish of trumpets; attendants carry him away

[2. 2.] *A room in the palace of Rousillon*

COUNTESS *and* CLOWN

Countess. Come on, sir. I shall now put you to the height of your breeding.

Clown. I will show myself highly fed and lowly taught. I know my business is but to the court.

Countess. To the court! why, what place make you special, when you put off that with such contempt? 'But to the court!'

Clown. Truly, madam, if God have lent a man any manners, he may easily put it off at court: he that cannot make a leg, put off's cap, kiss his hand, and say nothing, 10 has neither leg, hands, lip, nor cap; and, indeed, such a fellow, to say precisely, were not for the court. But for me, I have an answer will serve all men.

Countess. Marry, that's a bountiful answer that fits all questions.

Clown. It is like a barber's chair that fits all buttocks—the pin-buttock, the quatch-buttock, the brawn-buttock, or any buttock.

Countess. Will your answer serve fit to all questions?

Clown. As fit as ten groats is for the hand of an 20 attorney, as your French crown for your taffety punk, as Tib's rush for Tom's forefinger, as a pancake for Shrove Tuesday, a morris for May-day, as the nail to his hole, the cuckold to his horn, as a scolding quean to a wrangling knave, as the nun's lip to the friar's mouth, nay, as the pudding to his skin.

Countess. Have you, I say, an answer of such fitness for all questions?

Clown. From below your duke to beneath your constable, it will fit any question. 30

Countess. It must be an answer of most monstrous size that must fit all demands.

Clown. But a trifle neither, in good faith, if the learned should speak truth of it: here it is, and all that belongs to't. Ask me if I am a courtier, it shall do you no harm to learn.

Countess. To be young again, if we could...I will be a fool in question, hoping to be the wiser by your answer. I pray you, sir, are you a courtier?

40 *Clown.* O Lord, sir!—There's a simple putting off: more, more, a hundred of them.

Countess. Sir, I am a poor friend of yours, that loves you.

Clown. O Lord, sir!—Thick! thick! spare not me.

Countess. I think, sir, you can eat none of this homely meat.

Clown. O Lord, sir!—Nay, put me to't, I warrant you.

Countess. You were lately whipped, sir, as I think.

Clown. O Lord, sir!—Spare not me.

Countess. Do you cry, 'O Lord, sir!' at your whipping,

50 and 'spare not me'? Indeed, your 'O Lord, sir!' is very sequent to your whipping; you would answer very well to a whipping, if you were but bound to't.

Clown. I ne'er had worse luck in my life in my 'O Lord, sir!' I see things may serve long, but not serve ever.

Countess. I play the noble housewife with the time,
To entertain it so merrily with a fool.

Clown. O Lord, sir!—Why, there't serves well again.

Countess. An end, sir, to your business: give
Helen this,

60 And urge her to a present answer back.
Commend me to my kinsmen and my son.
This is not much.

Clown. Not much commendation to them?

Countess. Not much employment for you. You understand me?

Clown. Most fruitfully. I am there before my legs.

Countess. Haste you again.

[*they go out by different doors*

[2. 3.] *A room in the King's palace at Paris; at the back two chairs of state*

BERTRAM, LAFEU, *and* PAROLLES

Lafeu. They say miracles are past, and we have our philosophical persons, to make modern and familiar, things supernatural and causeless. Hence is it that we make trifles of terrors, ensconcing ourselves into seeming knowledge, when we should submit ourselves to an unknown fear.

Parolles. Why, 'tis the rarest argument of wonder that hath shot out in our latter times.

Bertram. And so 'tis.

Lafeu. To be relinquished of the artists— 10

Parolles. So I say.

†*Lafeu.* Both of Galen and Paracelsus.

Parolles. So I say.

Lafeu. Of all the learned and authentic fellows—

Parolles. Right, so I say.

Lafeu. That gave him out incurable—

Parolles. Why, there 'tis, so say I too.

Lafeu. Not to be helped—

Parolles. Right, as 'twere a man assured of a—

Lafeu. Uncertain life, and sure death. 20

Parolles. Just, you say well: so would I have said.

Lafeu. I may truly say, it is a novelty to the world.

Parolles. It is, indeed: if you will have it in showing, you shall read it in †what-do-ye-call't there?

Lafeu [*takes a ballad from his belt*]. 'A showing of a heavenly effect in an earthly actor.'

Parolles. That's it, I would have said the very same.

Lafeu. Why, your dolphin is not lustier: 'fore me I speak in respect—

30 *Parolles*. Nay, 'tis strange, 'tis very strange, that is the brief and the tedious of it, and he's of a most facinerious spirit that will not acknowledge it to be the—

Lafeu. Very hand of heaven.

Parolles. Ay, so I say.

Lafeu. In a most weak—

Parolles. And debile minister, great power, great transcendence, which should, indeed, give us a further use to be made than alone the recovery of the king, as 40 to be—

Lafeu. Generally thankful.

The KING *enters with* HELENA *and attendants*

Parolles. I would have said it. You say well... Here comes the king.

Lafeu. Lustick! as the Dutchman says: I'll like a maid the better, whilst I have a tooth in my head: why, he's able to lead her a coranto.

Parolles. Mort du vinaigre! Is not this Helen?

Lafeu. 'Fore God, I think so.

King. Go, call before me all the lords in court.

[*an attendant goes*

50 Sit, my preserver, by thy patient's side,

[*he leads her to the chairs of state*

And with this healthful hand, whose banished sense
Thou hast repealed, a second time receive
The confirmation of my promised gift,
Which but attends thy naming.... [*they sit*

'Enter three or four lords'; they stand before the King, BERTRAM *joining them*

Fair maid, send forth thine eye—this youthful parcel
Of noble bachelors stand at my bestowing,
O'er whom both sovereign power and father's voice
I have to use: thy frank election make,
Thou hast power to choose, and they none to forsake.

Helena. To each of you one fair and virtuous mistress 60
Fall, when Love please! marry, to each but one!

(*Lafeu* [*at a distance, to Parolles*]. I'd give bay Curtal and his furniture,
My mouth no more were broken than these boys',
And writ as little beard.

King. Peruse them well:
Not one of those but had a noble father.

Helena [*rises*]. Gentlemen,
Heaven hath, through me, restored the king to health.

All. We understand it, and thank heaven for you.

Helena. I am a simple maid, and therein wealthiest
That I protest I simply am a maid... 70
Please it your majesty, I have done already:
The blushes in my cheeks thus whisper me,
'We blush that thou shouldst choose; but, be refused...
Let the white death sit on thy cheek for ever,
We'll ne'er come there again.'

King. Make choice and see,
Who shuns thy love shuns all his love in me.

Helena. Now, Dian, from thy altar do I fly,
And to imperial Love, that god most high,
Do my sighs stream...['*she addresses her to a lord*'] Sir, will you hear my suit?

1 *Lord*. And grant it.

Helena. Thanks, sir—all the rest is mute. 80
[*he bows*

(*Lafeu*. I had rather be in this choice, than throw ames-ace for my life.

Helena [*passes to another lord*]. The honour, sir, that flames in your fair eyes,
Before I speak, too threat'ningly replies:
Love make your fortunes twenty times above
Her that so wishes and her humble love!

2 *Lord*. No better, if you please.

Helena. My wish receive,
Which great Love grant! and so, I take my leave.
[*she passes on*

(*Lafeu*. Do all they deny her? An they were sons of
90 mine, I'd have them whipped, or I would send them to th' Turk to make eunuchs of.

Helena [*to the third lord*]. Be not afraid that I your hand should take,
I'll never do you wrong for your own sake:
Blessing upon your vows! and in your bed
Find fairer fortune, if you ever wed! [*she passes on*

(*Lafeu*. These boys are boys of ice, they'll none have her: sure, they are bastards to the English, the French ne'er got 'em.

Helena [*to the fourth lord*]. You are too young, too happy, and too good,
100 To make yourself a son out of my blood.

4 *Lord*. Fair one, I think not so. [*she passes on*

(*Lafeu*. There's one grape yet—I am sure thy father drunk wine—but if thou be'st not an ass, I am a youth of fourteen; I have known thee already.

Helena [*to Bertram*]. I dare not say I take you, but I give
Me and my service, ever whilst I live,
Into your guiding power...This is the man.

King. Why then, young Bertram, take her, she's thy wife.

Bertram. My wife, my liege? I shall beseech your highness,
In such a business give me leave to use 110
The help of mine own eyes.
King. Know'st thou not, Bertram,
What she has done for me?
Bertram. Yes, my good lord;
But never hope to know why I should marry her.
King. Thou know'st she has raised me from my sickly bed.
Bertram. But follows it, my lord, to bring me down
Must answer for your raising? I know her well;
She had her breeding at my father's charge:
A poor physician's daughter my wife! Disdain
Rather corrupt me ever!
King. 'Tis only title thou disdain'st in her, the which 120
I can build up...Strange is it, that our bloods,
Of colour, weight, and heat, poured all together,
Would quite confound distinction, yet stand off
In differences so mighty....If she be
All that is virtuous (save what thou dislik'st,
A poor physician's daughter) thou dislik'st
Of virtue for a name; but do not so:
From lowest place when virtuous things proceed,
The place is dignified by th'doer's deed:
Where great additions swell's, and virtue none, 130
It is a dropsied honour: good alone
Is good, without a name; vileness is so:
The property by what it is should go,
Not by the title....She is young, wise, fair;
In these to nature she's immediate heir;
And these breed honour: that is honour's scorn,
Which challenges itself as honour's born,

And is not like the sire: honours thrive,
When rather from our acts we them derive
140 Than our foregoers: the mere word's a slave,
Deboshed on every tomb, on every grave
A lying trophy, and as oft is dumb
Where dust and damned oblivion is the tomb
Of honoured bones indeed. What should be said?
If thou canst like this creature as a maid,
I can create the rest: virtue and she
Is her own dower; honour and wealth, from me.

Bertram. I cannot love her, nor will strive to do't.

King. Thou wrong'st thyself, if thou shouldst strive to choose.

150 *Helena.* That you are well restored, my lord, I'm glad;
Let the rest go.

King. My honour's at the stake, which to defeat,
I must produce my power. [*rises*] Here, take her hand,
Proud scornful boy, unworthy this good gift,
That dost in vile misprision shackle up
My love and her desert; that canst not dream,
We, poising us in her defective scale,
Shall weigh thee to the beam: that wilt not know,
It is in us to plant thine honour where
160 We please to have it grow. Check thy contempt:
Obey our will, which travails in thy good:
Believe not thy disdain, but presently
Do thine own fortunes that obedient right
Which both thy duty owes and our power claims,
Or I will throw thee from my care for ever
Into the staggers and the careless lapse
Of youth and ignorance; both my revenge and hate,
Loosing upon thee in the name of justice,

Without all terms of pity. Speak, thine answer!
Bertram. Pardon, my gracious lord; for I submit 170
My fancy to your eyes. When I consider
What great creation and what dole of honour
Flies where you bid it, I find that she which late
Was in my nobler thoughts most base, is now
The praiséd of the king—who, so ennobled,
Is as 'twere born so.
King. Take her by the hand,
And tell her she is thine: to whom I promise
A counterpoise; if not to thy estate,
A balance more replete.
Bertram. I take her hand.
King. Good fortune and the favour of the king 180
Smile upon this contract; whose ceremony
Shall seem expedient on the now-born brief,
And be performed to-night: the solemn feast
Shall more attend upon the coming space,
Expecting absent friends. As thou lov'st her,
Thy love's to me religious; else, does err.
[*all depart save Lafeu and Parolles who 'stay behind, commenting of this wedding'*
Lafeu. Do you hear, monsieur? a word with you.
Parolles. Your pleasure, sir?
Lafeu. Your lord and master did well to make his recantation. 190
Parolles. Recantation! My lord! my master!
Lafeu. Ay; is it not a language I speak?
Parolles. A most harsh one, and not to be understood without bloody succeeding. My master!
Lafeu. Are you companion to the Count Rousillon?
Parolles. To any count, to all counts: to what is man!
Lafeu. To what is count's man: count's master is of another style.

Parolles. You are too old, sir; let it satisfy you, you
200 are too old.

Lafeu. I must tell thee, sirrah, I write man; to which title age cannot bring thee.

Parolles [*his hand upon his sword*]. What I dare too well do, I dare not do.

Lafeu. I did think thee, for two ordinaries, to be a pretty wise fellow; thou didst make tolerable vent of thy travel—it might pass: yet the scarfs and the bannerets about thee did manifoldly dissuade me from believing thee a vessel of too great a burden. I have now
210 found thee—when I lose thee again, I care not: yet art thou good for nothing but taking up, and that thou'rt scarce worth.

Parolles. Hadst thou not the privilege of antiquity upon thee,—

Lafeu. Do not plunge thyself too far in anger, lest thou hasten thy trial; which if—Lord have mercy on thee for a hen! So, my good window of lattice, fare thee well, thy casement I need not open, for I look through thee....Give me thy hand.

220 *Parolles* [*does so*]. My lord, you give me most egregious indignity.

Lafeu [*shakes his hand*]. Ay, with all my heart, and thou art worthy of it.

Parolles. I have not, my lord, deserved it.

Lafeu. Yes, good faith, every dram of it, and I will not bate thee a scruple.

Parolles. Well, I shall be wiser.

Lafeu. E'en as soon as thou canst, for thou hast to pull at a smack o'th' contrary. If ever thou be'st bound in
230 thy scarf and beaten, thou shalt find what it is to be proud of thy bondage. I have a desire to hold my acquaintance with thee, or rather my knowledge, that I may say, in the default, he is a man I know.

Parolles. My lord, you do me most insupportable vexation.

Lafeu. I would it were hell-pains for thy sake, and my poor doing eternal: for doing I am past, as I will by thee, in what motion age will give me leave.

[*he passes him swiftly and goes out*

Parolles. Well, thou hast a son shall take this disgrace off me; scurvy, old, filthy, scurvy lord! Well, I must be 240 patient, there is no fettering of authority. I'll beat him, by my life, if I can meet him with any convenience, an he were double and double a lord. I'll have no more pity of his age than I would have of—I'll beat him, an if I could but meet him again.

LAFEU returns

Lafeu. Sirrah, your lord and master's married, there's news for you; you have a new mistress.

Parolles. I most unfeignedly beseech your lordship to make some reservation of your wrongs. He is my good lord—whom I serve above, is my master. 250

Lafeu. Who? God?

Parolles. Ay, sir.

Lafeu. The devil it is that's thy master. Why dost thou garter up thy arms o' this fashion? dost make hose of thy sleeves? do other servants so? Thou wert best set thy lower part where thy nose stands. By mine honour, if I were but two hours younger, I'd beat thee: methink'st thou art a general offence, and every man should beat thee: I think thou wast created for men to breathe themselves upon thee. 260

Parolles. This is hard and undeserved measure, my lord.

Lafeu. Go to, sir, you were beaten in Italy for picking a kernel out of a pomegranate, you are a vagabond and no true traveller; you are more saucy with lords and honourable personages than the commission of your birth and virtue gives you heraldry. You are not worth another word else I'd call you knave. I leave you.

[*he goes*

Parolles. Good, very good, it is so then: good, very

270 good, let it be concealed awhile.

BERTRAM *enters*

(*Bertram*. Undone, and forfeited to cares for ever!

Parolles. What's the matter, sweet-heart?

(*Bertram*. Although before the solemn priest I have sworn,

I will not bed her.

Parolles. What, what, sweet-heart?

Bertram. O my Parolles, they have married me:

I'll to the Tuscan wars, and never bed her.

Parolles. France is a dog-hole, and it no more merits

The tread of a man's foot: to th' wars!

280 *Bertram*. There's letters from my mother: what th'import is,

I know not yet.

Parolles. Ay, that would be known...To th' wars, my boy, to th' wars!

He wears his honour in a box unseen,

That hugs his kicky-wicky here at home,

Spending his manly marrow in her arms,

Which should sustain the bound and high curvet

Of Mars's fiery steed...To other regions!

France is a stable, we that dwell in't jades,

Therefore to th' war!

290 *Bertram*. It shall be so. I'll send her to my house,

Acquaint my mother with my hate to her,

And wherefore I am fled; write to the king

That which I durst not speak: his present gift
Shall furnish me to those Italian fields,
Where noble fellows strike: war is no strife
To the dark house and the detested wife.

Parolles. Will this capriccio hold in thee, art sure?

Bertram. Go with me to my chamber, and advise me.
I'll send her straight away: to-morrow
I'll to the wars, she to her single sorrow. 300

Parolles. Why, these balls bound, there's noise in it. 'Tis hard;
A young man married is a man that's marred:
Therefore away, and leave her bravely; go.
The king has done you wrong; but, hush, 'tis so.

[*they go*

[2.4.] *Another room in the King's palace*

'*Enter* HELENA *and* CLOWN'

Helena. My mother greets me kindly. Is she well?

Clown. She is not well, but yet she has her health, she's very merry, but yet she is not well: but thanks be given, she's very well and wants nothing i'th' world; but yet she is not well.

Helena. If she be very well, what does she ail, that she's not very well?

Clown. Truly, she's very well indeed, but for two things.

Helena. What two things? 10

Clown. One, that she's not in heaven, whither God send her quickly: the other, that she's in earth, from whence God send her quickly.

PAROLLES comes in

Parolles. Bless you, my fortunate lady!

Helena. I hope, sir, I have your good will to have mine own good fortunes.

Parolles. You had my prayers to lead them on, and to keep them on have them still. O, my knave, how does my old lady?

20 *Clown.* So that you had her wrinkles, and I her money, I would she did as you say.

Parolles. Why, I say nothing.

Clown. Marry, you are the wiser man; for many a man's tongue shakes out his master's undoing: to say nothing, to do nothing, to know nothing, and to have nothing, is to be a great part of your title—which is within a very little of nothing.

Parolles. Away, th'art a knave.

Clown. You should have said, sir, 'before a knave 30 th'art a knave,' that's, before me th'art a knave: this had been truth, sir.

Parolles. Go to, thou art a witty fool, I have found thee.

Clown. Did you find me in yourself, sir? or were you taught to find me?

†*Parolles.* In myself.

Clown. The search, sir, was profitable; and much fool may you find in you, even to the world's pleasure and the increase of laughter.

Parolles. A good knave, i' faith, and well fed.
40 Madam, my lord will go away to-night,
A very serious business calls on him:
The great prerogative and rite of love,
Which as your due time claims, he does acknowledge,
But puts it off to a compelled restraint;
Whose want, and whose delay, is strewed with sweets,
Which they distil now in the curbéd time,

To make the coming hour o'erflow with joy,
And pleasure drown the brim.

Helena. What's his will else?

Parolles. That you will take your instant leave o'th' king,
And make this haste as your own good proceeding, 50
Strengthened with what apology you think
May make it probable need.

Helena. What more commands he?

Parolles. That, having this obtained, you presently
Attend his further pleasure.

Helena. In every thing I wait upon his will.

Parolles. I shall report it so. [*goes*

Helena. I pray you.—Come, sirrah. [*they go*

[2. 5.] *Another room in the same*

'*Enter* LAFEU *and* BERTRAM'

Lafeu. But I hope your lordship thinks not him a soldier.

Bertram. Yes, my lord, and of very valiant approof.

Lafeu. You have it from his own deliverance.

Bertram. And by other warranted testimony.

Lafeu. Then my dial goes not true, I took this lark for a bunting.

Bertram. I do assure you, my lord, he is very great in knowledge, and accordingly valiant.

Lafeu. I have then sinned against his experience and 10 transgressed against his valour, and my state that way is dangerous, since I cannot yet find in my heart to repent...

Enter PAROLLES

Here he comes, I pray you make us friends, I will pursue the amity.

Parolles [*to Bertram*]. These things shall be done, sir.

Lafeu. Pray you, sir, who's his tailor?

Parolles. Sir?

Lafeu. O, I know him well. Ay sir, he, sir, 's a good
20 workman, a very good tailor.

(*Bertram.* Is she gone to the king?

(*Parolles.* She is.

(*Bertram.* Will she away to-night?

(*Parolles.* As you'll have her.

(*Bertram.* I have writ my letters, casketed my treasure,
Given order for our horses—and to-night,
When I should take possession of the bride,
End ere I do begin.

Lafeu. A good traveller is something at the latter end
30 of a dinner, but one that lies three thirds and uses a
known truth to pass a thousand nothings with, should
be once heard and thrice beaten....[*they turn to him*]
God save you, captain.

Bertram. Is there any unkindness between my lord
and you, monsieur?

Parolles. I know not how I have deserved to run into
my lord's displeasure.

Lafeu. You have made shift to run into't, boots and
spurs and all, like him that leaped into the custard; and
40 out of it you'll run again, rather than suffer question for
your residence.

Bertram. It may be you have mistaken him, my lord.

Lafeu. And shall do so ever, though I took him at's
prayers. Fare you well, my lord, and believe this of
me, there can be no kernel in this light nut; the soul of
this man is his clothes: trust him not in matter of heavy
consequence; I have kept of them tame and know their
natures....Farewell, monsieur, I have spoken better of
you than you have or will to deserve at my hand, but
50 we must do good against evil. [*he goes*

Parolles. An idle lord, I swear.
Bertram [*hesitates*]. I think so.
Parolles. Why, do you not know him?
Bertram. Yes, I do know him well, and
common speech
Gives him a worthy pass....

HELENA enters

Here comes my clog.
Helena. I have, sir, as I was commanded from you,
Spoke with the king, and have procured his leave
For present parting—only he desires
Some private speech with you.
Bertram. I shall obey his will.
You must not marvel, Helen, at my course, 60
Which holds not colour with the time, nor does
The ministration and requiréd office
On my particular. Prepared I was not
For such a business, therefore am I found
So much unsettled...This drives me to entreat you
That presently you take your way for home,
And rather muse than ask why I entreat you,
For my respects are better than they seem,
And my appointments have in them a need
Greater than shows itself at the first view 70
To you that know them not....[*gives a letter*] This to
my mother.
'Twill be two days ere I shall see you, so
I leave you to your wisdom.
Helena. Sir, I can nothing say,
But that I am your most obedient servant.
Bertram. Come, come, no more of that.
Helena. And ever shall
With true observance seek to eke out that

Wherein toward me my homely stars have failed
To equal my great fortune.

Bertram. Let that go:
My haste is very great. Farewell; hie home.

80 *Helena.* Pray, sir, your pardon.

Bertram. Well, what would you say?

Helena. I am not worthy of the wealth I owe,
Nor dare I say 'tis mine...and yet it is—
But like a timorous thief most fain would steal
What law does vouch mine own.

Bertram. What would you have?

Helena. Something, and scarce so much: nothing, indeed.
I would not tell you what I would, my lord...
Faith, yes—
Strangers and foes do sunder, and not kiss.

Bertram. I pray you stay not, but in haste to horse.

90 *Helena.* I shall not break your bidding, good my lord...

Bertram. Where are my other men, monsieur?— Farewell. [*Helena departs*
Go thou toward home, where I will never come,
Whilst I can shake my sword, or hear the drum...
Away, and for our flight.

Parolles. Bravely, coragio! [*they go*

[3. 1.] *Florence. Before the Duke's palace*

'*Flourish. Enter the* DUKE OF FLORENCE, *the two Frenchmen with a troop of soldiers*'

Duke. So that from point to point now have you heard
The fundamental reasons of this war;
Whose great decision hath much blood let forth,

And more thirsts after.
1 *Lord.* Holy seems the quarrel
Upon your grace's part; black and fearful
On the opposer.
Duke. Therefore we marvel much our cousin France
Would in so just a business shut his bosom
Against our borrowing prayers.
2 *Lord.* Good my lord,
The reasons of our state I cannot yield, 10
But like a common and an outward man,
That the great figure of a council frames
By self-unable motion—therefore dare not
Say what I think of it, since I have found
Myself in my incertain grounds to fail
As often as I guessed.
Duke. Be it his pleasure.
1 *Lord.* But I am sure the younger of our nature,
That surfeit on their ease, will day by day
Come here for physic.
Duke. Welcome shall they be:
And all the honours that can fly from us 20
Shall on them settle...You know your places well;
When better fall, for your avails they fell:
To-morrow to th' field! [*a flourish; they pass on*

[3. 2.] *A room in the palace of Rousillon*

The COUNTESS (*with a letter in her hand*) *and the* CLOWN

Countess. It hath happened all as I would have had it, save that he comes not along with her.
Clown. By my troth, I take my young lord to be a very melancholy man.
Countess. By what observance, I pray you?

Clown. Why, he will look upon his boot and sing, mend the ruff and sing, ask questions and sing, pick his teeth and sing: I know a man that had this trick of melancholy sold a goodly manor for a song.

10 *Countess.* Let me see what he writes, and when he means to come. [*she opens the letter*

Clown. I have no mind to Isbel, since I was at court. Our old ling and our Isbels o'the country are nothing like your old ling and your Isbels o'the court: the brains of my Cupid's knocked out, and I begin to love, as an old man loves money, with no stomach.

Countess. What have we here?

Clown. E'en that you have there. [*he goes*

Countess [*reads*]. 'I have sent you a daughter-in-law.
20 She hath recovered the king, and undone me: I have wedded her, not bedded her, and sworn to make the 'not' eternal. You shall hear I am run away, know it before the report come. If there be breadth enough in the world, I will hold a long distance. My duty to you.

Your unfortunate son,

BERTRAM.'

This is not well, rash and unbridled boy,
To fly the favours of so good a king,
To pluck his indignation on thy head,
30 By the misprising of a maid too virtuous
For the contempt of empire.

The CLOWN *returns*

Clown. O madam, yonder is heavy news within between two soldiers and my young lady.

Countess. What is the matter?

Clown. Nay, there is some comfort in the news, some comfort—your son will not be killed so soon as I thought he would.

Countess. Why should he be killed?

Clown. So say I, madam, if he run away, as I hear he does. The danger is in standing to't, that's the loss of men, though it be the getting of children. Here they come will tell you more. For my part, I only hear your son was run away. 40

HELENA enters with two gentlemen

1 *Gentleman.* Save you, good madam.

Helena. Madam, my lord is gone, for ever gone.
[*she sobs*

2 *Gentleman.* Do not say so.

Countess [*takes her in her arms*]. Think upon patience.
Pray you, gentlemen,
I have felt so many quirks of joy and grief,
That the first face of neither, on the start,
Can woman me unto't...Where is my son, I
pray you? 50

2 *Gentleman.* Madam, he's gone to serve the Duke
of Florence.
We met him thitherward, for thence we came:
And after some dispatch in hand at court
Thither we bend again.

Helena. Look on his letter, madam, here's
my passport.
[*reads*] 'When thou canst get the ring upon my finger, which never shall come off, and show me a child begotten of thy body that I am father to, then call me husband: but in such a 'then' I write a 'never'.'
This is a dreadful sentence. 60

Countess. Brought you this letter, gentlemen?

1 *Gentleman.* Ay, madam,
And for the contents' sake are sorry for our pains.

Countess. I prithee lady have a better cheer,

If thou engrossest all the griefs are thine,
Thou robb'st me of a moiety...He was my son,
But I do wash his name out of my blood,
And thou art all my child....Towards Florence is he?
2 *Gentleman.* Ay, madam.
Countess. And to be a soldier?
2 *Gentleman.* Such is his noble purpose, and, believe't,
70 The duke will lay upon him all the honour
That good convenience claims.
Countess. Return you thither?
1 *Gentleman.* Ay, madam, with the swiftest wing of speed.
Helena [*reads*]. 'Till I have no wife, I have nothing in France.'
'Tis bitter.
Countess. Find you that there?
Helena. Ay, madam.
1 *Gentleman.* 'Tis but the boldness of his hand, haply, which his heart was not consenting to.
Countess. Nothing in France, until he have no wife!
There's nothing here that is too good for him
But only she, and she deserves a lord
80 That twenty such rude boys might tend upon
And call her hourly mistress. Who was with him?
1 *Gentleman.* A servant only, and a gentleman
Which I have sometime known.
Countess. Parolles, was it not?
1 *Gentleman.* Ay, my good lady, he.
Countess. A very tainted fellow, and full of wickedness.
My son corrupts a well-derivéd nature
With his inducement.
1 *Gentleman.* Indeed, good lady,

The fellow has a deal of that too much,
Which holds him much to have.
Countess. Y'are welcome, gentlemen. 90
I will entreat you, when you see my son,
To tell him that his sword can never win
The honour that he loses: more I'll entreat you
Written to bear along.
2 *Gentleman.* We serve you, madam,
In that and all your worthiest affairs.
Countess. Not so, but as we change our courtesies.
Will you draw near?
[*the Countess goes out with the gentlemen;*
the Clown follows
Helena. 'Till I have no wife, I have nothing
in France.'
Nothing in France, until he has no wife!
Thou shalt have none, Rousillon, none in France, 100
Then hast thou all again....Poor lord! is't I
That chase thee from thy country and expose
Those tender limbs of thine to the event
Of the none-sparing war? and is it I
That drive thee from the sportive court, where thou
Wast shot at with fair eyes, to be the mark
Of smoky muskets? O you leaden messengers,
That ride upon the violent speed of fire,
†Fly with false aim, move the still-piecing air
That sings with piercing, do not touch my lord! 110
Whoever shoots at him, I set him there.
Whoever charges on his forward breast,
I am the caitiff that do hold him to't.
And, though I kill him not, I am the cause
His death was so effected: better 'twere
I met the ravin lion when he roared
With sharp constraint of hunger: better 'twere

That all the miseries which nature owes
Were mine at once. No, come thou home, Rousillon,
120 Whence honour but of danger wins a scar,
As oft it loses all....I will be gone:
My being here it is that holds thee hence—
Shall I stay here to do't? no, no, although
The air of paradise did fan the house,
And angels officed all: I will be gone,
That pitiful rumour may report my flight,
To consolate thine ear. Come night! end day!
For with the dark, poor thief, I'll steal away. [*she goes*

[3. 3.] *Florence. Before the Duke's palace*

Flourish. Enter the DUKE OF FLORENCE, BERTRAM, PAROLLES, *officers, soldiers, drum and trumpets*

Duke. The general of our horse thou art, and we,
Great in our hope, lay our best love and credence
Upon thy promising fortune.
Bertram. Sir, it is
A charge too heavy for my strength, but yet
We'll strive to bear it for your worthy sake
To th'extreme edge of hazard.
Duke. Then go thou forth,
And fortune play upon thy prosperous helm,
As thy auspicious mistress!
Bertram. This very day,
Great Mars, I put myself into thy file!
10 Make me but like my thoughts, and I shall prove
A lover of thy drum, hater of love. [*they march off*

[3.4.] *A room in the palace of Rousillon*

COUNTESS *and* STEWARD

Countess. Alas! and would you take the letter of her?
Might you not know she would do as she has done,
By sending me a letter? Read it again.
Steward [*reads*]. 'I am S. Jaques' pilgrim, thither gone:
Ambitious love hath so in me offended,
That barefoot plod I the cold ground upon,
With sainted vow my faults to have amended.
Write, write, that from the bloody course of war
My dearest master, your dear son, may hie:
Bless him at home in peace, whilst I from far 10
His name with zealous fervour sanctify:
His taken labours bid him me forgive;
I, his despiteful Juno, sent him forth
From courtly friends with camping foes to live,
Where death and danger dogs the heels of worth.
He is too good and fair for death and me,
Whom I myself embrace to set him free.'
Countess. Ah, what sharp stings are in her mildest words!
Rinaldo, you did never lack advice so much,
As letting her pass so: had I spoke with her, 20
I could have well diverted her intents,
Which thus she hath prevented.
Steward. Pardon me, madam.
If I had given you this at over-night,
She might have been o'erta'en: and yet she writes,
Pursuit would be but vain.
Countess. What angel shall

Bless this unworthy husband? he cannot thrive,
Unless her prayers, whom heaven delights to hear
And loves to grant, reprieve him from the wrath
Of greatest justice....Write, write, Rinaldo,
30 To this unworthy husband of his wife,
Let every word weigh heavy of her worth
That he does weigh too light: my greatest grief,
Though little he do feel it, set down sharply.
Dispatch the most convenient messenger.
When haply he shall hear that she is gone,
He will return, and hope I may that she,
Hearing so much, will speed her foot again,
Led hither by pure love: which of them both
Is dearest to me, I have no skill in sense
40 To make distinction...Provide this messenger...
My heart is heavy and mine age is weak,
Grief would have tears, and sorrow bids me speak.
[*they go*

[3. 5.] *Without the walls of Florence*

Enter an old WIDOW *of Florence, her daughter* DIANA, *and* MARIANA, *with other citizens; 'a tucket afar off'*

Widow. Nay come, for if they do approach the city, we shall lose all the sight.

Diana. They say the French count has done most honourable service.

Widow. It is reported that he has taken their great'st commander, and that with his own hand he slew the duke's brother...[*tucket*] We have lost our labour, they are gone a contrary way—hark! you may know by their trumpets.

10 *Mariana*. Come, let's return again, and suffice our-

selves with the report of it....[*they turn*] Well, Diana, take heed of this French earl. The honour of a maid is her name, and no legacy is so rich as honesty.

Widow. I have told my neighbour how you have been solicited by a gentleman his companion.

Mariana. I know that knave, hang him! one Parolles, a filthy officer he is in those suggestions for the young earl. Beware of them, Diana: their promises, enticements, oaths, tokens, and all these engines of lust, are not the things they go under: many a maid hath been 20 seduced by them. And the misery is, example, that so terrible shows in the wrack of maidenhood, cannot for all that dissuade succession, but that they are limed with the twigs that threaten them. I hope I need not to advise you further, but I hope your own grace will keep you where you are, though there were no further danger known but the modesty which is so lost.

Diana. You shall not need to fear me.

HELENA approaches disguised as a pilgrim

Widow. I hope so...Look, here comes a pilgrim, I know she will lie at my house, thither they send one 30 another. I'll question her.
God save you, pilgrim! whither are you bound?

Helena. To S. Jaques le Grand.
Where do the palmers lodge, I do beseech you?

Widow. At the S. Francis here, beside the port.

Helena. Is this the way?

Widow. Ay, marry, is't....[*'a march afar'*] Hark
you! they come this way.
If you will tarry, holy pilgrim,
But till the troops come by,
I will conduct you where you shall be lodged, 40
The rather for I think I know your hostess?

As ample as myself.

Helena. Is it yourself?

Widow. If you shall please so, pilgrim.

Helena. I thank you, and will stay upon your leisure.

Widow. You came, I think, from France?

Helena. I did so.

Widow. Here you shall see a countryman of yours,
That has done worthy service.

Helena. His name, I pray you.

Diana. The Count Rousillon: know you such a one?

Helena. But by the ear, that hears most nobly of him:
50 His face I know not.

Diana. Whatsome'er he is,
He's bravely taken here. He stole from France,
As 'tis reported, for the king had married him
Against his liking. Think you it is so?

Helena. Ay, surely, the mere truth. I know his lady.

Diana. There is a gentleman that serves the count
Reports but coarsely of her.

Helena. What's his name?

Diana. Monsieur Parolles.

Helena. O, I believe with him,
In argument of praise, or to the worth
Of the great count himself, she is too mean
60 To have her name repeated—all her deserving
Is a reservéd honesty, and that
I have not heard examined.

Diana. ...Alas, poor lady!
'Tis a hard bondage to become the wife
Of a detesting lord.

Widow. I warrant, good creature, wheresoe'er she is,
Her heart weighs sadly: this young maid might do her

A shrewd turn, if she pleased.

Helena. How do you mean?

May be the amorous count solicits her

In the unlawful purpose.

Widow. He does indeed,

And brokes with all that can in such a suit 70

Corrupt the tender honour of a maid:

But she is armed for him, and keeps her guard

In honestest defence.

Mariana. The gods forbid else!

Widow. So, now they come...

The Florentine army draws near with colours flying and drums beating; BERTRAM and PAROLLES in the foremost ranks

That is Antonio, the duke's eldest son,

That, Escalus.

Helena. Which is the Frenchman?

Diana [points]. He—

That with the plume—'tis a most gallant fellow.

I would he loved his wife: if he were honester

He were much goodlier. Is't not a handsome gentleman?

Helena. I like him well. 80

Diana. 'Tis pity he is not honest: yond's that same knave

That leads him to these places: were I his lady,

I would poison that vile rascal.

Helena. Which is he?

Diana. That jack-an-apes with scarfs. Why is he melancholy?

Helena. Perchance he's hurt i'th' battle.

Parolles [mutters]. Lose our drum! well.

Mariana. He's shrewdly vexed at something. Look, he has spied us. [*Parolles doffs his hat*

Widow. Marry, hang you!

90 *Mariana.* And your curtsy, for a ring-carrier!

[*the soldiers pass on*

Widow. The troop is past...Come, pilgrim, I will bring you

Where you shall host: of enjoined penitents

There's four or five, to great S. Jaques bound,

Already at my house.

Helena. I humbly thank you:

Please it this matron and this gentle maid

To eat with us to-night, the charge and thanking

Shall be for me; and, to requite you further,

I will bestow some precepts of this virgin

Worthy the note.

Both. We'll take your offer kindly.

[*they walk towards the city*

[3. 6.] *The camp before Florence*

BERTRAM *and the two French Lords approach*

2 *Lord.* Nay, good my lord, put him to't; let him have his way.

1 *Lord.* If your lordship find him not a hilding, hold me no more in your respect.

2 *Lord.* On my life, my lord, a bubble.

Bertram. Do you think I am so far deceived in him?

2 *Lord.* Believe it, my lord, in mine own direct knowledge, without any malice, but to speak of him as my kinsman, he's a most notable coward, an infinite

10 and endless liar, an hourly promise-breaker, the owner of no one good quality worthy your lordship's entertainment.

1 *Lord.* It were fit you knew him, lest reposing too far in his virtue which he hath not, he might at some great and trusty business in a main danger fail you.

Bertram. I would I knew in what particular action to try him.

1 *Lord.* None better than to let him fetch off his drum, which you hear him so confidently undertake to do.

2 *Lord.* I, with a troop of Florentines, will suddenly surprise him; such I will have, whom I am sure he knows not from the enemy: we will bind and hoodwink him so, that he shall suppose no other but that he is carried into the leaguer of the adversaries, when we bring him to our own tents...Be but your lordship present at his examination—if he do not, for the promise of his life and in the highest compulsion of base fear, offer to betray you and deliver all the intelligence in his power against you, and that with the divine forfeit of his soul upon oath, never trust my judgement in any thing. 20 30

1 *Lord.* O, for the love of laughter, let him fetch his drum. He says he has a stratagem for't: when your lordship sees the bottom of his success in't, and to what metal this counterfeit lump of ore will be melted, if you give him not John Drum's entertainment, your inclining cannot be removed. Here he comes.

PAROLLES draws near, affecting melancholy

(2 *Lord.* O, for the love of laughter, hinder not the honour of his design, let him fetch off his drum in any hand.

Bertram. How now, monsieur! this drum sticks sorely in your disposition. 40

1 *Lord.* A pox on't, let it go, 'tis but a drum.

Parolles. 'But a drum!' is't 'but a drum'? A drum so lost! There was excellent command—to charge in with our horse upon our own wings, and to rend our own soldiers!

1 *Lord.* That was not to be blamed in the command of the service: it was a disaster of war that Cæsar himself could not have prevented, if he had been there to
50 command.

Bertram. Well, we cannot greatly condemn our success: some dishonour we had in the loss of that drum: but it is not to be recovered.

Parolles. It might have been recovered.

Bertram. It might, but it is not now.

Parolles. It is to be recovered. But that the merit of service is seldom attributed to the true and exact performer, I would have that drum or another, or 'hic jacet.'

60 *Bertram.* Why, if you have a stomach, to't monsieur: if you think your mystery in stratagem can bring this instrument of honour again into his native quarter, be magnanimous in the enterprise, and go on—I will grace the attempt for a worthy exploit: if you speed well in it, the duke shall both speak of it, and extend to you what further becomes his greatness, even to the utmost syllable of your worthiness.

Parolles. By the hand of a soldier, I will undertake it.

70 *Bertram.* But you must not now slumber in it.

Parolles. I'll about it this evening, and I will presently pen down my dilemmas, encourage myself in my certainty, put myself into my mortal preparation; and by midnight look to hear further from me.

Bertram. May I be bold to acquaint his grace you are gone about it?

Parolles. I know not what the success will be, my lord, but the attempt I vow.

Bertram. I know, th'art valiant—and, to the possibility of thy soldiership, will subscribe for thee...Farewell. 80

Parolles. I love not many words. [*he goes*

2 *Lord*. No more than a fish loves water....Is not this a strange fellow, my lord, that so confidently seems to undertake this business—which he knows is not to be done—damns himself to do, and dares better be damned than to do't.

1 *Lord*. You do not know him, my lord, as we do. Certain it is, that he will steal himself into a man's favour and for a week escape a great deal of discoveries, but when you find him out you have him ever after. 90

Bertram. Why, do you think he will make no deed at all of this that so seriously he does address himself unto?

2 *Lord*. None in the world, but return with an invention, and clap upon you two or three probable lies: but we have almost embossed him, you shall see his fall to-night; for indeed he is not for your lordship's respect.

1 *Lord*. We'll make you some sport with the fox ere we case him. He was first smoked by the old lord Lafeu. When his disguise and he is parted, tell me what a sprat you shall find him, which you shall see this very night. 100

2 *Lord*. I must go look my twigs, he shall be caught.

Bertram. Your brother, he shall go along with me.

2 *Lord*. As't please your lordship: I'll leave you. [*he goes*

Bertram. Now will I lead you to the house, and show you
The lass I spoke of.

1 *Lord*. But you say she's honest.

Bertram. That's all the fault: I spoke with her but once,
And found her wondrous cold, but I sent to her,
By this same coxcomb that we have i'th' wind,

Tokens and letters which she did re-send,
110 And this is all I have done...She's a fair creature,
Will you go see her?
  1 *Lord.* With all my heart, my lord.
[*they walk away*

[3.7.] *A room in the Widow's house at Florence*

Enter HELENA *and* WIDOW

Helena. If you misdoubt me that I am not she,
I know not how I shall assure you further,
But I shall lose the grounds I work upon.
  Widow. Though my estate be fall'n, I was well born,
Nothing acquainted with these businesses,
And would not put my reputation now
In any staining act.
  Helena. Nor would I wish you.
First give me trust the count he is my husband,
And what to your sworn counsel I have spoken
10 Is so from word to word; and then you cannot,
By the good aid that I of you shall borrow,
Err in bestowing it.
  Widow. I should believe you,
For you have showed me that which well approves
Y'are great in fortune.
  Helena. Take this purse of gold,
And let me buy your friendly help thus far,
Which I will over-pay and pay again
When I have found it....[*she gives it*] The count he wooes your daughter,
Lays down his wanton siege before her beauty,
Resolved to carry her: let her in fine consent,
20 As we'll direct her how 'tis best to bear it:
Now his important blood will nought deny

That she'll demand: a ring the county wears,
That downward hath succeeded in his house
From son to son, some four or five descents
Since the first father wore it: this ring he holds
In most rich choice; yet in his idle fire,
To buy his will, it would not seem too dear,
Howe'er repented after.

Widow. Now I see
The bottom of your purpose.

Helena. You see it lawful then. It is no more 30
But that your daughter, ere she seems as won,
Desires this ring; appoints him an encounter;
In fine, delivers me to fill the time,
Herself most chastely absent: after this,
To marry her, I'll add three thousand crowns
To what is past already.

Widow. I have yielded:
Instruct my daughter how she shall persever,
That time and place with this deceit so lawful
May prove coherent. Every night he comes
With musics of all sorts and songs composed 40
To her unworthiness: it nothing steads us
To chide him from our eaves, for he persists
As if his life lay on't.

Helena. Why then to-night
Let us assay our plot, which if it speed,
Is wicked meaning in a lawful deed,
And lawful meaning in a lawful act,
Where both not sin, and yet a sinful fact:
But let's about it. [*they go*

[4. 1.] *A field near the Florentine camp*

The second French Lord, 'with five or six other soldiers, in ambush'; one bearing a drum

2 *Lord.* He can come no other way but by this hedge-corner...When you sally upon him, speak what terrible language you will: though you understand it not yourselves, no matter: for we must not seem to understand him, unless some one among us whom we must produce for an interpreter.

1 *Soldier.* Good captain, let me be th'interpreter.

2 *Lord.* Art not acquainted with him? knows he not thy voice?

10 1 *Soldier.* No, sir, I warrant you.

2 *Lord.* But what linsey-woolsey hast thou to speak to us again?

1 *Soldier.* E'en such as you speak to me.

2 *Lord.* He must think us some band of strangers i'the adversary's entertainment. Now he hath a smack of all neighbouring languages; therefore we must every one be a man of his own fancy; not to know what we speak one to another, so we seem to know, is to know straight our purpose: choughs' language, gabble enough,
20 and good enough. As for you, interpreter, you must seem very politic. But couch, ho! here he comes—to beguile two hours in a sleep, and then to return and swear the lies he forges.

PAROLLES comes along the hedge

Parolles. Ten o'clock: within these three hours 'twill be time enough to go home. What shall I say I have done? It must be a very plausive invention that carries it. They begin to smoke me, and disgraces have of late knocked too often at my door...I find my tongue is too foolhardy, but my heart hath the fear of Mars before it and of his creatures, not daring the reports of my 30 tongue.

2 Lord. This is the first truth that e'er thine own tongue was guilty of.

Parolles. What the devil should move me to undertake the recovery of this drum, being not ignorant of the impossibility, and knowing I had no such purpose? I must give myself some hurts, and say I got them in exploit...Yet slight ones will not carry it. They will say, 'Came you off with so little?' And great ones I dare not give. Wherefore, what's the instance? Tongue, I must 40 put you into a butter-woman's mouth, and buy myself another of Bajazet's †mate, if you prattle me into these perils.

2 Lord. Is it possible he should know what he is, and be that he is?

Parolles. I would the cutting of my garments would serve the turn, or the breaking of my Spanish sword.

2 Lord. We cannot afford you so.

Parolles. Or the baring of my beard, and to say it was in stratagem.

2 Lord. 'Twould not do. 50

Parolles. Or to drown my clothes, and say I was stripped.

2 Lord. Hardly serve.

Parolles. Though I swore I leaped from the window of the citadel—

2 Lord. How deep?

Parolles. Thirty fathom.

2 Lord. Three great oaths would scarce make that be believed.

Parolles. I would I had any drum of the enemy's, 60 I would swear I recovered it.

(2 *Lord.* You shall hear one anon.

Parolles. A drum now of the enemy's—

[*they strike up the drum and rush upon him*

2 *Lord.* Throca movousus, cargo, cargo, cargo.

All. Cargo, cargo, cargo, villianda par corbo, cargo.

Parolles. O! ransom, ransom! Do not hide mine eyes.

[*they bind him and blindfold his eyes in his scarf*

1 *Soldier.* Boskos thromuldo boskos.

Parolles. I know you are the Muskos' regiment.
And I shall lose my life for want of language.
70 If there be here German, or Dane, low Dutch,
Italian, or French, let him speak to me,
I will discover that which shall undo
The Florentine.

1 *Soldier.* Boskos vauvado—
I understand thee, and can speak thy tongue:
Kerelybonto, sir,
Betake thee to thy faith, for seventeen poniards
Are at thy bosom.

Parolles. O!

1 *Soldier.* O, pray, pray, pray!
Manka revania dulche.

2 *Lord.* Oscorbidulchos volivorco.

80 1 *Soldier.* The general is content to spare thee yet,
And, hoodwinked as thou art, will lead thee on
To gather from thee. Haply thou mayst inform
Something to save thy life.

Parolles. O, let me live!
And all the secrets of our camp I'll show,
Their force, their purposes: nay, I'll speak that
Which you will wonder at.

1 *Soldier.* But wilt thou faithfully?

Parolles. If I do not, damn me.

1 *Soldier.* Acordo linta.

Come on, thou art granted space.

[*the interpreter and other soldiers carry off Parolles, the drum beating*

2 *Lord*. Go, tell the Count Rousillon, and my brother,
We have caught the woodcock, and will keep him muffled 90
Till we do hear from them.

2 *Soldier*. Captain, I will.

2 *Lord*. A' will betray us all unto ourselves—
Inform 'em that.

2 *Soldier*. So I will, sir.

2 *Lord*. Till then, I'll keep him dark, and safely locked. [*they go*

[4. 2.] *A room in the Widow's house at Florence*

BERTRAM *and* DIANA

Bertram. They told me that your name was Fontibell.

Diana. No, my good lord, Diana.

Bertram. Titled goddess!
And worth it, with addition...But, fair soul,
In your fine frame hath love no quality?
If the quick fire of youth light not your mind,
You are no maiden but a monument.
When you are dead, you should be such a one
As you are now, for you are cold and stern;
And now you should be as your mother was
When your sweet self was got. 10

Diana. She then was honest.

Bertram. So should you be.

Diana. No:
My mother did but duty—such, my lord,
As you owe to your wife.

Bertram. No more o' that:
I prithee, do not strive against my vows:
I was compelled to her, but I love thee
By love's own sweet constraint, and will for ever
Do thee all rights of service.
Diana. Ay, so you serve us
Till we serve you: but when you have our roses,
You barely leave our thorns to prick ourselves,
20 And mock us with our bareness.
Bertram. How have I sworn!
Diana. 'Tis not the many oaths that makes the truth,
But the plain single vow that is vowed true:
What is not holy, that we swear not by,
But take the High'st to witness: then, pray you, tell me,
If I should swear by Jove's great attributes
I loved you dearly, would you believe my oaths
When I did love you ill? This has no holding,
To swear by Him whom I protest to love,
That I will work against Him. Therefore your oaths
30 Are words and poor, conditions but unsealed,
At least in my opinion.
Bertram. Change it, change it;
Be not so holy-cruel: love is holy,
And my integrity ne'er knew the crafts
That you do charge men with...Stand no more off,
But give thyself unto my sick desires,
Who then recover. Say thou art mine, and ever
My love as it begins shall so persever.
Diana. †I see that men make rope's in such a scarre,
That we'll forsake ourselves. Give me that ring.
40 *Bertram.* I'll lend it thee, my dear; but have no power
To give it from me.
Diana. Will you not, my lord?

Bertram. It is an honour 'longing to our house,
Bequeathèd down from many ancestors,
Which were the greatest obloquy i'th' world
In me to lose.
Diana. Mine honour's such a ring,
My chastity's the jewel of our house,
Bequeathèd down from many ancestors,
Which were the greatest obloquy i'th' world
In me to lose. Thus your own proper wisdom
Brings in the champion Honour on my part, 50
Against your vain assault.
Bertram. Here, take my ring.
My house, mine honour, yea, my life be thine,
And I'll be bid by thee. [*she takes the ring*
Diana. When midnight comes, knock at my chamber-window:
I'll order take my mother shall not hear.
Now will I charge you in the band of truth,
When you have conquered my yet maiden bed,
Remain there but an hour, nor speak to me:
My reasons are most strong, and you shall know them
When back again this ring shall be delivered: 60
And on your finger in the night I'll put
Another ring, that what in time proceeds
May token to the future our past deeds.
Adieu till then, then fail not: you have won
A wife of me, though there my hope be done.
Bertram. A heaven on earth I have won by wooing thee.
Diana. For which live long to thank both heaven and me! [*he goes*
You may so in the end.
My mother told me just how he would woo,
As if she sat in's heart. She says all men 70

Have the like oaths: he had sworn to marry me
When his wife's dead; therefore I'll lie with him
When I am buried. Since Frenchmen are so braid,
Marry that will, I live and die a maid:
Only in this disguise I think't no sin
To cozen him that would unjustly win. [*she goes*

[4. 3.] *A tent in the Florentine camp*

The two French Lords, and two or three soldiers

2 *Lord.* You have not given him his mother's letter?

1 *Lord.* I have delivered it an hour since. There is something in't that stings his nature; for on the reading it he changed almost into another man.

2 *Lord.* He has much worthy blame laid upon him for shaking off so good a wife and so sweet a lady.

1 *Lord.* Especially he hath incurred the everlasting displeasure of the king, who had even tuned his bounty to sing happiness to him. I will tell you a thing, but
10 you shall let it dwell darkly with you.

2 *Lord.* When you have spoken it, 'tis dead, and I am the grave of it.

1 *Lord.* He hath perverted a young gentlewoman here in Florence, of a most chaste renown, and this night he fleshes his will in the spoil of her honour: he hath given her his monumental ring, and thinks himself made in the unchaste composition.

2 *Lord.* Now, God †lay our rebellion! as we are ourselves, what things are we!

20 1 *Lord.* Merely our own traitors. And as in the common course of all treasons, we still see them reveal themselves, till they attain to their abhorred ends; so he that in this action contrives against his own nobility in his proper stream o'erflows himself.

2 *Lord.* Is it not meant damnable in us, to be trumpeters of our unlawful intents? We shall not then have his company to-night?

1 *Lord.* Not till after midnight; for he is dieted to his hour.

2 *Lord.* That approaches apace: I would gladly have 30 him see his company anatomized, that he might take a measure of his own judgement, wherein so curiously he had set this counterfeit.

1 *Lord.* We will not meddle with him till he come; for his presence must be the whip of the other.

2 *Lord.* In the mean time, what hear you of these wars?

1 *Lord.* I hear there is an overture of peace.

2 *Lord.* Nay, I assure you, a peace concluded.

1 *Lord.* What will Count Rousillon do then? will he travel higher, or return again into France? 40

2 *Lord.* I perceive, by this demand, you are not altogether of his council.

1 *Lord.* Let it be forbid, sir, so should I be a great deal of his act.

2 *Lord.* Sir, his wife some two months since fled from his house: her pretence is a pilgrimage to S. Jaques le Grand; which holy undertaking with most austere sanctimony she accomplished: and, there residing, the tenderness of her nature became as a prey to her grief; in fine, made a groan of her last breath, and now she 50 sings in heaven.

1 *Lord.* How is this justified?

2 *Lord.* The stronger part of it by her own letters, which makes her story true, even to the point of her death: her death itself, which could not be her office to say is come, was faithfully confirmed by the rector of the place.

1 *Lord.* Hath the count all this intelligence?

2 *Lord.* Ay, and the particular confirmations, point
60 from point, to the full arming of the verity.

1 *Lord.* I am heartily sorry that he'll be glad of this.

2 *Lord.* How mightily sometimes we make us comforts of our losses!

1 *Lord.* And how mightily some other times we drown our gain in tears! The great dignity that his valour hath here acquired for him shall at home be encountered with a shame as ample.

2 *Lord.* The web of our life is of a mingled yarn, good and ill together: our virtues would be proud, if our
70 faults whipped them not, and our crimes would despair, if they were not cherished by our virtues.

A servant comes in

How now! where's your master?

Servant. He met the duke in the street, sir, of whom he hath taken a solemn leave; his lordship will next morning for France. The duke hath offered him letters of commendations to the king.

2 *Lord.* They shall be no more than needful there, if they were more than they can commend.

1 *Lord.* They cannot be too sweet for the king's
80 tartness.

BERTRAM enters

Here's his lordship now. How now, my lord, is't not after midnight?

Bertram. I have to-night dispatched sixteen businesses, a month's length a-piece, by an abstract of success: I have congied with the duke, done my adieu with his nearest, buried a wife, mourned for her, writ to my lady mother I am returning, entertained my convoy, and between these main parcels of dispatch, effected many nicer needs: the last was the greatest, but that I have not
90 ended yet.

2 *Lord.* If the business be of any difficulty, and this morning your departure hence, it requires haste of your lordship.

Bertram. I mean, the business is not ended, as fearing to hear of it hereafter...But shall we have this dialogue between the Fool and the Soldier? Come, bring forth this counterfeit module, has deceived me like a double-meaning prophesier.

2 *Lord.* Bring him forth. [*a soldier goes out*] Has sat i'th' stocks all night, poor gallant knave. 100

Bertram. No matter, his heels have deserved it, in usurping his spurs so long. How does he carry himself?

2 *Lord.* I have told your lordship already; the stocks carry him. But to answer you as you would be understood, he weeps like a wench that had shed her milk. He hath confessed himself to Morgan, whom he supposes to be a friar, from the time of his remembrance to this very instant disaster of his setting i'th' stocks: and what think you he hath confessed?

Bertram. Nothing of me, has a'? 110

2 *Lord.* His confession is taken, and it shall be read to his face. If your lordship be in't, as I believe you are, you must have the patience to hear it.

Soldiers bring in PAROLLES, *with his Interpreter*

Bertram. A plague upon him! muffled! he can say nothing of me.

1 *Lord.* Hush! hush! Hoodman comes! Portotartarossa.

Interpreter. He calls for the tortures. What will you say without 'em?

Parolles. I will confess what I know without constraint. If ye pinch me like a pasty, I can say no more. 120

Interpreter. Bosko chimurcho.

1 *Lord.* Boblibindo chicurmurco.

Interpreter. You are a merciful general...Our general bids you answer to what I shall ask you out of a note.

Parolles. And truly, as I hope to live.

Interpreter. 'First demand of him how many horse the duke is strong.' What say you to that?

Parolles. Five or six thousand, but very weak and
130 unserviceable: the troops are all scattered, and the commanders very poor rogues, upon my reputation and credit, and as I hope to live.

Interpreter. Shall I set down your answer so?

Parolles. Do, I'll take the sacrament on't, how and which way you will. [*the interpreter writes*

(*Bertram.* All's one to him. What a past-saving slave is this!

(1 *Lord.* Y'are deceived, my lord, this is Monsieur Parolles, the gallant militarist—that was his own
140 phrase—that had the whole theoric of war in the knot of his scarf, and the practice in the chape of his dagger.

(2 *Lord.* I will never trust a man again for keeping his sword clean, nor believe he can have every thing in him by wearing his apparel neatly.

Interpreter [*looks up*]. Well, that's set down.

Parolles. Five or six thousand horse, I said—I will say true—or thereabouts, set down, for I'll speak truth.

(1 *Lord.* He's very near the truth in this.

(*Bertram.* But I con him no thanks for't, in the nature
150 he delivers it.

Parolles. Poor rogues, I pray you, say.

Interpreter. Well, that's set down.

Parolles. I humbly thank you, sir—a truth's a truth—the rogues are marvellous poor.

Interpreter. 'Demand of him, of what strength they are a-foot.' What say you to that?

Parolles. By my troth, sir, if I were to †leave this

present hour, I will tell true. Let me see—Spurio a hundred and fifty, Sebastian so many, Corambus so many, Jaques so many; Guiltian, Cosmo, Lodowick, 160 and Gratii, two hundred and fifty each: mine own company, Chitopher, Vaumond, Bentii, two hundred and fifty each: so that the muster-file, rotten and sound, upon my life, amounts not to fifteen thousand poll, half of the which dare not shake the snow from off their cassocks, lest they shake themselves to pieces.

⟨*Bertram*. What shall be done to him?

⟨1 *Lord*. Nothing, but let him have thanks. [*to interpreter*] Demand of him my condition, and what credit I have with the duke. 170

Interpreter. Well, that's set down.
'You shall demand of him, whether one Captain Dumain be i'th' camp, a Frenchman: what his reputation is with the duke, what his valour, honesty, and expertness in wars; or whether he thinks it were not possible, with well-weighing sums of gold, to corrupt him to a revolt.'
What say you to this? what do you know of it?

Parolles. I beseech you, let me answer to the particular of the inter'gatories. Demand them singly. 180

Interpreter. Do you know this Captain Dumain?

Parolles. I know him, a' was a botcher's prentice in Paris, from whence he was whipped for getting the shrieve's fool with child—a dumb innocent, that could not say him nay. [*Dumain is about to strike him*

⟨*Bertram*. Nay, by your leave, hold your hands, though I know his brains are forfeit to the next tile that falls.

Interpreter. Well, is this captain in the Duke of Florence's camp? 190

Parolles. Upon my knowledge he is, and lousy.

(1 *Lord.* Nay, look not so upon me; we shall hear of your lordship anon.

Interpreter. What is his reputation with the duke?

Parolles. The duke knows him for no other but a poor officer of mine, and writ to me this other day to turn him out o'th' band. I think I have his letter in my pocket.

Interpreter. Marry, we'll search. [*he does so*

200 *Parolles.* In good sadness, I do not know—either it is there, or it is upon a file with the duke's other letters in my tent.

Interpreter. Here 'tis, here's a paper, shall I read it to you?

Parolles. I do not know if it be it or no.

(*Bertram.* Our interpreter does it well.

(1 *Lord.* Excellently.

Interpreter [*reads the paper*]. 'Dian, the count's a fool, and full of gold'—

Parolles. That is not the duke's letter, sir; that is an

210 advertisement to a proper maid in Florence, one Diana, to take heed of the allurement of one Count Rousillon, a foolish idle boy: but for all that very ruttish. I pray you, sir, put it up again.

Interpreter. Nay, I'll read it first, by your favour.

Parolles. My meaning in't, I protest, was very honest in the behalf of the maid: for I knew the young count to be a dangerous and lascivious boy, who is a whale to virginity, and devours up all the fry it finds.

(*Bertram.* Damnable both-sides rogue!

220 *Interpreter* [*reads*]. 'When he swears oaths, bid him drop gold, and take it;

After he scores, he never pays the score:
Half won is match well made, match and well make it,
He ne'er pays after-debts, take it before.

And say a soldier, Dian, told thee this:
Men are to mell with, boys are but to kiss:
For count of this, the count's a fool, I know it,
Who pays before, but not when he does owe it.
Thine, as he vowed to thee in thine ear,
PAROLLES.'

(*Bertram*. He shall be whipped through the army with 230
this rhyme in's forehead.

(2 *Lord*. This is your devoted friend, sir, the manifold
linguist, and the armipotent soldier.

(*Bertram*. I could endure any thing before but a cat,
and now he's a cat to me.

Interpreter. I perceive, sir, by the general's looks, we
shall be fain to hang you.

Parolles. My life, sir, in any case! not that I am afraid
to die, but that my offences being many I would repent
out the remainder of nature. Let me live, sir, in a 240
dungeon, i'th' stocks, or any where, so I may live.

Interpreter. We'll see what may be done, so you
confess freely; therefore, once more to this Captain
Dumain: you have answered to his reputation with the
duke and to his valour: what is his honesty?

Parolles. He will steal, sir, an egg out of a cloister:
for rapes and ravishments he parallels Nessus. He
professes not keeping of oaths, in breaking 'em he
is stronger than Hercules. He will lie, sir, with such
volubility, that you would think truth were a fool: 250
drunkenness is his best virtue, for he will be swine-
drunk, and in his sleep he does little harm, save to his
bed-clothes about him; but they know his conditions
and lay him in straw. I have but little more to say, sir,
of his honesty—he has every thing that an honest man
should not have; what an honest man should have, he
has nothing.

(1 *Lord*. I begin to love him for this.

(*Bertram*. For this description of thine honesty? A
260 pox upon him for me, he's more and more a cat.

Interpreter. What say you to his expertness in war?

Parolles. Faith, sir, has led the drum before the English tragedians; to belie him, I will not, and more of his soldiership I know not, except in that country he had the honour to be the officer at a place there called Mile-end, to instruct for the doubling of files. I would do the man what honour I can, but of this I am not certain.

(1 *Lord*. He hath out-villained villainy so far, that
270 the rarity redeems him.

(*Bertram*. A pox on him, he's a cat still.

Interpreter. His qualities being at this poor price, I need not to ask you, if gold will corrupt him to revolt.

Parolles. Sir, for a cardecue he will sell the fee-simple of his salvation, the inheritance of it; and cut th'entail from all remainders, and a perpetual succession for it perpetually.

Interpreter. What's his brother, the other Captain Dumain?

280 (2 *Lord*. Why does he ask him of me?

Interpreter. What's he?

Parolles. E'en a crow o'th' same nest; not altogether so great as the first in goodness, but greater a great deal in evil. He excels his brother for a coward, yet his brother is reputed one of the best that is. In a retreat he outruns any lackey; marry, in coming on he has the cramp.

Interpreter. If your life be saved, will you undertake to betray the Florentine?

290 *Parolles*. Ay, and the captain of his horse, Count Rousillon.

Interpreter. I'll whisper with the general, and know his pleasure.

(*Parolles.* I'll no more drumming, a plague of all drums. Only to seem to deserve well, and to beguile the supposition of that lascivious young boy, the count, have I run into this danger: yet, who would have suspected an ambush where I was taken?

Interpreter. There is no remedy, sir, but you must die: the general says, you that have so traitorously discovered 300 the secrets of your army and made such pestiferous reports of men very nobly held, can serve the world for no honest use; therefore you must die. Come, headsman, off with his head.

Parolles. O Lord, sir, let me live, or let me see my death!

Interpreter. That shall you, and take your leave of all your friends... [*he plucks the scarf from his eyes*
So, look about you. Know you any here?

Bertram. Good morrow, noble captain. 310

2 *Lord.* God bless you, Captain Parolles.

1 *Lord.* God save you, noble captain.

2 *Lord.* Captain, what greeting will you to my Lord Lafeu? I am for France.

1 *Lord.* Good captain, will you give me a copy of the sonnet you writ to Diana in behalf of the Count Rousillon? an I were not a very coward, I'd compel it of you, but fare you well.

[*Bertram and the Lords leave the tent*

Interpreter. You are undone, captain, all but your scarf—that has a knot on't yet. 320

Parolles. Who cannot be crushed with a plot?

Interpreter. If you could find out a country where but women were that had received so much shame, you might begin an impudent nation. Fare ye well, sir, I am for France too, we shall speak of you there. [*he goes*

Parolles. Yet am I thankful: if my heart were great,
'Twould burst at this...Captain I'll be no more,
But I will eat and drink, and sleep as soft
330 As captain shall: simply the thing I am
Shall make me live. Who knows himself a braggart,
Let him fear this; for it will come to pass
That every braggart shall be found an ass.
Rust, sword! cool, blushes! and, Parolles, live
Safest in shame! being fooled, by foolery thrive!
There's place and means for every man alive.
I'll after them. [*he goes*

[4. 4.] *The room in the Widow's house at Florence*

HELENA, WIDOW, and DIANA

Helena. That you may well perceive I have not wronged you,
One of the greatest in the Christian world
Shall be my surety: 'fore whose throne 'tis needful,
Ere I can perfect mine intents, to kneel.
Time was, I did him a desiréd office,
Dear almost as his life, which gratitude
Through flinty Tartar's bosom would peep forth,
And answer, thanks. I duly am informed
His grace is at Marseillës, to which place
10 We have convenient convoy...You must know,
I am supposéd dead: the army breaking,
My husband hies him home, where, heaven aiding,
And by the leave of my good lord the king,
We'll be before our welcome.

Widow. Gentle madam,
You never had a servant to whose trust

Your business was more welcome.

Helena. Nor you, mistress,
Ever a friend whose thoughts more truly labour
To recompense your love: doubt not but heaven
Hath brought me up to be your daughter's dower,
As it hath fated her to be my motive 20
And helper to a husband. But, O strange men,
That can such sweet use make of what they hate,
When saucy trusting of the cozened thoughts
Defiles the pitchy night! so lust doth play
With what it loathes, for that which is away.
But more of this hereafter...You, Diana,
Under my poor instructions yet must suffer
Something in my behalf.

Diana. Let death and honesty
Go with your impositions, I am yours
Upon your will to suffer.

Helena. Yet, I pray you... 30
†But with the word, that time will bring on summer,
When briars shall have leaves as well as thorns,
And be as sweet as sharp...We must away,
Our waggon is prepared, and time revives us.
'All's well that ends well,' still the fine's the crown;
Whate'er the course, the end is the renown. [*they go*

[4. 5.] *A room in the palace of Rousillon*

COUNTESS, LAFEU, and CLOWN

Lafeu. No, no, no, your son was misled with a snipt-taffeta fellow there, whose villanous saffron would have made all the unbaked and doughy youth of a nation in his colour: your daughter-in-law had been alive at this hour, and your son here at home, more advanced by the king than by that red-tailed humble-bee I speak of.

Countess. I would I had not known him—it was the death of the most virtuous gentlewoman that ever nature had praise for creating. If she had partaken of
10 my flesh, and cost me the dearest groans of a mother, I could not have owed her a more rooted love.

Lafeu. 'Twas a good lady, 'twas a good lady. We may pick a thousand salads ere we light on such another herb.

Clown. Indeed, sir, she was the sweet-marjoram of the salad, or rather, the herb of grace.

Lafeu. They are †knot-herbs, you knave, they are nose-herbs.

Clown. I am no great Nebuchadnezzar, sir, I have
20 not much skill in grass.

Lafeu. Whether dost thou profess thyself, a knave or a fool?

Clown. A fool, sir, at a woman's service, and a knave at a man's.

Lafeu. Your distinction?

Clown. I would cozen the man of his wife, and do his service.

Lafeu. So you were a knave at his service, indeed.

Clown. And I would give his wife my bauble, sir,
30 to do her service.

Lafeu. I will subscribe for thee, thou art both knave and fool.

Clown. At your service.

Lafeu. No, no, no.

Clown. Why, sir, if I cannot serve you, I can serve as great a prince as you are.

Lafeu. Who's that? a Frenchman?

Clown. Faith, sir, a' has an English name, but his fisnamy is more hotter in France than there.

40 *Lafeu.* What prince is that?

Clown. The Black Prince, sir, alias the prince of darkness, alias the devil.

Lafeu. Hold thee, there's my purse. I give thee not this to suggest thee from thy master thou talk'st of—serve him still.

Clown. I am a woodland fellow, sir, that always loved a great fire, and the master I speak of ever keeps a good fire. But, sure, he is the prince of the world, let his nobility remain in's court. I am for the house with the narrow gate, which I take to be too little for pomp to 50 enter: some that humble themselves may, but the many will be too chill and tender, and they'll be for the flowery way that leads to the broad gate and the great fire.

Lafeu. Go thy ways, I begin to be aweary of thee, and I tell thee so before, because I would not fall out with thee. Go thy ways, let my horses be well looked to, without any tricks.

Clown. If I put any tricks upon 'em, sir, they shall be jades' tricks, which are their own right by the law 60 of nature. [*he goes*

Lafeu. A shrewd knave and an unhappy.

Countess. So a' is. My lord that's gone made himself much sport out of him: by his authority he remains here, which he thinks is a patent for his sauciness, and indeed he has no pace, but runs where he will.

Lafeu. I like him well, 'tis not amiss...And I was about to tell you, since I heard of the good lady's death and that my lord your son was upon his return home, I moved the king my master to speak in the behalf of 70 my daughter—which, in the minority of them both, his majesty out of a self-gracious remembrance did first propose. His highness hath promised me to do it—and, to stop up the displeasure he hath conceived against your son, there is no fitter matter. How does your ladyship like it?

Countess. With very much content, my lord, and I wish it happily effected.

Lafeu. His highness comes post from Marseilles, of
80 as able body as when he numbered thirty—a' will be here to-morrow, or I am deceived by him that in such intelligence hath seldom failed.

Countess. It rejoices me, that I hope I shall see him ere I die. I have letters that my son will be here to-night: I shall beseech your lordship to remain with me till they meet together.

Lafeu. Madam, I was thinking with what manners I might safely be admitted.

Countess. You need but plead your honourable
90 privilege.

Lafeu. Lady, of that I have made a bold charter, but I thank my God it holds yet.

CLOWN *returns*

Clown. O madam, yonder's my lord your son with a patch of velvet on's face—whether there be a scar under't or no, the velvet knows, but 'tis a goodly patch of velvet—his left cheek is a cheek of two pile and a half, but his right cheek is worn bare.

Lafeu. A scar nobly got, or a noble scar, is a good livery of honour—so belike is that.

100 *Clown*. But it is your carbonadoed face.

Lafeu. Let us go see your son, I pray you. I long to talk with the young noble soldier.

Clown. Faith, there's a dozen of 'em, with delicate fine hats and most courteous feathers, which bow the head, and nod at every man. [*they go*

[5. 1.] *A street in Marseilles*

'*HELENA, WIDOW, and DIANA, with two attendants*'

Helena. But this exceeding posting day and night
Must wear your spirits low—we cannot help it:
But since you have made the days and nights as one,
To wear your gentle limbs in my affairs,
Be bold you do so grow in my requital
As nothing can unroot you.

'*Enter a gentle astringer*'

In happy time—
This man may help me to his majesty's ear,
If he would spend his power. God save you, sir.
Gentleman. And you.
Helena. Sir, I have seen you in the court of France. 10
Gentleman. I have been sometimes there.
Helena. I do presume, sir, that you are not fall'n
From the report that goes upon your goodness,
And therefore, goaded with most sharp occasions,
Which lay nice manners by, I put you to
The use of your own virtues, for the which
I shall continue thankful.
Gentleman. What's your will?
Helena. That it will please you
To give this poor petition to the king,
And aid me with that store of power you have 20
To come into his presence. [*she gives him a paper*
Gentleman. The king's not here.
Helena. Not here, sir!
Gentleman. Not indeed,
He hence removed last night, and with more haste
Than is his use.

Widow. Lord, how we lose our pains!
Helena. 'All's well that ends well' yet,
Though time seem so adverse and means unfit....
I do beseech you, whither is he gone?
Gentleman. Marry, as I take it, to Rousillon,
Whither I am going.
Helena. I do beseech you, sir,
30 Since you are like to see the king before me,
Commend the paper to his gracious hand,
Which I presume shall render you no blame
But rather make you thank your pains for it.
I will come after you with what good speed
Our means will make us means.
Gentleman. This I'll do for you.
Helena. And you shall find yourself to be well thanked,
Whate'er falls more. We must to horse again.
Go, go, provide. [*they hurry away*

[5. 2.] *In the park near the palace of Rousillon*

CLOWN *and* PAROLLES

Parolles. Good Master Lavache, give my Lord Lafeu this letter. I have ere now, sir, been better known to you, when I have held familiarity with fresher clothes; but I am now, sir, muddied in fortune's mood, and smell somewhat strong of her strong displeasure.

Clown. Truly, fortune's displeasure is but sluttish, if it smell so strongly as thou speak'st of: I will henceforth eat no fish of fortune's butt'ring. Prithee, allow the wind.

10 *Parolles.* Nay, you need not to stop your nose, sir; I spake but by a metaphor.

Clown. Indeed, sir, if your metaphor stink, I will

stop my nose, or against any man's metaphor. Prithee, get thee further.

Parolles. Pray you, sir, deliver me this paper.

Clown. Foh! prithee, stand away: a paper from fortune's close-stool to give to a nobleman! Look, here he comes himself.

LAFEU approaches

Here is a pur of fortune's, sir, or of fortune's cat—but not a musk-cat—that has fallen into the unclean 20 fishpond of her displeasure, and, as he says, is muddied withal: pray you, sir, use the carp as you may, for he looks like a poor, decayed, †ingenerous, foolish, rascally knave. I do pity his distress in my similes of comfort, and leave him to your lordship. [*he goes off*

Parolles. My lord, I am a man whom fortune hath cruelly scratched.

Lafeu. And what would you have me to do? 'tis too late to pare her nails now. Wherein have you played the knave with fortune, that she should scratch you, who 30 of herself is a good lady and would not have knaves thrive long under her? There's a cardecue for you [*he gives him a coin*]: let the justices make you and fortune friends; I am for other business. [*he passes on*

Parolles. I beseech your honour to hear me one single word.

Lafeu [*turns*]. You beg a single penny more: come, you shall ha't—save your word.

[*he gives him another coin*

Parolles. My name, my good lord, is Parolles.

Lafeu. You beg more than one word then. Cox my 40 passion! give me your hand...How does your drum?

Parolles. O my good lord, you were the first that found me.

Lafeu. Was I, in sooth? and I was the first that lost thee.

Parolles. It lies in you, my lord, to bring me in some grace, for you did bring me out.

Lafeu. Out upon thee, knave! dost thou put upon me at once both the office of God and the devil? one
50 brings thee in grace and the other brings thee out. [*trumpets sound*] The king's coming, I know by his trumpets. Sirrah, inquire further after me. I had talk of you last night—though you are a fool and a knave, you shall eat. Go to, follow. [*he hurries away*

Parolles. I praise God for you. [*he follows*

[5. 3.] *A room in the palace of Rousillon*

Flourish. Enter KING, COUNTESS, LAFEU, *lords, gentlemen, guards, &c.*

King. We lost a jewel of her, and our esteem
Was made much poorer by it: but your son,
As mad in folly, lacked the sense to know
Her estimation home.

Countess. 'Tis past, my liege,
And I beseech your majesty to make it
Natural rebellion, done i'th' blaze of youth,
When oil and fire, too strong for reason's force,
O'erbears it and burns on.

King. My honoured lady,
I have forgiven and forgotten all,
10 Though my revenges were high bent upon him,
And watched the time to shoot.

Lafeu. This I must say—
But first I beg my pardon—the young lord
Did to his majesty, his mother and his lady
Offence of mighty note; but to himself

The greatest wrong of all. He lost a wife
Whose beauty did astonish the survey
Of richest eyes, whose words all ears took captive,
Whose dear perfection hearts that scorned to serve
Humbly called mistress.

King. Praising what is lost
Makes the remembrance dear. Well, call him hither— 20
We are reconciled, and the first view shall kill
All repetition: let him not ask our pardon,
The nature of his great offence is dead,
And deeper than oblivion we do bury
Th'incensing relics of it. Let him approach,
A stranger, no offender; and inform him
So 'tis our will he should.

Gentleman. I shall, my liege. [*he goes out*

King. What says he to your daughter? have you spoke?

Lafeu. All that he is hath reference to your highness.

King. Then shall we have a match. I have letters sent me, 30
That sets him high in fame.

BERTRAM enters and stands by the door, awaiting his summons

Lafeu. He looks well on't.

King. I am not a day of season,
For thou mayst see a sunshine and a hail
In me at once: but to the brightest beams
Distracted clouds give way—so stand thou forth,
The time is fair again.

Bertram [*kneels before him*]. My high-repented blames,
Dear sovereign pardon to me.

King. All is whole,

Not one word more of the consumèd time.
Let's take the instant by the forward top:
40 For we are old, and on our quick'st decrees
Th'inaudible and noiseless foot of Time
Steals ere we can effect them. You remember
The daughter of this lord?
Bertram. Admiringly, my liege. At first
I stuck my choice upon her, ere my heart
Durst make too bold a herald of my tongue:
Where the impression of mine eye infixing,
Contempt his scornful perspective did lend me,
Which warped the line of every other favour,
50 Scorned a fair colour or expressed it stol'n,
Extended or contracted all proportions
To a most hideous object. Thence it came
That she whom all men praised and whom myself,
Since I have lost, have loved, was in mine eye
The dust that did offend it.
King. Well excused:
That thou didst love her, strikes some scores away
From the great compt: but love that comes too late,
Like a remorseful pardon slowly carried,
To the great sender turns a sour offence,
60 Crying 'That's good that's gone'...Our rash faults
Make trivial price of serious things we have,
Not knowing them, until we know their grave.
Oft our displeasures, to ourselves unjust,
Destroy our friends and after weep their dust:
Our own love waking cries to see what's done,
While shameful hate sleeps out the afternoon.
Be this sweet Helen's knell, and now forget her.
Send forth your amorous token for fair Maudlin.
The main consents are had, and here we'll stay
70 To see our widower's second marriage-day.

Countess. Which better than the first, O dear heaven, bless!
Or, ere they meet, in me, O nature, cesse!
Lafeu. Come on, my son, in whom my house's name
Must be digested, give a favour from you,
To sparkle in the spirits of my daughter,
That she may quickly come....[*Bertram gives a ring*]
By my old beard,
And every hair that's on't, Helen that's dead
Was a sweet creature: such a ring as this,
The last that e'er I took her leave at court,
I saw upon her finger.
Bertram. Hers it was not. 80
King. Now pray you, let me see it; for mine eye,
While I was speaking, oft was fastened to't...
[*he takes it from Lafeu and sets it upon his finger*
This ring was mine, and when I gave it Helen
I bade her, if her fortunes ever stood
Necessitied to help, that by this token
I would relieve her. Had you that craft, to reave her
Of what should stead her most?
Bertram. My gracious sovereign,
Howe'er it pleases you to take it so,
The ring was never hers.
Countess. Son, on my life,
I have seen her wear it, and she reckoned it 90
At her life's rate.
Lafeu. I am sure I saw her wear it.
Bertram. You are deceived, my lord, she never saw it:
In Florence was it from a casement thrown me,
Wrapped in a paper, which contained the name
Of her that threw it: noble she was, and thought
I stood ungaged: but when I had subscribed

To mine own fortune and informed her fully
I could not answer in that course of honour
As she had made the overture, she ceased
100 In heavy satisfaction and would never
Receive the ring again.
King. Plutus himself,
That knows the tinct and multiplying med'cine,
Hath not in nature's mystery more science
Than I have in this ring. 'Twas mine, 'twas Helen's,
Whoever gave it you: then, if you know
That you are well acquainted with yourself,
Confess 'twas hers, and by what rough enforcement
You got it from her. She called the saints to surety,
That she would never put it from her finger,
110 Unless she gave it to yourself in bed—
Where you have never come—or sent it us
Upon her great disaster.
Bertram. She never saw it.
King. Thou speak'st it falsely, as I love mine honour;
And mak'st conjectural fears to come into me,
Which I would fain shut out. If it should prove
That thou art so inhuman—'twill not prove so...
And yet I know not—thou didst hate her deadly,
And she is dead, which nothing but to close
Her eyes myself could win me to believe,
120 More than to see this ring. Take him away.
[*guards seize Bertram*
My fore-past proofs, howe'er the matter fall,
Shall tax my fears of little vanity,
Having vainly feared too little. Away with him,
We'll sift this matter further.
Bertram. If you shall prove
This ring was ever hers, you shall as easy

Prove that I husbanded her bed in Florence,
Where yet she never was. [*the guards lead him away*
King. I am wrapped in dismal thinkings.

A gentleman enters and presents a paper

Gentleman. Gracious sovereign,
Whether I have been to blame or no, I know not,
Here's a petition from a Florentine, 130
Who hath for four or five removes come short
To tender it herself. I undertook it,
Vanquished thereto by the fair grace and speech
Of the poor suppliant, who by this I know
Is here attending: her business looks in her
With an importing visage, and she told me,
In a sweet verbal brief, it did concern
Your highness with herself.
King [*reads*]. 'Upon his many protestations to marry me when his wife was dead, I blush to say it, he won 140 me. Now is the Count Rousillon a widower, his vows are forfeited to me, and my honour's paid to him. He stole from Florence, taking no leave, and I follow him to his country for justice: grant it me, O king! in you it best lies, otherwise a seducer flourishes and a poor maid is undone. DIANA CAPULET.'
Lafeu. I will buy me a son-in-law in a fair, and toll for this. I'll none of him.
King. The heavens have thought well on thee, Lafeu,
To bring forth this discov'ry. Seek these suitors... 150
[*the gentleman goes*
Go, speedily and bring again the count.
[*attendants hurry forth*
I am afeard the life of Helen, lady,
Was foully snatched.
Countess. Now, justice on the doers!

The guards return with BERTRAM

King. I wonder, sir, sith wives are monsters to you,
And that you fly them as you swear them lordship,
Yet you desire to marry.

The gentleman returns with WIDOW *and* DIANA

What woman's that?

Diana. I am, my lord, a wretched Florentine,
Derivéd from the ancient Capulet.
My suit, as I do understand, you know,
160 And therefore know how far I may be pitied.

Widow. I am her mother, sir, whose age and honour
Both suffer under this complaint we bring,
And both shall cease, without your remedy.

King. Come hither, count—do you know these women?

Bertram. My lord, I neither can nor will deny
But that I know them. Do they charge me further?

Diana. Why do you look so strange upon your wife?

Bertram. She's none of mine, my lord.

Diana. If you shall marry,
You give away this hand, and that is mine;
170 You give away heaven's vows, and those are mine;
You give away myself, which is known mine;
For I by vow am so embodied yours,
That she which marries you must marry me,
Either both or none.

Lafeu. Your reputation comes too short for my daughter, you are no husband for her.

Bertram. My lord, this is a fond and desp'rate creature,
Whom sometime I have laughed with: let your highness
Lay a more noble thought upon mine honour,

Than for to think that I would sink it here. 180

King. Sir, for my thoughts, you have them ill to friend
Till your deeds gain them: fairer prove your honour
Than in my thought it lies.

Diana. Good my lord,
Ask him upon his oath, if he does think
He had not my virginity.

King. What say'st thou to her?

Bertram. She's impudent, my lord,
And was a common gamester to the camp.

Diana. He does me wrong, my lord; if I were so,
He might have bought me at a common price.
Do not believe him. O, behold this ring, 190
Whose high respect and rich validity
Did lack a parallel; yet for all that
He gave it to a commoner o'th' camp,
If I be one.

Countess. He blushes, and 'tis it!
Of six preceding ancestors, that gem,
Conferred by testament to th' sequent issue,
Hath it been owed and worn. This is his wife,
That ring's a thousand proofs.

King. Methought you said
You saw one here in court could witness it.

Diana. I did, my lord, but loath am to produce 200
So bad an instrument. His name's Parolles.

Lafeu. I saw the man to-day, if man he be.

King. Find him, and bring him hither.

[*Lafeu goes out*

Bertram. What of him?
He's quoted for a most perfidious slave,
With all the spots o'th' world taxed and deboshed;
Whose nature sickens but to speak a truth.

Am I or that or this for what he'll utter,
That will speak any thing?

King. She hath that ring of yours.

Bertram. I think she has: certain it is I liked her,
210 And boarded her i'th' wanton way of youth:
She knew her distance, and did angle for me,
Madding my eagerness with her restraint—
As all impediments in fancy's course
Are motives of more fancy—and in fine
Her infinite cunning with her modern grace
Subdued me to her rate. She got the ring,
And I had that which any inferior might
At market-price have bought.

Diana. I must be patient:
You that turned off a first so noble wife,
220 May justly diet me. I pray you yet—
Since you lack virtue I will lose a husband—
Send for your ring, I will return it home,
And give me mine again.

Bertram. I have it not.

King. What ring was yours, I pray you?

Diana. Sir, much like
The same upon your finger.

King. Know you this ring? this ring was his of late.

Diana. And this was it I gave him, being abed.

King. The story then goes false, you threw it him
Out of a casement?

Diana. I have spoke the truth.

LAFEU returns with PAROLLES

230 *Bertram.* My lord, I do confess, the ring was hers.

King. You boggle shrewdly, every feather starts you...
Is this the man you speak of?

Diana. Ay, my lord.
King. Tell me, sirrah, but tell me true, I charge you,
Not fearing the displeasure of your master—
Which on your just proceeding I'll keep off—
By him and by this woman here what know you?
Parolles. So please your majesty, my master hath been an honourable gentleman: tricks he hath had in him, which gentlemen have.
King. Come, come, to th' purpose: did he love this 240 woman?
Parolles. Faith, sir, he did love her, but how?
King. How, I pray you?
Parolles. He did love her, sir, as a gentleman loves a woman.
King. How is that?
Parolles. He loved her, sir, and loved her not.
King. As thou art a knave, and no knave. What an equivocal companion is this!
Parolles. I am a poor man, and at your majesty's 250 command.
Lafeu. He's a good drum, my lord, but a naughty orator.
Diana. Do you know he promised me marriage?
Parolles. Faith, I know more than I'll speak.
King. But wilt thou not speak all thou know'st?
Parolles. Yes, so please your majesty...I did go between them as I said—but more than that, he loved her, for indeed he was mad for her, and talked of Satan, and of Limbo, and of Furies, and I know not what: 260 yet I was in that credit with them at that time, that I knew of their going to bed, and of other motions, as promising her marriage, and things which would derive me ill will to speak of—therefore I will not speak what I know.

King. Thou hast spoken all already, unless thou canst say they are married. But thou art too fine in thy evidence, therefore stand aside....
This ring, you say, was yours?

Diana. Ay, my good lord.

270 *King.* Where did you buy it? or who gave it you?

Diana. It was not given me, nor I did not buy it.

King. Who lent it you?

Diana. It was not lent me neither.

King. Where did you find it then?

Diana. I found it not.

King. If it were yours by none of all these ways,
How could you give it him?

Diana. I never gave it him.

Lafeu. This woman's an easy glove, my lord, she goes off and on at pleasure.

King. This ring was mine, I gave it his first wife.

Diana. It might be yours or hers, for aught I know.

280 *King.* Take her away, I do not like her now,
To prison with her: and away with him.
Unless thou tell'st me where thou hadst this ring,
Thou diest within this hour.

Diana. I'll never tell you.

King. Take her away.

Diana. I'll put in bail, my liege.

King. I think thee now some common customer.

Diana [*to Lafeu*]. By Jove, if ever I knew man, 'twas you.

King. Wherefore hast thou accused him all this while?

Diana. Because he's guilty, and he is not guilty:
He knows I am no maid, and he'll swear to't:
290 I'll swear I am a maid, and he knows not.
Great king, I am no strumpet, by my life,
I am either maid, or else this old man's wife.

King. She does abuse our ears—to prison with her!
Diana. Good mother, fetch my bail....[*Widow goes*]
Stay, royal sir,
The jeweller that owes the ring is sent for,
And he shall surety me. But for this lord,
Who hath abused me, as he knows himself,
Though yet he never harmed me, here I quit him.
He knows himself my bed he hath defiled,
And at that time he got his wife with child: 300
Dead though she be, she feels her young one kick:
So there's my riddle—One that's dead is quick.
And now behold the meaning.

WIDOW returns with HELENA

King. Is there no exorcist
Beguiles the truer office of mine eyes?
Is't real that I see?
Helena. No, my good lord,
'Tis but the shadow of a wife you see,
The name and not the thing.
Bertram [*kneels*]. Both, both. O, pardon!
Helena. O, my good lord, when I was like this maid,
I found you wondrous kind. There is your ring,
And, look you, here's your letter: this it says, 310
'When from my finger you can get this ring,
And are by me with child,' &c. This is done.
Will you be mine, now you are doubly won?
Bertram. If she, my liege, can make me know
this clearly,
I'll love her dearly, ever, ever dearly.
Helena. If it appear not plain and prove untrue,
Deadly divorce step between me and you!
O, my dear mother, do I see you living?
Lafeu. Mine eyes smell onions, I shall weep anon:

320 [*to Parolles*] Good Tom Drum, lend me a handkercher: so, I thank thee. Wait on me home, I'll make sport with thee: let thy curtsies alone, they are scurvy ones.

King. Let us from point to point this story know,
To make the even truth in pleasure flow...
[*to Diana*] If thou be'st yet a fresh uncroppéd flower,
Choose thou thy husband, and I'll pay thy dower,
For I can guess that by thy honest aid
Thou kept'st a wife herself, thyself a maid.
Of that and all the progress, more and less,
330 Resolvedly more leisure shall express:
All yet seems well, and if it end so meet,
The bitter past, more welcome is the sweet.

A flourish. The King advances to speak the Epilogue

Epilogue

The king's a beggar now the play is done.
All is well ended, if this suit be won,
That you express content; which we will pay,
With strife to please you, day exceeding day:
Ours be your patience then, and yours our parts,
Your gentle hands lend us, and take our hearts.
[*they go*

THE COPY FOR
ALL'S WELL THAT ENDS WELL, 1623

The play here edited is one of the most neglected in the canon. There is no money in it, since it is never read in schools and very rarely in universities; and the commentators have therefore for the most part either given it the go-by or (if they were committed to 'The Complete Works') merely scratched the surface. Dr Johnson is, as ever, the most enlightening; but he disliked the play and even his grip on the dialogue seems slack at times. Of modern critics I owe most to Mr A. E. Thistleton. He really lays his mind alongside his problems, sometimes with fruitful results, and though his determination to justify everything he finds in the F. text leads him into absurdities—he goes so far as to give a dramatic explanation of 'legegs' (2. 2. 66) which is palpably a misprint for 'legges'—his conservatism is at least bracing. I have profited too from the editions of the play by Professor J. L. Lowes in the American *Tudor Shakespeare* and by Mr W. O. Brigstocke in the English *Arden Shakespeare*, while Professor Herford's pithy footnotes in *The Eversley Shakespeare* are always worth pondering. Yet, when all is said, I found a very great deal to do—to do, that is, merely by way of exegesis, quite apart from textual problems. How much the play has been neglected may be gauged from the fact that it contains over thirty passages upon which I believe I have been able to throw new light, and that a large proportion of these have never been annotated before[1]. Needless to

[1] The more important of these are: When it was out (1. 2. 58); pluck (1. 3. 87); the surplice of humility etc. (1. 3. 92–3); left off (1. 3. 238); higher Italy (2. 1. 12); the last monarchy (2. 1. 14); questant (2. 1. 16); the forehorse

say, the ultimate source of this light is in most cases *The New English Dictionary*, which, now happily complete, constitutes the greatest critical instrument that a Shakespearian commentator has ever had at his disposal. Most pleasing of all perhaps is its service when it enables one to justify a reading like 'this captious and inteemable sieve' (1. 3. 199) which has not appeared in print since F 1, or 'may justly diet me' (5. 3. 220) which has puzzled everyone and is roundly condemned by the *Arden* editor as 'undoubtedly corrupt.'

All this means that both the space and time available for the editing of this play have of necessity been largely taken up with the work of commentary, and that the discussion of the nature of the 'copy' which follows is even more tentative than usual. 'As he proceeds,' I wrote in the Textual Introduction to the edition as a whole, 'the textual editor...will attempt some *provisional* definition of the "copy" for each of the original Shakespearian texts.' In this the twelfth volume it is as well to reiterate that word 'provisional,' which has been overlooked by some critics. In any event here I can do little more than set down general impressions, arrived at after such close scrutiny of the text as no conscientious editor can avoid, and influenced of course by the findings in previous volumes. That they are not entirely idle I am encouraged to believe by their close correspondence with the conclusions of my co-editor, as expounded in

to a smock (2. 1. 30); Stay: the king (2. 1. 49); dearest issue (2. 1. 106); put it off (2. 2. 9); good for nothing but taking up (2. 3. 211); picking a kernel out of a pomegranate (2. 3. 263–64); to a compelled restraint (2. 4. 44); distil now in the curbéd time (2. 4. 46); who's his tailor? (2. 5. 17); an idle lord (2. 5. 51); the great figure of a council etc. (3. 1. 12); old ling (3. 2. 13); passport (3. 2. 55); 'a short alarum within' (4. 1. 88); rebellion (4. 3. 18); dieted to his hour (4. 3. 28–9); how and which way you will (4. 3. 134–35); mell with (4. 3. 225); knot-herbs (4. 5. 17); a pur of fortune's (5. 2. 19); turns a sour offence (5. 3. 59).

his Introduction, conclusions reached upon independent enquiry and not communicated to me until my own general impressions had been formulated. I go rather further than he does in some directions, as will be seen, but it was thought better to let such divergencies stand than to jettison what might prove suggestive points in his essay or mine for the sake of a seemingly perfect editorial unanimity.

The First Folio gives us 'our only text and a vile one,' as the Introduction states. It is indeed the worst we have so far encountered, its only possible rival being that of *Measure for Measure*, a text to which it is akin in many ways. Here as there, for instance, the 'corruption frequently suggests the carelessness of some hasty transcriber[1].' Our notes will reveal a number of errors —verbal transpositions and the like—which seem easier to attribute to a copyist than to a compositor (e.g. 1. 3. 161, 209; 2. 1. 43, 141, 144, 192; 2. 3. 24; 3. 2. 9; 4. 4. 34; 5. 3. 79). There are, too, many omissions, including one of a whole speech (2. 4. 35). Furthermore, there is much carelessness in the distribution of speeches. This is specially noticeable in rapid dialogue such as we get at 2. 3. 11–13, and in several instances the first sentence or the first words of a speech have somehow got detached and assigned to another speaker (v. notes 1. 1. 57; 2. 2. 39; 4. 3. 116, 136; 5. 3. 242). This is not an unnatural accident in some types of transcript since a transcriber often seems to have written out the text first and to have added the speakers' prefixes later[2]. In any case, we can hardly doubt the existence of a hasty transcriber, and in my notes and emendations I do not hesitate to allow for him throughout.

To quote the Introduction again, '*All's Well* is largely

[1] *Measure for Measure*, p. 97.
[2] I owe this sentence to Dr W. W. Greg.

a palimpsest and overwritten upon juvenile work after a considerable interval of time.' Clearly there are at least two textual layers, and in places some very obvious joins. The most glaring of these occurs at I. I. 165 which is a broken and, as it stands, meaningless line beginning a verse-speech of Helena's, itself so abrupt, obscure and disconnected with the prose-speech of Parolles just before it, that Dr Johnson throws up the sponge with the cry 'I know not what to do with the passage,' while Professor Herford writes: 'Probably the preceding dialogue (from l. 108) has been clumsily pieced with the context, involving the loss of at least several lines.' This, we do not doubt, is the true explanation[1]. But if it be, it involves important consequences, seeing that this passage of prose dialogue (ll. 108–64) 'clumsily pieced with the context,' which is verse at both ends, is just that 'idle chat' on the subject of virginity between Parolles and Helena which is picked out in our Introduction as degrading to her, and has been condemned as 'a blot on the play' (to use Clark and Wright's words) by almost every editor who has handled the text. The obscurity of Helena's speech beginning with l. 165 is partly due to the fact that, though its theme is the ladies Bertram will find and love at court, it is not till we get to the word 'court' in l. 177 that we can see this. A similar textual join may be seen, I think, at I. 3. 125. Suddenly, in the middle of a speech, the Countess changes from prose to verse. As the change marks a passage from talk with her steward to soliloquy it is perhaps natural. But why does the Folio begin the verse section with a fresh speech-heading? And why after

[1] Dr A. W. Pollard suggests (privately) that the whole prose passage (ll. 108–64) may have been written upon one leaf at the time of revision and inserted between two leaves of original verse and that the necessary readjustment at the beginning of the second of these two leaves was not completed.

using the abbreviation '*Cou.*' in the scene hitherto does the F. from this point onwards for 40 or 50 lines head the speeches '*Old Cou.*'? There has been 'piecing' as in 1. 1.; only, as we shall presently see, in this case the verse (at any rate the rhyming verse ll. 125–32) has probably been pieced on to the prose. There are many other indications of patchwork and adaptation besides these, among which it is sufficient here to mention the occurrence from time to time of passages in fragmentary blank verse which have patently been cut about to allow of structural changes, and the double entry given for Parolles in 5. 3. together with a statement by the King concerning him for which there is no support in what has gone before (v. notes 5. 3. 156, 198–99). It cannot, I think, be denied by any candid enquirer that there have been some pretty considerable alterations of the text here and there.

There are clues too which, in my opinion, point to a handling of the play at two different periods of time, quite apart from the manifest inconsistencies of style which have been almost universally accepted as evidence of a later recension of early work. Critics on the whole agree that the text must have reached its present form round about 1605, and this date finds support in two hitherto unnoticed topical allusions, the one as I believe to the Gunpowder Plot (v. notes 1. 1. 122–23; 4. 3. 22), and the other to Bancroft's enforcement of the surplice upon the puritan clergy in 1604–5 (v. note 1. 3. 92–3). On the other hand, there is a passage at the beginning of 2. 1. which so exactly mirrors the situation of the young favourites of Elizabeth, sighing for action and the wars, and all the while

> kept a coil with
> 'Too young,' and 'the next year,' and ''tis too early,'

that it can scarcely have been written after 1603. The expression 'the forehorse to a smock' (v. note 2. 1. 30) might have been dangerous on the Elizabethan stage, but it would have been pointless on the Jacobean. Yet though *All's Well* as we now have it is undoubtedly an Elizabethan play revised in the reign of James I, I am inclined to suspect that the textual problems it presents arose from a more complicated situation than Shakespearian revision of a Shakespearian original would involve.

The most obvious feature of *All's Well* to one interested in the classification of Shakespearian texts is its striking similarity, dramatic, stylistic, textual, with *Measure for Measure*. In almost every respect they are twin phenomena, and what explains one will assuredly go some way towards explaining the other. Indeed so closely are they allied that it is probable a more thorough examination of *All's Well* than can here be undertaken would lead us to modify in some particulars the conclusions as regards *Measure for Measure* arrived at when we considered that text in isolation. For the present, however, we must be content to work the other way round and to make what use we can of our findings in *Measure for Measure*[1] for the elucidation of *All's Well*.

The verse of the former play, we discovered, belonged to two strongly marked types. First there was blank verse in the late Shakespearian manner, full of difficult constructions and of unusual words, but packed with imagery and above all packed with meaning. *All's Well* contains a quantity of blank verse which obviously belongs to the same period, and scenes in the two plays which deal with similar situations, such as the temptation of Isabella by Angelo and of Diana by Bertram, might have been written by Shakespeare in the same year, so strongly do they resemble each other. On the other hand, it may be noted in passing, unlike *Measure for Measure*, except perhaps in 5. 1. of that play, *All's Well* occasionally gives us blank verse of a much simpler kind,

[1] v. Note on 'The Copy for *Measure for Measure*, 1623.'

presumably belonging to the Elizabethan stratum of the text. The best example is 3. 4., which with its sonnet-letter reminds us of *Romeo and Juliet*. Naturally enough, since rhyme is a characteristic feature of Shakespeare's early plays, critics have been ready to assign the couplets, of which there are a large quantity in *All's Well*, to this same stratum. Some of them may be, though whether they are Shakespeare's is another problem, to be viewed in the light of the remarkable fact that, as Mr J. M. Robertson[1] has cogently pointed out, the rhyming dialogue of 80 lines between Helena and the King (2. 1. 130–210) bears an extraordinary resemblance to the style both of Robert Greene and of the Gonzago play in *Hamlet*, while even the hardiest conservative among us must hesitate to credit Shakespeare himself with a rhyme like 'finisher...minister' (ll. 136–37) or with mechanical fustian like the following (2. 1. 161–68):

> Ere twice the horses of the sun shall bring
> Their fiery torcher his diurnal ring,
> Ere twice in murk and occidental damp
> Moist Hesperus hath quenched her sleepy lamp;
> Or four and twenty times the pilot's glass
> Hath told the thievish minutes how they pass;
> What is infirm from your sound parts shall fly,
> Health shall live free, and sickness freely die.

Now whether these couplets are early or late, Shakespearian or not, and whatever may lie behind their patent connexion with *Hamlet*, one thing is indisputable, viz. that most of the rhyming couplets of *All's Well*, at any rate outside the second half of 2. 1., are identical in style with those we were obliged to ascribe in *Measure for Measure* to some non-Shakespearian reviser. The

[1] *The Shakespeare Canon*, pt. iii. pp. 41–2. It is so difficult to secure agreement, even between two 'disintegrators,' on points of style that it may be worth noting that I had myself observed these resemblances before consulting Mr Robertson's essay on *All's Well*.

rhymed verse in *Measure for Measure*—the second of its strongly marked types of verse—was very stiff, we found, and sometimes very clumsy, with rhymes that were often forced, construction that was generally strained, and meaning which, when it was possible to discover it behind the tortuous diction, was invariably banal and commonplace. But meaning was clearly of secondary importance with its author to a desire to create an effect of oracular and riddling moralising. For a taste of its quality may be quoted:

> This is his pardon, purchased by such sin
> For which the pardoner himself is in:
> Hence hath offence his quick celerity,
> When it is borne in high authority....
> When vice makes mercy, mercy's so extended,
> That for the fault's love is th'offender friended.
>
> (4. 2. 107–12.)

Set beside this cryptic sententious rubbish the following from *All's Well* (5. 3. 63–6):

> Oft our displeasures, to ourselves unjust,
> Destroy our friends and after weep their dust:
> Our own love waking cries to see what's done,
> While shameful hate sleeps out the afternoon—

and it will be at once clear that they are by the same writer. *Can* it be Shakespeare? Dr Johnson at any rate found it difficult to believe it, for in his note on the second of this pair of couplets he observes, 'These lines I should be glad to call an interpolation of a player; they are ill-connected with the former, and not very clear or proper in themselves.' But is the first couplet any better? The truth is that no one has really been able to extract much sense from any of the four lines. As to 'interpolation,' omit them all and the context not only gains but becomes intelligible for the first time. Here it is, printed so that ll. 55–62, 67 run straight on:

> *King.* Well excused:
> That thou didst love her, strikes some scores away

From the great compt: but love that comes too late,
Like a remorseful pardon slowly carried,
To the great sender turns a sour offence,
Crying 'That's good that's gone'...Our rash faults
Make trivial price of serious things we have,
Not knowing them, until we know their grave.
Be this sweet Helen's knell, and now forget her.

The soft rhyme 'have...grave' gives a perfect suggestion for the 'knell' of a lover about to be forgotten. By introducing his peal of jingling bells in ll. 63–6 the reviser has spoilt the whole effect.

One of the features of the reviser's couplets in *Measure for Measure* is that, like the four we have just been considering, they are readily detachable from their Shakespearian context. This is also true of a good many in *All's Well*; but not of all, a distinction which indicates, I think, that the process of revision was not quite the same in both plays. There are indeed a much larger quantity of couplets in *All's Well* than in *Measure for Measure*, and some of them are so essential to the plot or to the speeches in which they occur, as to suggest collaboration rather than revision proper[1]. But, if so, then an examination of the prose equally suggests that the collaborator and not Shakespeare had the final word.

Differences of style in verse are hard enough to establish; those in prose are harder still. Nevertheless, we found good reasons for thinking there were two hands at work in the prose of *Measure for Measure*, and for identifying one of these hands with the author of the couplets. I think, too, that anyone who has gone with us so far will be prepared to discover the same hand in the prose of *All's Well*. There can, indeed, be little reasonable doubt about it. Contradictions in the subject-matter of the first 111 lines of 1. 2. in *Measure for Measure* led us to set aside the opening half of this prose

[1] Collaboration is also suggested by the remarkable S.D. at 2. 3. 186 (v. note).

dialogue as belonging to the non-Shakespearian reviser. It is sorry fooling, mostly turning on the topic of venereal disease; and in reference to this one character says to another:

> Thou art good velvet; thou'rt a three-piled piece, I warrant thee...I had as lief be a list of an English kersey, as be piled, as thou art piled, for a French velvet....Do I speak feelingly now? (1. 2. 32–5.)

Almost exactly the same unsavoury jest is made by the Clown in *All's Well* (4. 5. 93–7): 'O madam,' he says, speaking of the returned Bertram,

> Yonder's my lord your son with a patch of velvet on's face—whether there be a scar under't or no, the velvet knows, but 'tis a goodly patch of velvet—his left cheek is a cheek of two pile and a half, but his right cheek is worn bare.

If the first is non-Shakespearian, so must the second be. And if we can relieve Shakespeare, on purely objective grounds, of responsibility for these dreary jests about syphilis, is it not common sense also to relieve him of the tedious bawdy chat already dealt with between Helena and Parolles in the opening scene, which Clark and Wright[1] and many others have suspected to be an interpolation? In view of the clumsy piecing of this dialogue with the verse that follows, I think we may do so with a clear conscience. Indeed, once the presence of a collaborator or reviser, with a passion for sententious couplets and a mind running on sexual disease, be admitted, his handiwork becomes evident all over the play, and we begin to ask ourselves how Shakespeare can ever have been credited with some of the prose it contains, so poor is its quality, so empty its meaning. The writer's ideas are limited and he is forced to repeat them time and again. We have seen how he makes use of the 'velvet' jest in two different plays. At 2. 3. 209

[1] v. note 1. 1. 112–64.

in *All's Well* Lafeu informs Parolles 'I have now found thee [i.e. found you out]—when I lose thee again, I care not,' and this quip seemed so precious to its author that he placed it in the mouth of a second character at 2. 4. 33, and in that of Lafeu again at 5. 2. 44. Further, we find the Clown quibbling on the proverb 'Better fed than taught' at 2. 2. 3–4, and Parolles quibbling on exactly the same proverb at 2. 4. 39. Moreover, the reviser is prone to repetitions of an even more trivial nature than these. Is it possible, for instance, to saddle Shakespeare with sentences like the following: '*Well*, thou hast a son shall take this disgrace off me...*Well*, I must be patient' (2. 3. 239–41); '*I hope* I need not to advise you further, but *I hope* your own grace will keep you where you are, though there were no further danger known but the modesty which is so lost' (3. 5. 24–7)? Only if we give him also the sententious prose in *Measure for Measure*, which patently belongs to the same mint. Or once more, could Shakespeare be guilty of such dramatic somnolence as to begin two consecutive speeches with an expression like 'O, for the love of laughter' (3. 6. 31, 37), when there was no point whatever in the repetition?

I am not of course contending that all the prose in the play is non-Shakespearian. On the contrary I feel sure that here, as in the verse, and as in the prose of *Measure for Measure*, there has been a process of expansion by some inferior dramatist who, having a Shakespearian basis to go upon, was set the task of completing it or of filling it out to the required length for a public performance. Thus, to take the three chief prose characters, viz. Parolles, Lafeu and the Clown, I find a Shakespearian kernel, so to speak, in each. The Clown in 1. 3., for instance, is surely more than cater-cousin to that 'material fool' Touchstone[1], while his famous speech

[1] In this connexion it is interesting to notice that a textual 'join' occurs in 1. 3. (v. pp. 104–105) in the middle of a speech, the first half of which is in prose (presumably Shake-

in 4. 5. on 'the house with the narrow gate' and 'the flowery way that leads to the broad gate and the great fire' bears the very stamp of the master's hand. Whatever again may be thought as drama and as prose of the scene in which Parolles is unmasked, the world will not be easily persuaded that it lacks a Shakespearian basis or that the concluding soliloquy in verse with its memorable phrase 'simply the thing I am/Shall make me live' is not at any rate in part Shakespeare's. As for Lafeu, the reviser uses him much as he uses a very different character, Lucio, in *Measure for Measure*, viz. as a kind of chorus[1]; and yet the old man has at times a charm about him which once more it is difficult to believe he derives from anyone but Shakespeare.

Who then is this reviser? It is safer to refrain from speculation until we have more evidence about him. But the evidence, it should be observed, is accumulating. We have now found him at work not only in *Measure for Measure* and *All's Well* but also, it will be remembered, in and around the Hymen episode of *As You Like It* (ibid. p. 108, and notes 5. 4. 18–25, 104 S.D., 127, 138–43, 145). His presence in the last-named is proclaimed not only by its stiff and obscure couplets, not only by a clumsy piece of repetition, exactly like those quoted above from *All's Well*, viz. 'to make all this matter even...To make these doubts all even' (5. 4. 18–25), but also by the occurrence of that repeated phrase itself. The word 'even,' used apparently in a commercial sense and referring to the balancing of accounts, seems to have been a favourite one with the reviser, for it occurs no less than three times in the present text (v. G.) and once in *Measure for Measure*. Other curious expressions, worth noting as clues to authorship, are 'wear' (sb.) meaning fashion and 'to bare the beard' meaning

speare's) and the second half in rhyme. This rhyme (ll. 125–32) looks like patchwork by the reviser linking together two originally separate Shakespearian scenes.

[1] *Measure for Measure*, pp. 98–9.

to shave; both of which are found in *Measure for Measure* (v. G.) and *All's Well* (v. G.). Lastly, the verb 'to hold' in the peculiar sense of 'uphold' may be mentioned as characteristic, for though it only occurs in *All's Well* it does so there on four separate occasions (v. note 1. 1. 9). More careful search would no doubt bring to light yet further clue-expressions.

But enough for the time. All this Note attempts to do is to outline the general character of the text of *All's Well* and to suggest its close affinity with that of *Measure for Measure*.

To sum up, the editing of this play leaves us with the strong impression that the F. text is the product of a Jacobean revision (c. 1605) of an Elizabethan play perhaps by Shakespeare but if so probably containing pre-Shakespearian elements, and that this revision was undertaken by Shakespeare and a collaborator, the bulk of the work devolving upon the latter who was indeed left to carry out the final shaping of the play and to finish off many scenes begun by his great fellow-worker. Nowhere perhaps is this process more evident than in the final scene, most of which is indubitable Shakespeare, but which concludes with such grating upon a 'scrannel pipe of wretched straw' that it is hard to tell whether the verse or the sentiment it conveys is the more nauseating.

The detailed working-out or checking of this thesis must be left to another occasion or to other hands. By that time perhaps we shall be in possession of the findings of Professor Lowes who is known to have 'a thorough study' of the text and problems of *All's Well* in preparation for the press. An outline of his theory is to be found in the Introduction to his edition of the play in *The Tudor Shakespeare* (pp. viii–x)—an outline which sets our appetite keenly on edge for the complete exposition.

[1929] D.W.

NOTES

All significant departures from the Folio are recorded; the name of the critic or text first responsible for the accepted reading being placed in brackets. Illustrative spellings and misprints are quoted from the Good Quarto texts, or from the Folio where no Good Quarto exists. The line-numeration for reference to plays not yet issued in this edition is that used in Bartlett's *Concordance*.

F., unless otherwise specified, stands for the First Folio; T.I. for the Textual Introduction, to be found in the *Tempest* volume; N.E.D. for *The New English Dictionary*; Sh. Eng. for *Shakespeare's England*; Brigstocke for the edition of the play by W. Osborne Brigstocke in *The Arden Shakespeare*; Lowes for the edition by J. L. Lowes in *The Tudor Shakespeare* (see also p. 113); Herford for the edition by C. H. Herford in *The Eversley Shakespeare*; Thistleton for *Some Textual Notes on All's Well* by A. E. Thistleton (1900); Tilley for *Elizabethan Proverb Lore* by M. P. Tilley (1926); Ham. Sp. and Misp. for *Spellings and Misprints in the Second Quarto of Hamlet* (Essays and Studies, Eng. Assoc. vol. x); S.D. for stage-direction; G. for Glossary.

Characters in the Play. A list was first supplied by Rowe. Most edd. include in the list the name of *Violenta*, who is given an entry in the S.D. at the beginning of 3. 5., but there is nothing to indicate that she was intended to be a real character in the text as it stands. It is difficult to ascribe the occurrence of this name with assurance to any one of the several agents presumably responsible for this complicated text. It would be natural to suppose, for instance, that 'Violenta' was a character in the play at some earlier stage and that she had been thrown overboard in the process of revision. On the other hand, I think it equally likely that it was just a mistake for Diana made by a playhouse scribe (transcriber or 1605 reviser, if they are not the same person) who was by a natural trick of memory led to substitute the name of a character in another play acted by the boy who impersonated Diana. It tends to support this theory that the name Violenta is found instead of Viola in a stage-direction of 1. 5. of F. text of *Twelfth Night*.

We follow Pope and mod. edd. in the form *Rousillon*, though it should be noted that the F. spelling 'Rossillion' comes very close to the Italian 'Rossiglione,' which appears in Boccaccio's story and Paynter's translation, whence the plot of the play was drawn (v. Introd.), while the curious form Rosignoll which once occurs (v. note 1. 2. 18) may also have been suggested by the Italian. The name *Helena* occurs three or four times in the F. S.D.s, and once in the dialogue (1. 1. 52), but everywhere else she is called 'Hellen'; we suspect the latter to be the name Shakespeare thought of her by, more especially as he invariably uses that spelling in the verse. For 'waiting-gentlewoman' v. note 1. 3. 67. *Parolles* is clearly intended as a play upon the Fr. 'paroles' = words (cf. notes 2. 4. 26; 3. 6. 81–2; 5. 2. 40).

This text shows considerable inconsistency in its treatment of character-names in S.D.s and speech-headings, e.g. the Countess of Rousillon is styled 'Mother' in the speech-headings of 1. 1., 'Countess' or 'Old Countess' in those of 1. 3., and after that 'Lady' or 'Old Lady,' while her son is described now as 'Bertram' and now as 'Rossillion.' On the other hand, in the handling of 'two French gentlemen' the text displays a mixture of consistency with inconsistency which clearly marks it out as prompt-copy. Dramatically they are vaguely conceived, and play much the same part in this drama as Lucio's 'two gentlemen' do in *Measure for Measure*, being little more than pegs to hang information on. They begin as 'Lords' in 1. 2.; 2. 1. Later in 3. 1. and 3. 2. they have become 'the two Frenchmen' sans phrase, in which character they appear first with the troop of the Duke of Florence. Finally in 3. 6. they are gazetted 'Captain' and, though one of them turns 'Lord' again in 4. 1., when we reach 4. 3. they remain 'Captains,' and we are even informed that their name is Dumain. It is in striking contrast with all this apparent vacillation that from beginning to end the letters E and G distinguish them in their speech-headings, letters which as Capell long ago pointed out almost certainly indicate the names of the actors playing the parts, and Clark and Wright have suggested that G may stand for the 'Gilburne' or 'Goughe' and E for the 'Ecclestone' who figure in the list of players at the beginning of F1.

Acts and Scenes. The F. gives no scene-divisions, but marks the five acts.

Punctuation. Moderately good, but not especially dramatic. The grammatical full-stop, for instance, is employed so frequently that we have found it impossible to record its appearance in the notes.

Stage-directions. All original S.D.s are quoted in the notes. For S.D.s of special interest v. notes 2. 3. 186; 3. 6. head; 5. 3. 156 and p. 105.

1. 1.

S.D. F. 'Eneer yong Bertram Count of Roffillion, his Mother, and Helena, Lord Lafew, all in blacke.' For 'Rousillon' v. p. 116.

5. *in ward* This is an important point, too little emphasised by commentators; cf. 2. 3. 56–8, 162–64, 4. 5. 71, and Sh. Eng. i. 386–87, 'The Lord of a vassal who held by military tenure was guardian of the vassal's orphan...until in the case of males the ward attained twenty-one, or in the case of females, sixteen years....During the infancy the guardian had the right of marrying the ward to anyone he pleased of equal rank.' The story of Bertram and Helena ignores this

last condition. Shakespeare's own patron, the Earl of Southampton, was such a ward.

9. *hold* i.e. uphold. This sense occurs four times in this play (cf. 1. 1. 79; 2. 3. 231; 3. 2. 89)—not found I think elsewhere in Shakespeare.

9–11. *whose worthiness...abundance* i.e. 'even if the king lacked kindness, your worthiness would stir it up; how much more then shall you find it, where it is already present in abundance' (Lowes).

11. *lack* Theobald plausibly suggested 'slack'; 'lack' seems pointless, but parts of the prose dialogue in this play are conspicuously pointless, e.g. the strained notion of 'persecuting time with hope' (ll. 15–16).

19. *sad a passage* The word 'had' reminds the Countess of the recent death of her own husband, and the word is made to stand for the notion (of 'passing away') which it conveys. 'Passage' is used quibblingly, v. G.

20. *honesty;* F. 'honeſtie,'

35. *fistula* v. G. Charles V of France suffered from a thoracic fistula, v. Sh. Eng. i. 433. The fistula is mentioned of course in Paynter.

41. *promises: her dispositions* F. 'promiſes her diſpoſitions'

43. *virtuous qualities* i.e. qualities of 'virtu,' accomplishments, 'qualities of good breeding and erudition' (Warburton). The contrast is between inherited disposition, the 'honesty' she derives from her birth, and the qualities and accomplishments she has acquired by education.

49. *best brine...season* A homely metaphor. 'To season has here a culinary sense: to preserve by salting' (Malone).

53–4. *affect a sorrow* i.e. you are in love with sorrow (cf. *Tw. Nt.* 2. 5. 28). Helena, of course, quibbles on the ordinary meaning of the word in her reply—the grief which she affects for her father is really for Bertram.

54. *to have*— So F. There seems no point in this interruption. Capell boldly read 'have it' and the *Globe* follows suit. But lack of point in this text unfortunately affords no ground for suspecting corruption.

57. *How understand we that?* F. and all edd. give this question, as a separate speech to Lafeu, placing it after l. 61 (*Ber.* Madam, I desire your holy wishes.). No one has ever been able to explain it; for Kinnear's suggestion that it is a 'humourous allusion to the possibility of the Countess's wishes being anything but holy' need not be taken seriously—how could the actor make so recondite a jest clear to the audience? By placing the words at the beginning of Lafeu's previous speech all is made clear, and if we suppose that the transcriber first omitted the question and then added it in the margin with insufficient direction as to its insertion, its position in the F. text is explained. I owe this solution to a suggestion by Mr. A. W. Ayling. Cf. p. 103. [1952]

59–60. *If the living...soon mortal.* A passage much commented upon, but its meaning seems simple enough: 'if we keep a firm hand upon ourselves,' says the Countess in effect, 'the transports of sorrow are soon over.' Malone aptly quotes *R. & J.* 2. 6. 9–10:

> These violent delights have violent ends,
> And in their triumph die.

Cf. also *Ham.* 3. 2. 206–207:

> The violence of either grief or joy
> Their own enactures with themselves destroy—

and for the psychological truth of all this v. Spearman, *Abilities of Man*, p. 107.

61. *Madam, I desire* etc. Bertram abruptly checks this tedious discussion about the grief of a waiting-gentlewoman.

62–71. *Be thou blest, Bertram*, etc. The Countess's advice closely resembles that of Polonius to Laertes, though she is less windy.

65. *Share with* Generally explained 'be equal to,' a meaning N.E.D. labels 'rare.' Is it not better to take it in its ordinary sense? 'Goodness' and 'birthright' are but 'blood and virtue' over again, which after contending for empire, were to reign as partners, sharing it between them.

68. *key:* F. 'key.'

73. *the best* i.e. the best advice.

74. *his lord* F. 'his loue' No one has made sense of the F. reading, and Craig (*Arden Shakespeare*) suggests 'this lord,' taking 'he' as the antecedent of 'that.' We think it simpler and easier to read 'his lord' (i.e. the French king who was legally 'lord' of the ward, Bertram). Lafeu reassures the Countess—'The unseasoned courtier will have the benefit of the best counsel to be found in the French court.' The emendation also explains the Countess's 'Heaven bless him,' which is now seen to refer to the sick monarch, but which, as the F. stands, must refer to Bertram, awkwardly enough with 'Farewell, Bertram' immediately following. The two words 'lord' and 'loue' might easily be confused in MS, cf. the converse misprint *Ham.* (Q2) 3. 2. 179.

75. S.D. F. gives no 'exit.'

76–7. *The best wishes...servants to you!* Most edd. follow Rowe and make the whole speech an address to Helena; but Thistleton is assuredly right in taking this first sentence as Bertram's parting words to his mother; it would be dramatically most inappropriate if spoken to Helena.

79. *hold* v. note 1. 1. 9.

80. S.D. F. gives no 'exeunt.'

82–3. *And these great tears...shed for him.* These tears (which I shed for Bertram) seem to grace my father's memory more than those I actually wept for him.

84. *forgot him:* F. 'forgott him.'

85. *Carries no favour in't* 'Favour' used in two

senses here (*a*) face, image, v. G., (*b*) the token one lover 'carries' in memory of the other.

89. *above me:* F. 'aboue me'

90–1. *In his...collateral light...not in his sphere.* Shakespeare uses technical astronomical (or rather astrological) terms: stars set in different spheres moved collaterally; the radiance of one was visible from the others, but they could never touch.

95–7. *to sit and draw...heart's table* v. G. 'table.' Malone quotes *Son.* xxiv. 1–2:

> Mine eye hath played the painter and hath stelled
> Thy beauty's form in table of my heart.

100. S.D. F. 'Enter Parrolles.'

103. *a great way fool, solely a coward* i.e. mostly fool and wholly coward.

105. *take place* i.e. come off (as we say in mod. slang); cf. G. 'place.' Parolles is a companionable rogue.

steely bones How well this hits off the uncompromising jaw and cheekbones of the precisian!

106. *Look* (Rowe) F. 'Lookes'

107. *Cold...superfluous folly* 'Cold' = naked; 'superfluous' = overclothed. Parolles was certainly 'superfluous' in this sense.

109. *monarch* Steevens suggests that this refers to 'Monarcho,' a crazy Italian, whom Queen Elizabeth kept among her retinue to amuse her with his fantastic megalomania. v. *L.L.L.* G. 'Monarcho,' and Stopes, *Shakespeare's Environment*, pp. 270 et seq.

112–64. *Are you meditating on virginity?* Herford writes: 'This passage has been with reason suspected... there is evidence of patching at l. 165, and the passage is probably a relic of the earlier play.' And the comment of the Cambridge editors (1863) is: 'If it were not for the

> Pretty, fond, adoptious christendoms,
> That blinking Cupid gossips,

[lines which fall outside the section here under consideration] we should be inclined to suppose that the whole passage was by another hand. Indeed all the foregoing dialogue between Helena and Parolles is a blot on the play. Mr Badham (*Cambridge Essays*, 1856, p. 256) would strike out the whole passage (112–164)... as an interpolation.' For our own view v. p. 104.

113. *some stain of soldier* a dash of soldier in you. Some suppose that she refers to the colour of Parolles' coat, which was apparently red, or faced with red; cf. 'red-tailed humble-bee' (4. 5. 6).

118. *valiant in the defence, yet* F. 'valiant, in the defence yet'

120. *setting down* v. G. There is, of course, a quibble upon 'sitting down' which most edd. read.

122–23. *Bless...from underminers and blowers up!* This reads like an allusion to the Gunpowder Plot, November 5, 1605, which attempted the undermining and blowing up of Parliament. Cf. note 1. 3. 92–3.

130. *virgin got* (F2) F. 'Virgin goe'

131. *mettle* F. 'mettall' The two forms were not differentiated in Shakespeare's day. There was probably an alchemical meaning attached to the 'mettle' sense. Cf. 2. 1. 41 and v. *Meas.* G.

138–39. *To speak...accuse your mothers* Tilley (452) quotes *Euphues* 'If thy mother had been of that mind [i.e. not to marry] when she was a maiden, thou hadst not now been born to be of this mind to be a maiden.'

140. *He that hangs himself* etc. i.e. virgins and suicides are self-destroyers.

145. *his own stomach* = its own stomach.

147. *Keep it not* etc. A commercial metaphor: 'keep' = hoard, and 'out with't' = put it out to interest.

148–49. *within ten year...ten* (Hanmer) F. 'within ten yeare...two' Malone points to l. 132 'Virginity by being once lost may be ten times found.'

153. *ill* i.e. one must do ill.

154. *'Tis a commodity...lying.* Cf. *Shrew*, 2. 1. 321 "'Twas a commodity lay fretting by you.'

156. *vendible;* F. 'vendible.'

answer the time of request i.e. respond to the economic demand.

158. *suited* trimmed, decked.

158–59. *the brooch and the toothpick* Cf. *L.L.L.* 5. 2. 616–18 'a brooch of lead...worn in the cap of a tooth-drawer.'

159. *wear* (Capell) F. 'were' Cf. p. 112.

Your date etc. A quibble, 'date' meaning (*a*) time of life, (*b*) fruit. In the days before sugar became plentiful and cheap, dates were the cook's stand-by for sweetening. Cf. *Troil.* 1. 2. 280.

165. *Not my virginity yet* For the explanation of this fragmentary line v. p. 104.

166. *There* We discover at l. 177, but not before, that Helena is speaking of the court.

167. *A mother* etc. The catalogue that follows clearly consists of the titles that young courtiers were apt to give their inamoratas in love-letters and poems. Most of these 'adoptious christendoms' are plain enough, e.g. 'mistress,' 'friend' (= 'lover' in Shakespeare), 'guide,' 'goddess,' 'sovereign,' 'dear,' while titles chiming with another mood are 'enemy,' 'traitress,' 'jarring concord,' 'discord dulcet,' 'sweet disaster.' 'Phœnix' is of course a variant of paragon, and 'captain' is a natural title in a soldier's mouth (cf. *Oth.* 2. 1. 74 'She that I spake of, our great captain's captain'). The only difficulty is 'mother,' which seems the last name a suitor would apply to his mistress. Herford suggests that the word intended is 'mauther,' a dialect word for 'girl' or 'maiden,' which Ben Jonson uses and which was often spelt 'mother' or 'modder'; but the term seems nearly always to imply an overgrown or awkward girl, a meaning most inappropriate here. Graphically the reading 'motion' (sp. 'motyon') is possible; cf. *Two Gent.* 2. 1.

90 'O excellent motion! O exceeding puppet!' (referring to Silvia).

172. *concord,* F. 'concord:'

174–75. *Of pretty, fond, adoptious...gossips* i.e. christian names of adopted children for which Cupid stands godfather. v. G. 'christendom,' 'gossip.' 'Blinking,' of course, means 'blind,' but the word converts the blind love-god into an old crone (gossip).

181–86. *That wishing...thanks.* The contrast is between wishing and fulfilling, thinking and showing; and the emphatic words are 'effects,' 'show,' 'think.' Would we could confer, says Helena, upon our friends the good things (effects) which we in our poverty can only think for them and so fail to earn their thanks. The phraseology is astrological.

186. S.D. F. 'Enter Page.'

187. S.D. F. gives no 'exit.'

195. *wars have* (Pope) F. 'warres hath'

197–98. *predominant...retrograde* v. G.

204. *a virtue of a good wing* A bird, or arrow, of a good wing, is one with a swift and strong flight.

204–205. *I like the wear* i.e. I like the fashion. Cf. l. 157 above, *Meas.* 3. 2. 73–4 'it is not the wear' and p. 112.

213. *money* (Williams) F. 'none' The F. makes nonsense, as Brigstocke notes, and 'monie', written a minim or two short, might be read as 'none'

214. S.D. F. gives no 'exit.'

215–18. *Our remedies...dull* Cf. *J.C.* 1. 2. 140–41:

> The fault, dear Brutus, is not in our stars,
> But in ourselves, that we are underlings.

217. *scope;* F. 'ſcope,'

221 et seq. *The mightiest space* etc. The verse, like the rhyming couplets in the second half of 2. 1., is strongly reminiscent of that in the Gonzago play of *Hamlet*. The first two lines are so obscure as altogether

to baffle Dr Johnson, but Malone paraphrases, 'The affections given us by nature often unite persons between whom fortune or accident has placed the greatest distance or disparity; and cause them to join, like likes (*instar parium*), like persons in the same situation or rank of life.' Cf. p. 107.

222. *likes*, F. 'likes;'

224. *That weigh their pains in sense* i.e. that count the cost, as common sense sees it.

225. *hath been* etc. Hanmer read 'hath not been can't be' which makes much better sense.

cannot be: F. 'cannot be.'

227. *The king's disease—* F. '(The Kings diſeaſe)'

228. S.D. F. 'Exit.'

I. 2.

S.D. F. 'Flouriſh Cornets. Enter the King of France with Letters, and diuers Attendants.'

1. *Senoys* the people of Sienna. Paynter speaks of 'the Florentines and the Senois.'

3. 1 *Lord*. F. '1 Lo.G.' For this and '2 Lo.E.' (l. 15) v. pp. 116–17. It is to be remarked that these two lords, who play a prominent rôle in the play that follows, are given no special entry in the F. S.D.

17. S.D. F. 'Enter Bertram, Lafew, and Parolles.'

18. *Count Rousillon* F. 'Count Roſignoll' The F. sp. is always 'Roſſillion' elsewhere. This aberration is characteristic of the carelessness of the text. Cf. *Characters in the Play*, p. 116.

26–7. *He did look...time* 'he had keen insight in the affairs of war' (Herford).

28. *bravest:* F. 'braueſt.'

29. *on us...steal on* For the use of a double preposition v. Abbott, *Shak. Gram.* § 407, and cf. *A.Y.L.* 2. 7. 138–39 'The scene wherein we play in.'

34. *Till their...unnoted* i.e. Till their own jokes are

so stale that they fail to recognise them when they hear them on another's lips.

35. *hide their levity in honour* 'Jocose follies,' remarks Dr Johnson, 'are only allowed by mankind in him that over-powers them by great qualities.'

36–7. *So like a courtier...sharpness* Cf. Newman (*Idea of a University*, viii. 10) 'It is almost a definition of a gentleman to say that he is one who never inflicts pain.'

40. *speak*, F. 'ſpeake:'

41. *his hand* i.e. the hands of the clock; in other words, the dictates of honour.

42. *another place* The context makes it clear that the sense required is 'a higher place,' and Williams accordingly conj. 'a nobler place,' which however is difficult to justify graphically; but 'neyer' (a common 16th cent. sp. of 'nigher') would not be unlike 'nother' in a careless hand of the period, and *a nigher place* i.e. a place nearer himself, is equivalent to 'a higher place.'

45. *he humble* F. 'he humbled' The F. reading is generally recognised as corrupt, but no satisfactory emendation has yet been advanced, though Brigstocke's suggestion 'so humbled' gives the meaning required. Our reading involves a minimum of graphical change ('humble' for 'humbld'—an *e* : *d* misreading, v. T.I. p. xli) while 'he humble' balances 'them proud' in the previous line.

50. *So in approof...epitaph* 'the truth of his epitaph is in no way so fully confirmed' (Onions).

53. *Methinks...now;* F. '(Me thinkes...now)'

54–5. *He scattered...bear* Knight quotes, from one of the collects at the end of the Communion Service in the *Book of Common Prayer*, words which must have suggested these lines to Shakespeare: 'Grant...that the words which we have heard...with our outward ears, may...be so grafted inwardly in our hearts, that they may bring forth in us the fruit of good living.'

55. *bear—* F. 'beare:'

56. *Thus* (Pope) F. 'This'

57–8. *On the catastrophe...out* No one seems to have noticed that 'it' refers to 'heel,' and that the 'pastime' therefore is 'out at heel.' We paraphrase: 'when he lost or got tired of some game.' Perhaps Shakespeare is thinking of an unsuccessful day at the chase, which is apt to induce melancholy in sportsmen.

out— F. 'out:'

61–2. *whose judgements...garments* i.e. 'who have no other use of their faculties than to invent new modes of dress' (Dr Johnson).

63. *wished:* F. 'wiſh'd.' 64. *too,* F. 'too:'—transposed pointing.

67. *You are* (Capell) F. 'You'r' N.B. The usual Shakespearian form is 'y'are.' Cf. 1. 3. 41.

68. *lend it you* it' is 'love'

76. S.D. F. 'Exit/Flouriſh.'

1. 3.

S.D. F. 'Enter Counteſſe, Steward, and Clowne.'

3–7. *Madam...publish them.* 'The Steward beats about the bush, because he has the delicacy to shrink from making known his discovery to the Countess in the presence of a third party—and such a third party too! The word 'publish' is a strong hint to her to dismiss the Clown, which she promptly takes. The Clown, however, makes the most of his privileges, and airs his wit before he goes' (Thistleton).

10. *believe:* F. 'beleeue,'

18. *go to the world* i.e. get married. v. G.

19. *and I will* (F2) F. 'and w will'

23. *In Isbel's case* etc. The Clown is quibbling on the use of 'case' to denote the body as distinct from the soul; cf. *A. & C.* 4. 15. 89.

23–4. *Service is no heritage* Commentators note this as 'proverbial' but do not explain what it means. The notion seems to be that if he cannot get wealth by service, he can 'get children by marriage.

31. *other holy reasons* He reminds the Countess that his first 'reason' is to be found in the marriage service.

39. *wife's* F. 'wiues'—as often in F.

41. *in great friends* Hanmer put a full-stop after 'madam' and read 'E'en great friends,' and Malone approved of a reading which is undoubtedly forcible and easily justified (cf. note 3. 2. 18). But the F. reading makes good sense as it stands, i.e. 'you know nothing about great friends.'

44. *in the crop* F. 'Inne the crop' i.e. harvest or store the crop.

50–1. *Chairbonne...Poisson* F. 'Charbon...Poysam' Malone first suggested 'Poisson' (= fish) symbolising the papist's observance of fast-days, and Aldis Wright and Easy suggested independently of each other 'Chairbonne' (= good flesh) typifying the puritan's contempt for fasting. Shakespeare probably wrote 'Charbon' and 'Poyson,' the F. form of the latter being one of the usual *a* : *o* misreadings, v. T.I. p. xli.

58. *the next way* i.e. the nearest way.

59–62. *For I the ballad* etc. F. prints this as prose. Steevens found 'something like' this ballad in John Grange's *Garden*, 1577:

Content yourself as well as I, let reason rule your minde,
As cuckoldes come by destinie, so cuckowes sing by kinde.

62. *by kind* i.e. by nature, without being taught.

67. *my gentlewoman* This marks Helena's position in the Countess's household; she was a waiting-gentlewoman, as Nerissa was in Portia's.

71–2. *Fond done...joy?* F. prints this in one line and clearly omits one or two words necessary to the sense and the metre, which had no doubt some reference to Paris. Malone notes *The Lamentation of Hecuba and the*

Ladyes of Troye (entered Stat. Reg. 1585) as possibly the original from which the Clown quotes.

73. *With that...stood* F. prints the word *bis* in italics at the end of this line, to denote repetition. It is noteworthy that N.E.D., which describes 'bis' as a musical direction, quotes no instance of its use in England before 1819.

75–8. *And gave this sentence then* etc. F. prints this as prose. It is clear of course from the Countess's words that the Clown misquotes the song and that the original concluded with the lines

If one be bad amongst nine good
There's yet one bad in ten.

Warburton suggested that the 'sentence' was spoken by Hecuba in reference to her ten sons, of whom Paris, King Priam's favourite, was the bad one.

85. *but or* (Capell) F. 'but ore' Or = before. Thistleton notes: 'The star announces that the birth has taken place, while...the earthquake is to synchronise with the birth.' Other readings for the F. 'ore' are 'on' (Rann), 'ere' and 'one' (Collier), ''fore' (Staunton).

87. *pluck* i.e. draw (in a lottery). v. G. The Clown has in mind a draw from a pack of cards.

91. *honesty* with its usual Shakespearian meaning of 'chastity.' The impudent rascal is of course referring to himself.

92–3. *wear the surplice...over the black gown* Conforming puritan clergy in Shakespeare's day compromised with their conscience thus, combining the surplice, which they detested as a rag of popery but which the law compelled them to wear, with the black gown of Geneva.

This reference to ecclesiastical vestments seems, like that to 'underminers and blowers up' (I. I. 122–23) to point to the year 1605, since the issue of the canons of 1604 followed by legal measures against ministers refusing to conform, made the surplice very much the talk of the day and there must have been thousands of 'big hearts' wearing the detested garment for the first time in 1605. v. Frere, *Hist. Ch. Eng.* 1558–1625, ch. xviii.

93. *a big heart* a proud spirit.

95. S.D. F. 'Exit.'

100. *without other advantage* apart from other claims.

111–12. *where qualities were level* where the two parties were of equal rank.

112. *level; Diana no queen* (Theobald) F. 'leuell, Queene' Theobald's addition is necessary to make sense, but Clark and Wright suggest that more than two words have been omitted, perhaps even a whole line.

113. *her poor knight* Cf. *Ado*, 5. 3. 12–13:

> Pardon, goddess of the night,
> Those that slew thy virgin knight—

which lends strong support to Theobald's emendation in l. 112.

124. S.D. F. 'Exit Steward.'/'Enter Hellen.'

125–32. *Even so it was* etc. v. pp. 104–105. Most edd. give Helena her entry at l. 132. 'The Countess may be supposed to be observing Helena earnestly as she enters with slow step and downcast eye. Her words have thus more force and point' (Clark and Wright). But the pause is awkward and may be due to interpolation.

126. *these* i.e. the pangs of love. So we can gather as we read, but an audience could hardly be expected to do the like. Cf. pp. 104–105.

128. *Our blood...born* As we are born with blood in our veins, so this is born of our passion ('blood').

132. *or then we thought them none* i.e. or rather at that time we did not think them faults.

134–35. *You know...to you.* F. prints in one line.

136–37. *Nay...said 'a mother'* F. again prints in one line.

said F. 'ſed'—a common sp. but not found in the Qq.

142–43. *choice breeds...seeds* i.e. choice breeds, as native cuttings of plants grown from foreign seeds. Perhaps in special reference to fruit, of which the apricot, almond, gooseberry, raspberry, melon and currant were not grown in England before Tudor times (v. Sh. Eng. i. 372).

146. *God's mercy, maiden!* F. prints this within brackets. *does* F. 'dos'—a sp. not found in the Qq.

148. *distempered* v. G.

149. *The many-coloured Iris* etc. Henley quotes *Lucr.* 1586–87:

> And round about her tear-distained eye
> Blue circles streamed like rainbows in the sky.

150. *Why? that you are* etc. F. begins this line with a long dash which Thistleton explains as 'due to the Countess pausing at the end of the preceding line for a reply, failing which she puts a further question.'

160. *both our mothers* the mother of us both. A common construction with Sh.

161. *I care no more for't* F. 'I care no more for' Everyone, even Thistleton, suspects corruption in this line. The addition of a *t* is the simplest possible emendation, and makes the sense clear and straightforward. Cf. note 2. 3. 24. Capell read 'I'd care no more for't' It is of course Helena's backhanded way of saying that to share mothers with Bertram (without being his sister) would be very heaven.

162. *Can't* = Can it.

165–66. *daughter...pulse* So nervous are you become 'twixt love and dread of the name of daughter.

168. *loneliness* (Theobald) F. 'louelinesse' The emendation, which involves a very slight graphical change, has been almost universally accepted, though

Thistleton adheres to 'loveliness' which he explains as 'the state of being in love.' Theobald quotes 'Alone she was, and did communicate to herself' (ll. 105–106 above).

169. *gross...* The F. colon marks the pause before the accusation. Most edd. give no stop at all.

174. *th'one to th'other* (Knight) F. ''ton tooth to th'other' Shakespeare probably wrote 'ton tooth tother' (v. N.E.D. 'tone,' 'tother').

176. *in their kind* after their fashion; cf. *Two Gent.* 3. 1. 90 'in their silent kind.'

179. *wound a goodly clew* i.e. you have made a pretty tangle of it! Cf. *Two Gent.* 3. 2. 51–3, and *Book of Sir Thomas More* (Malone Soc. Rep. p. 79, ll. 20–2):

> And let this be thy maxim—to be great
> Is, when the thread of hazard is once spun,
> A bottom great wound up, greatly undone.

180. *forswear't:* F. 'forſweare't'

186. *disclose* F. 'diſcloſe:'

188. *appeached* informed against you. The Countess speaks as to a traitor who, after spies or turncoats have proved his guilt, is asked to make a clean breast of it.

191. *I love your son.* F. prints this with l. 190.

199. *this captious and inteemable sieve* F. 'this captious and intemible Siue.' A much discussed passage, many emendations being offered, the earliest being 'intenible' for 'intemible' in F2, which all editions have since followed. The first thing to notice, though apparently it has escaped notice so far, is that 'this sieve' is 'hope,' the last thing mentioned in the preceding line. Grasp this, and the point of 'captious' becomes clear, for the primary meaning of 'captious' is 'fallacious, specious, sophistical' (v. N.E.D.), while no doubt Shakespeare was also conscious of the word's connexion with L. *capere*. Hope then is a sieve which, when one tries to fill it, 'takes in' in both senses. And 'inteemable'

(our normalised spelling for the F. 'intemible') meaning 'that which cannot be emptied' (v. N.E.D. 'teem' vb. 2) is equally applicable, since though an 'inexhaustible sieve' would seem a contradiction in terms, Hope is just such a sieve. To paraphrase what Helen says herself in the following line: 'I go on pouring the waters of my love into it, and never lack more water to pour'; and Pope puts the same thought in his own way:

> Hope springs eternal in the human breast:
> Man never is, but always to be blest.

The full-stop after 'Siue' in F. is of course an error.

209. *Love...dearly* (Malone) F. 'Wiſh chaſtly, and loue dearely' The transcriber has obviously transposed 'wish' and 'love', thus making nonsense of the passage. No mod. ed. seems to have been bold enough to adopt Malone's conjecture.

209–10. *that your Dian...Love* i.e. that Diana and Venus were not two but one goddess. This is dramatically a very significant phrase, in view of what happens later on. Helena makes it clear that the side of love which interested Bertram most meant little or nothing to her.

214. *riddle-like...dies.* v. G. 'riddle-like.' Compare the story of Viola's imaginary sister, *Tw. Nt.* 2. 4. 110–18.

218. *my father left me...prescriptions* Dr John Hall who married Shakespeare's daughter Susannah in 1607 and was a well-known physician, collected notes of this kind which are now in the British Museum (Egerton MS 2065) and were translated from the Latin and printed after their author's death by Dr James Cooke in 1657 (v. Sh. Eng. i. pp. 419–20).

220. *manifest experience* Some take 'manifest' to be corrupt, and Collier suggested 'manifold.' Others interpret as 'well known.' May not the whole phrase mean 'knowledge of manifestations or phenomena he had actually seen' as contrasted with the 'reading' in l. 219?

221. *For general sovereignty* i.e. as 'sovereign remedies in all cases' (Herford).

222. *In heedfull'st...bestow them* Most edd. explain 'to put them away with the utmost care.' But the usual meaning of 'bestow' in Sh. is 'confer as a gift' and a better interpretation seems 'to bestow (or grant) their use only in very special need or for very important persons.'

223–24. *As notes...note* Usually explained 'as prescriptions more potent than was generally recognised'; but, as Herford observes, 'in note' refers strictly not to the prescriptions, which were not known at all, but to the remedies prescribed; and, apart from this confusion of thought, the repetition of 'note' in two different senses is extremely awkward. The word 'notes' is therefore suspect, and Gould has conjectured 'cures' to take its place. We suggest that the word Shakespeare wrote was 'motts' or 'motes,' i.e. devices or mottoes inscribed upon shields and coats of arms and expressing in pithy or riddling phrase the exploits or aspirations of the wearer. Such devices, one of which Shakespeare was himself called upon to compose for the Duke of Rutland in 1613 (Lee, *Life*, 455–57), were deliberately cryptic so that their 'faculties inclusive were more than they were in note,' i.e. they implied much more than appeared on the surface. In short the whole passage is a simile ('as' meaning 'like') probably suggested by the word 'reservation' in l. 222, which seems to have been a technical word for the composition of these mottoes; cf. *Sonn.* 85. 3.

232. *Haply* (Pope) F. 'Happily'

235. *help* v. G.

238. *Embowelled...doctrine* exhausted of their science. Embowelling, or as we should now call it disembowelling, was one of the features of public executions in Shakespeare's day.

left off i.e. given up as incurable. N.E.D. quotes

R. Mathew (1662) 'left off by a very honest and able Doctor.' Hitherto unexplained.

239. *hints* (Hanmer) F. 'in't' The change was approved by all the great 18th cent. edd., and is surely correct. It is not necessary to assume that the copy lacked an aspirate, since *y* and *h* being often very similar in the current hand 'hints' might have been misread as 'ynte.'

246. *day and hour* (F2) F. 'day, an houre'

253. S.D. F. 'Exeunt.'

2.1.

S.D. F. 'Enter the King with diuers yong Lords, taking leaue for the Florentine warre: Count, Roſſe, and Parrolles. Floriſh Cornets.'

'Count, Roſſe' is clearly meant for Count Rossillion. For 'yong Lords' v. note ll. 1, 2 below.

'*borne...chair*' In 1.2. we see the King leaning for support upon a courtier's arm. In the present scene the progress of his malady is marked by his entry in a chair. This is inferential, there being no F. S.D.s to guide us but it is clear from ll. 62–5 below that he could neither kneel nor stand. It is also clear that he swoons at l. 23 and has to be carried away for treatment, though his presence on the stage is once again evident at l. 49 (v. notes).

1, 2. *lords* Many edd. follow Hanmer and read 'lord' in both instances; but as Clark and Wright (*Camb. Shak.* iii. 260) well suggest, the young lords may be 'divided into two sections according as they intended to take service with the Florentines or the Sennoys, seeing that the King had freely granted them leave "to stand on either part"' (1. 2. 13–15). There was similarly a constant exodus of young lords 'sick for breathing and exploit' from the court of Elizabeth to take part in the wars in the Netherlands and in France. Cf. pp. 105–106.

3. *you. If both gain all,* (Johnson) F. 'you, if both gaine, all'

5. 1 *Lord* (Rowe) F. 'Lord G.' v. pp. 116–17.

6. *After, well-entered soldiers* F. 'After well entred souldiers,' Most explain 'after being thoroughly initiated as soldiers'—very awkwardly; and Abbott (*Shak. Gram.* § 418) 'cannot recall another instance' of such a construction. The addition of a comma, which enables us to take 'after' with 'return', makes all well.

9. *he owes* i.e. it owns.

12. *higher Italy* Much debated. A reference to a physical map of Italy removes the difficulty. It is simply another way of saying 'Tuscany,' which lay on the high ground south of the Lombard plain and of which Florence and Sienna were prominent cities. Cf. 'travel higher' (4. 3. 40).

13–14. *Those bated...monarchy* Also much discussed, the 'last monarchy' being interpreted variously as the Roman Empire and as the reign of the emperor Charles V. Surely the reference is to the decline of the great house of the Medici, after the death of Cosimo, Grand-duke of Tuscany, in 1574, a period lasting two or three decades, which *The Cambridge Modern History* (iii. 396) describes as one of 'social demoralisation,' when 'Florence was permeated by an atmosphere of adultery, violence, and pecuniary corruption.' We paraphrase therefore: 'except those Tuscans who adhere to the decadent fortunes and vices of the Medicis.' v. G. 'fall.' The brackets come from F.

15–17. *When...cry you loud* Hitherto unexplained. The metaphor is from the chase, when some dangerous animal is the quarry. 'Questant' (v. G.) is a coinage from 'quest' (= to seek for game) and means a hound on the scent. Fame blows the horn.

16. *shrinks,* F. 'ſhrinkes:'

23. *Come hither to me* F. gives no S.D. here. Combining suggestions from P. A. Daniel and Aldis Wright, we suppose that the king is seized with a sudden fainting-fit, summons his attendants, who bear him away in his chair to a couch in the 'alcove' at the back of the stage,

before which curtains are drawn only to be re-drawn at l. 48.

27–8. *I am commanded...too early*. Thus might the young Earl of Essex have talked, and after him the young Earl of Southampton, while the phrases Bertram is 'kept a coil' (= fussed about) with are just those constantly used by Queen Elizabeth to her favourites. Cf. note l. 30 and pp. 105–106.

29. F. prints this in two lines.

30. *the forehorse to a smock* A 'forehorse' is the leading horse of a team; but why 'smock'? Edd. explain the whole phrase as 'a lady's usher,' but surely the obvious meaning is 'the leader in a team of horses driven by a woman'? Taken with ll. 27–8, and 'steal away' (l. 33) which is what her favourites were always doing, the reference to Elizabeth seems palpable. Certainly it has nothing to do with a French king. Cf. pp. 105–106.

31. *on the plain masonry* i.e. on the palace floor instead of the rough battle-field.

32–3. *no sword...dance with* Cf. *Ant. & Cleo.* 3. 11. 35–6 'he at Philippi kept/His sword e'en like a dancer.' The reference is to the practice at dances of wearing dress swords, which were not intended to be drawn.

34. *honour in the theft* Steevens quotes *Macb.* 2. 3. 151–52 'there's warrant in that theft/Which steals itself.' Perhaps some proverb lies behind these quibbles.

36–7. *I grow to you...body*. 'We two growing together, and having, as it were, but one body ("like to a double cherry, seeming parted") our parting is a tortured body; i.e. cannot be effected but by the disruption of limbs which are now common to both' (Malone).

38. *Farewell* (F2) F. 'Farewll'

40. *heroes,* F. 'Heroes;'

41. *metals:* F. 'mettals.' One is tempted to print 'mettles' here; the forms were interchangeable with Shakespeare. Cf. note 1. 1. 131 and G. 'mettle.'

43. *with his cicatrice, an emblem* (Theobald) F. 'his ſicatrice, with an Embleme'—a simple case of transposition.

47–8. S.D. F. gives neither 'exeunt' nor entry. No entry was needed theatrically, as the actor has never left the stage.

49. *Stay: the king!* F. 'Stay the King.' F2 'Stay: the King.' (Capell added the S.D. 'Seeing him rise.') Pope, 'Stay; the king—' Collier, 'Stay with the king.' Edd. are divided in their interpretation of this speech. Pope, Johnson and others give the king an entry with Lafeu at l. 60, and paraphrase Bertram's words as 'I am going to stay. The king [*with a shrug*] will have it so.' Collier and Brigstocke follow the same arrangement, but one emends (v. above) and the other reads as F. and paraphrases 'support or attend upon the king.' Capell, on the other hand, followed by Malone, Aldis Wright and many others, prints 'Stay' with a colon or semicolon, interprets the speech as 'No more—here's the king,' and accordingly gives the king his re-entry at this point. This, we are convinced, is the correct version, partly because to read 'Stay' as 'Stay behind' flatly contradicts 'steal away' (l. 33), and partly for a reason which has in the minds of some told heavily against the introduction of the king here—we mean the long speech of Parolles which immediately follows and appears at first sight unseemly in the royal presence; v. next note.

50–7. *Use a more...farewell* This is an odd speech, which no one has attempted to explain. The young lords have gone off, after due leave-taking, and in excellent humour; why then this talk of 'too cold an adieu,' why these commands to curry favour with them? The answer surely is that the re-appearance of the king just as Bertram is about to speak of his scheme for 'stealing away' throws the pair into confusion, and that they slink off, Parolles (the ever-ready) covering their retreat with a verbal smoke-screen. To mark the speech 'aside to

Bertram' as Clark and Wright do is to spoil the effect; it should be uttered volubly and in a loud voice, though with face carefully averted from the king.

53. *wear themselves...time* i.e. are in the height of fashion. Cf. *Ham.* 2. 2. 233.

54. *muster true gait* i.e. learn proper deportment. *gait*, F. 'gate;'

55. *the most received star* i.e. the very latest and most predominant fashion. Fashions like stars were now in the ascendant and then retrograde.

60. S.D. F. 'Exeunt.'/'Enter Lafew.'

62. *I'll fee* (Theobald) F. 'Ile fee' Staunton conj. 'I'll sue' Emendation is more than usually risky in a piece of dialogue which seems to turn upon some quibble the point of which is lost. If 'fee' is right, then the King appears to mean 'Pardon shall be your fee if you will get up off your knees—so as to lend me an arm to rise myself,' while Lafeu's retort may be interpreted as 'I don't really need your pardon, because the news I bring is certain of your indulgence.'

63. *brought* Theobald conj. 'bought'

66–7. *I would...for't.* The King mentions the only conditions under which he would ask mercy of a subject.

67. *across* v. G.

67–72. F. divides 'Good faith...'tis thus,/Will... infirmitie?/No./O will...foxe?/Yes but...and if/My... medicine' We follow Capell's arrangement.

71. *My noble grapes* The 'my' is emphatic (Rolfe).

72. *a medicine* i.e. a physician.

76. *araise* v. G.

76–7. *Pepin...Charlemain* Names of kings dead long since. Cf. *L.L.L.* 4. 1. 119 'that was a man when King Pepin of France was a little boy.'

85. *Than...weakness* i.e. has filled me with more amazement than I dare set down to my dotage.

89. *take off thine* i.e. relieve thee of thine. The

earliest instance of 'take off' = imitate, mock, quoted in N.E.D. belongs to 1750; or that sense would suit here.

91. S.D. F. gives neither 'exit' nor re-entry for Lafeu. Theatrically he makes none; he goes to meet Helena at the stage-door and returns.

93. S.D. F. 'Enter Hellen.'—at l. 94.

97. *Cressid's uncle* Pandarus.

98. S.D. F. 'Exit.'

100–102. *Ay...well-found.* F. arrangement; it is idle to attempt re-arrangement as some do. We suspect it to be the remains of a longer speech, cut down.

101. *father;* F. 'father,'

106. *dearest issue* pet child. Cf. 'only darling' in next line.

108. *triple* third. v. G.

109. *two, more dear; I have so:* (Steevens) F. 'two: more deare I haue ſo,'

111. *cause* = disease. Cf. *Cor.* 3. 1. 235.

117. *The congregated College* A reference to the Royal College of Physicians (Thistleton), who were constantly employed in restraining quacks and charlatans from practice, even when these were countenanced by the Crown itself (Sh. Eng. i. 432).

118–19. *ransom...inaidible* Thistleton notes that one of the chief 'aids' due from a feudal tenant to his lord was to ransom him when taken prisoner.

124. *A senseless help* a stupid piece of quackery. v. G. 'help.'

past sense beyond reason.

128. *A modest one* lit. 'a moderate one,' i.e. 'moderate approval, a simple admission that her offer, though declined, was not out of place' (Herford).

135. *set up your rest* are set. v. G. 'rest.'

136–37. *finisher...minister* Cf. the burlesque rhymes in *M.N.D.*, e.g. 'sinister...whisper' (5. 1. 162–63); v. p. 107.

138–39. *So holy writ...been babes* Holt White takes

this to be a reference to the vindication of Susanna from the judgment of the elders by the 'young youth' Daniel, which story is also hinted at in *M.V.* 4. 1. 220. Malone thinks it refers to *Matth.* xi. 25. The infant Samuel and the doting Eli may be added to the list. In fact 'holy writ' is full of such 'babes.'

140–41. *great seas...denied* Holt White sees in this a reference to the passage of the Red Sea and the hardness of Pharaoh's heart.

141. *When...denied* The scansion of this line is difficult and would be eased if we read 'greatest' for 'the great'st.'

144. *fits* (Theobald) F. 'ſhifts' Both rhyme and sense seem to make the emendation certain, though it is difficult to account for the error on graphical grounds.

148. *Inspirèd merit...barred* The contrast is between divine inspiration and human breath (= words). The king turns her away, she hints, as the kings of old rejected prophets and apostles.

150. *square our guess by shows* i.e. shape our speculation concerning reality by material appearances only. Cf. *Meas.* 5. 1. 478.

155. *impostor* F. 'Impoſtrue' = misp. for 'Impoſture'

155–56. *that proclaim...aim* a tortuous way of saying 'who professes more than he can perform'; v. G. 'level.'

158. *past power* powerless to work the cure.

160. *The great'st grace lending grace* i.e. God willing. Brigstocke writes that this mouthful, following upon 'Hop'st thou my cure?' is 'impossible: it is difficult to believe Shakespeare wrote it.' Is it more difficult than to credit him, at any rate c. 1605, with the ridiculous description of the passage of time that follows in ll. 161–68? a description which is curiously paralleled in the burlesque Gonzago play of *Hamlet* (3. 2. 165–68). Cf. note 1. 1. 221 and p. 107.

164. *her sleepy* Most edd. follow Rowe and read

'his sleepy' We agree with Brigstocke that the mistake was probably in the original.

165. *pilot's glass* v. G. 170. *Tax* v. G.

173. *Seared; otherwise—ne...extended* F. 'Seard otherwise, ne...extended' A much discussed passage; many changes proposed. The simplest, the addition of a colon or semi-colon, suggested independently by both Hanmer and Johnson, seems to remove all difficulty, except the crabbedness inherent in the style. 'Let my name be dishonoured,' says Helena, 'or if not let me be put to death with torture, which cannot be worse than the worst, viz. dishonour.' The 'ne,' Herford declares, 'cannot be right, being obsolete in Shakespeare's time, except as a deliberate archaism.' But 'deliberate archaism' was, I think, a mark of the style of these couplets. Cf. note l. 160 above. v. G. 'ne.'

177–78. *And what...another way* 'That which seems impossible in the light of everyday reason, sounder reason may accept on other grounds' (Lowes).

180. *hath estimate* has value.

181. *Youth...all* Two syllables are lacking in this line, which have been variously supplied, e.g. 'virtue' (Theobald), 'honour' (Collier), 'health and' (Brigstocke).

183. *Thou this to hazard* etc. It is strained expressions like this, quite as much as the artificial diction, which makes Shakespeare's authorship of these couplets so difficult to credit.

187. *flinch in property* 'fall short in any detail of my promise' (Herford). v. G. 'property.'

191. *make it even* i.e. carry it out. Cf. 'makes these odds all even' *Meas.* 3. 1. 41, 'make these doubts all even' *A.Y.L.* 5. 4. 25, and *A.Y.L.* 5. 4. 18, 106; see also above 1. 3. 4 and below 5. 3. 324, and cf. p. 112.

192. *heaven* (Thirlby) F. 'helpe' Probably careless copying; the rhyme confirms the emendation.

198. *image* representative.

210. *thy deed* Dyce conj. and *Globe* reads 'thy meed'

S.D. F. 'Florifh. Exit.'

2. 2.

S.D. F. 'Enter Counteffe and Clowne.'

3–4. *highly fed and lowly taught* Alluding to the proverbial 'Better fed than taught' (Tilley, 221). Cf. note 2. 4. 39; v. p. 111.

9. *put it off* i.e. palm it off. He catches up 'put off' (l. 6) = brush aside; v. G. 'put off.'

16. *like a barber's chair* etc. Proverbial; Steevens quotes *More Fooles Yet* (1610):

> ...a barber's chayre;
> As fit for every Jacke and journeyman,
> As for a knight or worthy gentleman.

20. *ten groats* i.e. 3*s*. 4*d*., the attorney's fee.

22. *Tib's rush...forefinger* The rush ring was used in mock marriages among peasantry; cf. *A.Y.L.* G. 'cage of rushes.'

26. *the pudding to his skin* 'Pudding,' as often, means 'sausage' here.

33. *trifle* F. 'trifllc'

37. *To be young again* etc. i.e. learn to be young again, etc. The Clown has proposed the sort of game, in question and answer, that children play.

39. *I pray...courtier?* F. prints this as a separate speech with a special heading (*La.*) of its own. Cf. p. 103.

40. *O Lord, sir!* 'A foolish expletive of speech then in vogue at court' (Warburton). No doubt uttered with a leer or simper, which varies with each question; but it is silly stuff.

51–2. *answer...to a whipping* i.e. repay a whipping.

52. *bound to't* i.e. 'tied to the whipping-post,' but with a quibble upon 'bound on oath to answer,' e.g. like a witness in a law-court.

56–7. *I play...a fool.* The Countess is speaking ironically, of course. N.B. F. prints the speech as prose—and the scene now gradually passes into verse.

59. *An end* (Rowe) F. 'And end'

63. *Not much...them?* Theobald suggested the query, which is not in F.

66. *I am...legs.* The old quibble upon 'understand' and 'stand under.' Cf. *Tw. Nt.* 3. 1. 89 'My legs do better understand me, sir, than I understand what you mean' etc.

legs (F2) F. 'legegs' Cf. p. 101.

67. S.D. F. 'Exeunt.'

2. 3.

S.D. F. 'Enter Count, Lafew, and Parolles.' Lafeu's speeches in this scene are headed 'Ol. Laf.' or 'Old Laf.', while at l. 102 we get 'Ol. Lord'; probably the 'Old' prefix was to avoid confusion with the other 'Lords' (1. Lo. and 2. Lo.).

1–2. *our philosophical persons* Such as Sir Walter Raleigh and his circle, who were reputed to deny not only miracles but also the existence of God and the soul. Cf. *L.L.L.* Introd. pp. xxxii–xxxiv, and G. B. Harrison, *Willobie His Avisa*, app. iii.

6. *unknown fear* 'fear' is here 'an object of fear' (Johnson).

7. *argument* v. G. The dialogue between Parolles and Lafeu that follows is very similar to that between Osric and Hamlet.

8. *shot out* A phrase suggesting some comet or portent of the sky.

10. *artists* v. G.

11–13. *So I say...So I say.* (Clark and Wright: *Globe*) F. 'So I ſay both of Galen and Parcelſus'—assigning it to *Par.*

12. *Both of Galen and Paracelsus* i.e. of both schools of medical opinion. 'The Paracelsians, as against the

Galenists, laid stress upon chemical principles' (Sh. Eng. i. 418); cf. G. 'Galen,' 'Paracelsus.'

14. *authentic fellows* i.e. Fellows of the Royal College of Physicians. Cf. note 2. 1. 117, and G. 'authentic.'

23. *indeed: if* F. 'indeede if'

in showing Parolles' way of saying 'in print.'

24. *what-do-ye-call't* F. 'what do ye call' Shakespeare probably wrote 'calt' which was easily taken for 'call'. Cf. note 1. 3. 161 for similar misprint. Parolles, no doubt, motions to a specimen in Lafeu's hand of the inevitable ballad which followed hot upon every marvel of that age. Warburton first saw that Lafeu was intended to read the title of some ballad or pamphlet.

28. *your dolphin* The gambols of the dolphin are again referred to in *A. & C.* 5. 2. 89. Some edd. read 'Dauphin' which was commonly spelt 'Dolphin' by the Elizabethans, but (as Malone notes) Shakespeare would probably then have written 'the Dolphin' not 'your Dolphin.'

31. *the brief and the tedious of it* It would be beneath him to say 'the long and the short.'

32. *facinerious* The usual form is 'facinorous' (= wicked), and edd. suppose that either Parolles or the printer blundered. But N.E.D. gives it as a true form, cites 'facinorious' from Heywood, and traces it to O.F. 'facinereux.'

36–41. *In a most weak...thankful.* Clark and Wright (*Globe*) give all this to Lafeu, interspersing the bombast with pauses as if Lafeu dares Parolles to interrupt.

41. S.D. F. 'Enter King, Hellen, and attendants.'

44. *Lustick!* F. 'Lustique,' v. G.

45. *whilst I have a tooth* Tilley quotes *King John*, 1. 1. 213 'Sweet, sweet, sweet poison for the age's tooth'; *Hen. VIII*, 1. 3. 48 'Your colt's tooth is not cast yet' and *Euphues* 'I am now old, yet I have in my head a loose tooth.'

46. *coranto* F. 'Carranto'

47. *Mort du vinaigre!* F. 'Mor du vinager' Professor Saurat suggests (privately) that this strange oath may perhaps be a particularly blasphemous perversion of some common expletive such as 'Mort et Sang de Dieu,' the word 'vinaigre' being used as a slang equivalent to 'Sang,' the two expressions 'Mort du' and 'Mort et' being easily interchanged, and the use of a word like 'vinaigre' for the Holy Blood being likely to appeal to the soldiery.

48. *'Fore God, I think so.* Lafeu seems to be surprised. Yet he had known Helena at Rousillon, and had himself introduced her to the king. Perhaps he should speak the words mockingly to Parolles. But one is tempted to give the speech to Bertram.

54. S.D. F. 'Enter 3 or 4 Lords.' 'The scene must be so regulated that Lafeu and Parolles talk at a distance where they may see what passes between Helena and the lords, but not hear it, so that they know not by whom the refusal is made' (Dr Johnson). Mod. edd. seem to have missed this note. Yet though Johnson is assuredly right, even he has not completely understood. There are four young lords besides Bertram drawn up in a line in front of the chairs upon which the king and Helena sit. She rises and, after a blushing speech to them all, addresses each in turn, passing along the line as she does so. The irony of the situation, as is clear from their replies, is that all three lords who do speak are very ready to accept this delightful maid at the king's hands. So evident indeed is their intention in their eyes, that Helena is obliged to be abrupt with the first, and to put words of refusal as it were into the mouths of the other three. The fact that Lafeu, standing at a distance, misunderstands what is going on, has misled the commentators. That all the wards but Bertram should desire her is both good nature and good drama.

56–8. *stand...to use* Cf. note 1. 1. 5.

60. *mistress* F. 'Mistris;'

61. *to each but one!* The exception is of course the one who is to marry her—she refuses to describe herself as 'fair and virtuous.'

62–4. *I'd give...beard* It is noteworthy that these lines are the only ones in verse given to Lafeu in this verse section of the scene. His other speeches are, I suggest, additions by the reviser much in the fashion of the Lucio-speeches in 2. 2. of *Measure*. Cf. p. 112.

62. *bay Curtal and his furniture* i.e. my war-horse and his harness; v. G. 'Curtal.'

63. *broken* Lafeu is speaking of his teeth.

64. *writ* v. G. Cf. l. 201 below and 2 *Hen. IV*, 1. 2. 31 'as if he had writ man ever since his father was a bachelor.'

65. F. prints here the S.D. 'She addreſſes her to a Lord.' which edd. omit as inappropriate at this point. But it would suit well enough at l. 79 where she for the first time speaks to an individual, and it is noteworthy that the rhyming couplets begin just at this point. Perhaps the F. S.D. is a relic of the original text which has been displaced in revision.

66–7. *Gentlemen...health* F. prints this as prose. The metrically isolated 'Gentlemen' suggests textual adaptation.

73. *choose; but, be refused...* F. 'chooſe, but be refuſed;' The F. pause after 'refused' is a natural one.

79. S.D. v. note l. 65 above.

Sir, will you hear etc. So F. Thistleton proposes to read 'Sirs' here, on the ground that the speech, if addressed to one lord, would seem like a request for his hand, and supports the change by 'all the rest is mute' (l. 80) which he interprets as 'all the others are silent.' But 'all the rest is mute' (N.B. 'is' not 'are') is only a rather forced way (characteristic of these couplets) of saying 'I have nothing more to say to you,' as Steevens originally pointed out, quoting *Ham*. 5. 2. 369; while she only—a little archly no doubt—asks 1 Lord whether he will *hear* her suit, though when he eagerly replies that he will 'grant it,' she sees she has gone a little too far and passes quickly from him. Despite her blushes, Helena thoroughly enjoys this interview of the candidates for her hand, and to overlook her gaiety is to miss half the charm of the episode.

80. *all the rest is mute* v. previous note.

81–2. *throw ames-ace for my life* (v. G. 'ames-ace') i.e. escape death by the skin of my teeth. Hitherto misunderstood.

83. *The honour, sir, that flames* etc. It is, of course, his admiration that flames, though Helena finds it expedient to call it 'honour.'

87. *No better, if you please.* i.e. I desire nothing better than you.

88. *great Love* F. 'great loue' F3 and some edd. read 'great Ioue', which may be right. The difference between 'l' and 'I' in the F. type is very slight, and the letters might get mixed in the compositor's case. Cf. note 4. 3. 296.

96–7. *have her* (F2) F. 'haue heere'

99. *You are too young* etc. F. heads this 'La.', though all her other speeches are headed 'Hel.' 'La.', of course = Lady, and not 'Lafeu' as some have supposed.

101. *Fair one, I think not so.* This is frank enough. To take this and l. 87 as mere empty compliments is surely absurd; yet on the traditional interpretation of the scene we are forced to do so. Cf. note l. 54 S.D. above.

102. *There's one grape yet* etc. F. heads this 'Ol. Lord', v. head-note. Dr Johnson paraphrases: 'There is one yet, into whom his father put good blood—but I have known thee long enough to know thee for an ass.'

103. *wine—but* F. 'wine. But'

108. *Why...wife.* 111–14. *Know'st...sickly bed.* F. prints all these speeches as prose.

122. *Of colour, weight, and heat* This should be taken

after 'distinction', i.e. 'would confound distinction of colour, weight and heat.' No one seems to have observed this, though the passage has puzzled many, including Malone. Tilley quotes *Euphues* 'There is no difference of bloods in a basin.'

123. *distinction,* F. 'diſtinction:' *stand* (Rowe) F. 'ſtands'

125–26. *save...daughter* F. closes the bracket at 'diſlik'ſt'

127. *a name* (Collier) F. 'the name'

127–47. *but do not so...from me* Note that these twenty lines of rhyming couplets might be omitted without any loss to the context. Cf. pp. 108–109.

128. *place when* (Thirlby) F. 'place whence'

129. *deed:* F. 'deede.'

130. *great additions swell's* great titles swell us out.

131. *honour:* F. 'honour.'

132. *vileness is so* Add 'too' (understood) and the sense is clear. It would be difficult to imagine a more awkward way of expressing a very obvious thought, viz. that good and evil in men are independent of their wealth or station.

133–34. *The property...title* i.e. the particular quality should be judged ('should go') by what it is intrinsically and not by what it is called.

133. *what it is* (F2) F. 'what is is'

135. *In these...heir* i.e. she inherits by nature.

137. *challenges itself as* i.e. claims to be.

138. *honours thrive* F2 and many edd. read 'honours best thrive', 'not observing,' as Malone notes, 'that *sire* was used...as a dissyllable.'

141. *grave* F. 'graue:' 143. *tomb* F. 'Tombe.'

144. *indeed.* F. 'indeed,' The compositor clearly found great difficulty in punctuating these rhyming couplets. Thistleton makes a valiant but unconvincing effort to justify the F. pointing. The argument of the passage is that while Honour is 'a lying trophy' on the

grave of every unworthy person, too often 'honoured' (i.e. honourable) bones lie in 'dust and damned oblivion'. The F. full-stop at 'tomb' makes nonsense of the whole passage.

150. *I'm glad* F. 'I'me glad' This form of contraction is very rare in F.

152 et seq. *My honour's at the stake* etc. The rhymes are suddenly dropped and the verse becomes at once vigorous, forthright, full of pith, Shakespearian. But that Shakespeare was working over rhyming couplets (perhaps his own written in the 'nineties) is suggested by the fossil-rhymes 'dream...beam' (ll. 156–58), 'know...grow' (ll. 158–60), and 'eyes...Flies' (ll. 171–73). Cf. 3. 4. 24–5 (note).

which to defeat 'which' refers to the attack upon his honour.

155. *misprision* Rushton rightly detected a quibble here. v. G.

156–58. *that canst not...beam* who cannot understand that my love and her desert in the scale will make your scale kick the beam.

159. *in us* F. 'in Vs' The capital denotes an emphatic word.

162–64. *but presently...power claims* Cf. note 1. 1. 5.

166. *careless* Dyce emends 'cureless' and his reasons appear to be almost overwhelming, more especially as *a* : *u* misreadings are one of the commonest forms of misprint in Shakespeare. The reasons are: (i) the awkwardness of 'careless' with 'care' in l. 165. (ii) 'Lapse' = fall—Bertram is threatened with irreparable ruin, cf. *M.V.* 4. 1. 141–42 'Repair thy wit, good youth, or it will fall to cureless ruin.'

172. *great creation...dole* The two are contrasted: the king can at will create great titles or confer petty dignities.

178–79. *if not...replete* i.e. he promises to make her Bertram's equal in rank and fortune, if not his superior.

182. *Shall seem expedient on the now-born brief* i.e. shall swiftly follow on the signing of the legal papers, which are already prepared. The passage has puzzled most edd. (except Johnson); the clue is 'expedient', which means not 'proper' but, as always in Shakespeare, 'expeditious, swiftly performed.' We must imagine that the king and the parties to the contract leave for the signature at l. 186.

184. *Shall more...space* i.e. shall be less 'expedient.' 'Space' = time; cf. *Lear*, 5. 3. 53. Among the 'absent friends' was of course the Countess.

186. S.D. F. 'Exeunt.'/'Parolles and Lafew ſtay behind, commenting of this wedding.' Steevens declares that this last S.D. 'could only have been the marginal note of a prompter, and was never designed to appear in print.' Rather I think it may be a hint or instruction, perhaps by Shakespeare himself, to the collaborator for the writing of the prose dialogue that follows. Cf. p. 109.

196. *counts:* Thistleton supposes that Parolles in harping on the word 'count' intends a slur upon Lafeu's inferior rank.

197. *count's man* Lafeu takes 'man' in the sense of 'servant.' The speech means: 'You may be familiar with a count's servants, I am familiar with a count's master, viz. the king.'

201. *I write man* v. note l. 64 above.

205. *for two ordinaries* for two meals, v. G. *ordinaries*, F. 'ordinaries:'

206. *fellow;* F. 'fellow,'

210. *found..lose* 'found' = found out, v. G. 'Better lost than found' is proverbial, v. Tilley, 404. Cf. 2. 4. 32; 5. 2. 42–4 and p. 111.

211–12. *good for nothing...worth* The point of this has been missed, because 'taking up' (v. G.) has been misunderstood; it means here, not 'contradicting' or 'taking up short' as most have imagined, but (*a*) 'picking up' (as one hopes to do with something lost), and (*b*) 'enlisting as a common soldier' (cf. 2 *Hen. IV*, 2. 1. 199; 4. 2. 26), which is the point of 'and that thou'rt scarce worth.' *thou'rt* F. 'th'ourt' This is interesting in view of the suspect character of this dialogue; the normal Shakespearian form is 'th'art'. Cf. notes 1. 2. 67 and (below) l. 228.

217. *my good window of lattice* A reference to Parolles' face, which was red like the latticed window of an ale-house. Cf. 2 *Hen. IV*, 2. 2. 85–7 'A' calls me e'en now...through a red lattice, and I could discern no part of his face from the window.' v. G. 'lattice.'

218. *thy casement...open* with a quibble perhaps upon 'case' = body; i.e. I needn't make a hole in you with my sword, as you're transparent already.

228. *E'en* F. 'Eu'n' The normal Shakespearian form is 'ene'; cf. 'th'ourt' note ll. 211–12 and 'I'me' note l. 150 above.

228–29. *to pull...contrary* 'there's a dash of the opposite (i.e. folly) in the dram you have to drink' (Lowes).

230. *shalt find* (F2) F. 'ſhall finde'

231–32. *hold my acquaintance* v. note 1. 1. 9.

233. *in the default* Johnson explained 'at a need', and all edd. have followed suit, though N.E.D. gives no support, and this is apparently the only occasion in which the phrase occurs. We suggest that 'default' is a military term, meaning a 'failure to support one's friends or allies in battle.' A fear that Parolles may fail in this way is expressed at 3. 6. 13–15; cf. 1 *Hen. VI*, 2. 1. 60; 4. 4. 28.

237. *for doing I am past* Some see an indelicate allusion here and N.E.D. (v. 'doing' vbl. sb. 1b) supports.

237–38. *as I will by thee* 'A play on the word *past*', i.e. as I will pass by thee (Malone). *motion* = speed.

238. S.D. F. 'Exit.'

245. S.D. F. 'Enter Lafew.'

249. *make some reservation of your wrongs* i.e. restrain your insults a little.

257–58. *methink'st* So F. Mod. edd. follow Dyce and read 'methinks't', while those before Dyce followed Rowe and read 'methinks'. But there can be little doubt that Thistleton is right in diagnosing it as a case of attraction (= thou seemest to me), the impersonal verb being treated 'as if it were capable of the inflection of a personal verb.' Cf. 'think'st thee' *Ham.* 5. 2. 63, 'Where it think'st best' *Ric. III,* 3. 1. 63 (F.), and Abbott, § 297.

259–60. *breathe themselves* v. G. 'breathe' and cf. 'breathing' 1. 2. 17.

263–64. *for picking a kernel out of a pomegranate* i.e. for petty theft. This seems the natural interpretation of a hitherto unexplained passage; and 'you are a vagabond' etc. follows appropriately upon it.

268. S.D. F. 'Exit.'

270. S.D. F. 'Enter Count Roſſillion.'—at l. 268.

273–74. *Although...bed her.* F. prints as prose.

280–81. *There's letters...yet.* F. prints as prose, and mod. edd. follow; but Capell and most 18th cent. edd. arrange it as verse, which it palpably is. This fact and the broken line, taken with the prose-lining of verse noted in ll. 273–74, strongly suggest revision or adaptation. Parolles has not been given any verse before this.

284. *here at home* F. 'heare at home'

295. *war* (F2) F. 'Warres'

296. *To the dark house* i.e. in comparison with madness. Madmen were confined in darkness at this period; cf. *A.Y.L.* 3. 2. 391, *Tw. Nt.* 5. 1. 350. 'Bertram means that to live with a wife he detested would drive him out of his wits' (Thistleton).

detested wife (Rowe) F. 'detected wife' Both 'ct' and 'ſt' are ligatures in the F. and it is probable that the compositor's ligature boxes have got a little 'foul.'

298. *advise* (F2) F. 'aduice'

299. *to-morrow* Steevens read 'betimes to-morrow' Evidently some word has been omitted.

300. *her single sorrow* This makes an excellent end to the scene. I suspect the couplets that follow to be the reviser's addition.

301–302. *Why, these balls bound...marred* Sh. Eng. ii. 460 points out a very striking and, considering the date, curious parallel with this in *The Arte of English Poesie* (1589). The author illustrates the figure of Antanaclasis or the Rebound, as follows: 'Ye have another figure which by his nature we may call the Rebound, alluding to the tennis ball which being smitten with the racket reboundes backe againe, and where the last figure before [syneciosis] played with two words somewhat like, this playeth with one word written all alike but carrying divers sences as thus: The maide that soone married is, soone marred is.'

304. S.D. F. 'Exit.'

2.4.

S.D. F. 'Enter Helena and Clowne.'

1–3. The first three lines of the scene are verse. The verse begins again at l. 40.

11–13. *One...quickly*. The pointlessness of this speech makes it difficult to believe Shakespeare responsible for it. The allusion is, of course, to the belief that it is well with the dead, a belief on which the Elizabethans constantly quibbled.

13. S.D. F. 'Enter Parolles.'

16. *fortunes* (Capell) F. 'fortune' The 'them' in l. 17 makes the emendation secure.

21. *I would she did as you say* The 'did' is caught up from the 'does' of Parolles, but with a quibble also upon 'died,' the pronunciation of 'died' and 'did' being not unlike at this time. The Clown is still harping upon the death of the Countess.

23–4. *many...undoing* The idea is that the tongue by its wagging shakes out the secret which the serving-man intended to keep in (v. N.E.D. 'shake' vb. 20). In 'master's undoing' the Clown still seems to be glancing at the Countess's death.

26. *your title* i.e. what you are entitled to, your possessions, v. G. 'title.' Perhaps there is a quibble intended also upon the name of Parolles.

29. *before a knave* i.e. in a knave's presence.

30. *before me* A form of asseveration, meaning 'upon my soul.'

32. *found thee* Cf. 2. 3. 210, p. 111 and G. 'find.'

33. *in yourself* i.e. by yourself, without the help of others (v. N.E.D. 'in' prep. 22), and cf. *Ham.* 2. 1. 71 'Observe his inclination in yourself.'

35. Par. *In myself.* (Nicholson) This speech is not found in F. which however prints 'The search, sir,' etc. (ll. 36–8) as a separate speech with its own heading 'Clo.' It is obvious that some reply by Parolles to the Clown's questions is required to complete the sense of the passage. What the lost words are can of course only be guessed at, but that Nicholson's simple reading gives us the essence of them is certain.

39. *A good...fed* Once again a verse speech of Parolles begins with a passage of prose; cf. note 2. 3. 280–81. *well fed* i.e. better fed than taught; cf. note 2. 2. 3–4, and p. 111.

40. *Madam* etc. Directly we begin the verse section of the scene we find ourselves in an atmosphere indubitably Shakespearian.

44. *to a compelled restraint* Here, as often in Shakespeare, 'to' = in accordance with, (almost) in obedience to. Cf. 'mar it to the time' *Shrew*, 4. 3. 97. Many edd. read 'by a compelled restraint' with F3.

45–6. *Whose want...curbèd time* The antecedent to 'whose' is 'the great prerogative and rite of love.' The whole metaphor, hitherto unexplained, is drawn from the process of distillation, 'the curbéd time' being conceived as the confined vessel or still in which the process was carried on. Parolles means, of course, that delay, with all the delightful anticipation it brings with it, will only render the consummation the more joyous when it comes. Possibly 'curbéd' is used with a quibble upon curb = the brim of the still. Malone quotes *Troil.* 3. 2. 19–22.

56. S.D. F. 'Exit Par.'

S.D. F. 'Exit.'

2. 5.

S.D. F. 'Enter Lafew and Bertram.'

6–7. *lark...bunting* The two birds are very similar to the unpractised eye. For 'dial' v. G.

13. S.D. F. 'Enter Parolles.'—after l. 15.

16–17. *These things...tailor?* The point of this has, I think, been missed. Lafeu is insulting Parolles as usual. He pretends that the overdressed braggart is a tailor's servant who has called to tell Bertram that his orders have been put in hand by his master; and he enquires the latter's name from Bertram.

19. *well...a good* (Capell & Theobald) F. 'well, I ſir, hee ſirs a good'—which leaves the sense doubtful. Some edd. read 'well, I, sir; he, sir, 's a good'

28. *End* (Collier) F. 'And'

29. *A good traveller* etc. A continuation of Lafeu's theme at 2. 3. 205–12.

29–30. *at the latter end of a dinner* i.e. for after-dinner stories.

30. *but one* (Rowe) F. 'but on'—a common error. At this period words were often spelt without the final mute *e*. Cf. Ham. Sp. and Misp. p. 46.

32. *heard* (F2) F. 'hard'—another old spelling.

33. *God save...captain.* He affects to recognise Parolles for the first time.

39. *spurs and all,* F. 'spurres and all:' *him that...*

custard Theobald quotes Ben Jonson, *The Devil's an Ass*, 1. 1.:

> He may perchance, in tail of a sheriff's dinner,
> Skip with a rhyme o'the table, from New-nothing,
> And take his Almain-leap into a custard,
> Shall make my lady mayoress and her sisters
> Laugh all their hoods over their shoulders.

custard; F. 'Custard,'

41. *residence* v. G.

47. *I have kept of them tame* i.e. I have kept tame animals of this kind.

49. *have or will to deserve* F2 omits 'to' and many edd. follow, while Singer ingeniously proposed to insert 'or wit' before 'or will'. But Thistleton paraphrases 'have deserved or intend to deserve,' which seems to make all clear.

50. *we...evil* we must return good for evil.

51. *idle* i.e. cracked (as we should say), v. G.

52–3. *I think...him?* At first sight it is tempting to read as S. Walker suggests, and as Singer and Brigstocke read (viz. '*Ber.* I think not so. *Par.* Why, do you know him?'), on the supposition that the 'not' has been accidentally transferred from one line to the other. But this reading lands us in the absurdity that Parolles who travelled with Lafeu and Bertram to Paris (1. 1.) did not know that they were acquainted. On the other hand, let Bertram pronounce 'I think so' with hesitation, and there is no difficulty.

55. *Gives him a worthy pass* i.e. allows him for a worthy fellow.

S.D. F. 'Enter Helena.'

61–3. *nor does...particular* nor does the service required on my part accord with the time.

68. *respects* reasons, considerations. For 'appointments' v. G.

78–9. *Let that go...home* F. prints as prose.

81. *I owe* i.e. I own.

87. *Faith, yes—* F. prints this at the end of l. 86.

91. *Where are my other men...Farewell.* F. continues this as part of Helena's speech, and begins Bertram's with 'Go thou toward home' etc. Theobald first rectified this.

S.D. F. 'Exit.'

94. S.D. F. gives no 'exeunt.'

3. 1.

S.D. F. 'Flouriſh. Enter the Duke of Floreuce, the two Frenchmen, with a troope of Souldiers.' For 'the two Frenchmen' v. pp. 116–17; their speeches are headed '1. Lord.', 'Fren.E.' and 'Fren.G.' in this scene.

12–13. *That the great...motion* The general sense of this is clear, but commentators have missed the point of the metaphor, which hinges on 'figure', an astrological term. v. G. 'I am,' says 2. Lord, 'like an ordinary man who unlearned in politics seeks to determine the disposition of a Council of State by his own unaided intelligence.' The intentions of the Council are compared with the disposition of the heavenly bodies, as equally lofty and mysterious to the average man.

17. *nature* i.e. character, disposition; v. G.

22. *When better...fell* i.e. when better places fall vacant, they will have fallen vacant for you to fill.

23. S.D. F. 'Flouriſh.'

3. 2.

S.D. F. 'Enter Counteſſe and Clowne.'

6. *boot and sing,* F. 'boote, and ſing:'

7. *ruff* F. 'Ruffe' This is possibly a misprint for 'ruffle' (sp. 'rufle') but v. G.

9. *sold* (F3) F. 'hold' Since 'hold' and 'know' do not hang together grammatically, emendation of some kind is necessary. We might read 'I knew a man...held' or 'I know a man...held,' where 'hold' = wager. But it seems more likely that 'sold' was the original reading,

though if so the change to 'hold' can only be explained as sheer inadvertence on the part of the transcriber or compositor, *s* and *h* not being alike in 'secretary' hand.

13. *old ling* (F2) F. 'old Lings' This has puzzled 19th cent. edd.; those of the 18th pass it over in silence, probably because they understood it. Kinnear (1883) conj. 'codlings' (= raw youths), which attracts many and Brigstocke actually reads it. But 'old ling' is salted cod, and when it is remembered that 'salt' = lecherous, and that 'cod' also has a second meaning of which 'codpiece' is a familiar illustration, it becomes clear that the text is correct.

18. *E'en that* (Theobald) F. 'In that' The sp. 'in' for 'e'en' is common in Shakespearian texts; cf. *M.V.* 3. 5. 20, *Err.* 2. 2. 101, *A. & C.* 4. 15. 73.

S.D. F. 'exit.'

19. *I have sent* etc. F. heads this 'A letter' and omits speech-heading for the Countess. Cf. *M.V.* pp. 96–9.

21–2. *the 'not'* with a quibble upon 'knot'; cf. note 4. 5. 17.

31. *For the contempt of empire* i.e. for an emperor to despise.

S.D. F. 'Enter Clowne.'

43. *run away* Capell gave *Clo.* an 'exit' here, and is followed by all mod. edd. He may be right, but no 'exit' is necessary before l. 97.

S.D. F. 'Enter Hellen and two Gentlemen.' The speeches of the Gentlemen are headed 'Fren.E.' and 'Fren.G.' The next entry for E. and G. is in 3. 6., the head S.D. of which describes them as 'the Frenchmen, as at first.' This suggests that here they wore a different costume than in 3. 1. and 3. 6. and were intended to be taken as different characters. Cf. pp. 116–17.

50. *Can woman me unto't* i.e. can make me give way to it (or break down under it) like a woman. Thus Shakespeare draws attention to her calm bearing.

55. *passport* i.e. a beggar's permit. v. G. Helena is bitter.

59. F. prints 'but in ſuch a (then) I write a Neuer'—an excellent example of the inconsistency of the old punctuation, though the intention is clear enough.

61–2. *Ay, madam...pains.* F. prints as prose.

64–5. *engrossest...moiety* The metaphor is from commerce or the purchase of land; to 'engross' = to buy up so as to obtain a monopoly of a commodity, or so as unfairly to prevent others from purchasing a share. Possibly Shakespeare has the enclosure of land in mind.

82–3. *A servant...known.* F. prints as prose.

83. *Which* F. 'whlch'

87–95. *Indeed...affairs.* F. prints as prose. Capell first arranged as verse.

88–9. *a deal...to have* i.e. a deal of that superfluity (of naughtiness) which gives him a great reputation (with young sparks like your son). v. note 1. 1. 9. Addis conj. 'bolds' (= makes bold) for 'holds'.

96. *Not so...courtesies.* i.e. I will allow you to call yourselves servants only if you will permit *me* to offer you service in the form of entertainment.

97. S.D. F. 'Exit.'

109. *still-piecing* (Steevens) F. 'ſtill-peering' The Shakespearian sp. of 'piece' is 'peece,' and the graphical difference between 'peece' and 'peere' is small, while 'still-piecing' (= ever-repairing or continually joining up again) exactly fits the context.

116. *the ravin lion* Many suspect 'ravin' to be corrupt; but N.E.D. gives other instances of 'ravin' as an adjective.

119–21. *come thou home...I will be gone* These words confute the notion of some critics that Helena pursues Bertram to Italy. Cf. 3. 4. 8–11.

120. *Whence...scar* i.e. from the wars where honour wins nothing from danger except scars.

128. S.D. F. 'Exit.'

3. 3.

S.D. F. 'Flourish. Enter the Duke of Florence, Rossillion, drum and trumpets, soldiers, Parrolles.'

1. *general of our horse* Both Essex and Southampton held the position of Master of the Horse at different times in Elizabeth's reign; cf. note 2. 1. 27–8, 30 and pp. 105–106.

7. *fortune play...helm* A common expression with Shakespeare; cf. *R. III*, 5. 3. 79, 351; *A. & C.* 1. 3. 99–100; *Hen. V*, 4. 5. 5.

11. S.D. F. 'Exeunt omnes.'

3. 4.

S.D. F. 'Enter Countesse & Steward.'

4. *I am S. Jaques'* etc. F. heads this 'Letter.', gives no speech-heading for Steward and none for the Countess at l. 18. Cf. *M.V.* pp. 96–9. This sonnet-letter seems to belong to the same period as *R. & J.* and *L.L.L.*

S. Jaques No one has succeeded in identifying such a shrine in Italy, though there is the famous shrine of S. Jaques de Compostella in Spain.

7. *have* (F2) F. 'hane'

8–11. *Write, write* etc. Cf. note 3. 2. 119–21.

9–10. *hie: Bless...peace, whilst* (F3) F. 'hie, Blesse ...peace. Whilst'

12–13. *taken labours...despiteful Juno* alluding to the labours of Hercules and his persecution by Juno.

24–5. *o'erta'en...vain* Note the rhyme, and cf. 2. 3. 152 (note).

42. S.D. F. 'Exeunt.'

3. 5.

S.D. F. 'A Tucket afarre off./Enter old Widdow of Florence, her daughter, Violenta and Mariana, with other Citizens.' For 'Violenta' v. *Characters in the Play*, pp. 115–16.

1–15. F. prints these speeches in short lines like

verse. As they occur at the foot of the second column of p. 242 in F. and as on p. 243 the arrangement ceases, it is clearly due to the compositor's necessity of filling out the tail-end of his stint with insufficient matter.

17. *suggestions* temptations.

20. *go under* pretend to be.

23. *dissuade succession* dissuade other girls from following the same road.

24. *threaten* (Pope) F. 'threatens'

24–5. *I hope...I hope* Note the clumsy duplication. Cf. p. 111.

28. S.D. F. 'Enter Hellen.'

32–43. *God save...please so, pilgrim.* This fragmentary blank verse lying between prose (ll. 1–31) and regular blank verse (l. 44 et seq.) suggests that the scene has been revised.

33. *le Grand* (F3) F. 'la grand'

35. *At the S. Francis* i.e. a hostelry with the sign of S. Francis. *port* = gateway.

37. S.D. F. 'A march afarre.'—at l. 36.

50. *Whatsome'er* This form is characteristic of Shakespeare; cf. *A. & C.* 2. 6. 102, *Ham.* (Q2) 1. 2. 249 (both good texts).

51. *bravely taken* i.e. regarded a fine fellow.

52. *reported,* F. 'reported:'

54. *the mere truth* (Hanmer). F. 'meere the'—one of those transpositions to which all compositors are prone.

56. *coarsely* F. 'courſely' v. G.

58. *In argument...worth* i.e. if it's a question of praise, or in comparison with the worth.

61. *a reservéd honesty* a well-guarded chastity.

65. *I warrant* (Clark and Wright: *Globe*) F. 'I write' Most other edd. read 'Ay, right!' a reading which assumes oral transmission of some kind. 'I warrant' gives excellent sense and finds strong support in misprints like 'wit' and 'wait' for 'warrant' in *Ham.* (Q2), v. Ham. Sp. and Misp. p. 42.

74. S.D. F. 'Drumme and Colours./Enter Count Roſſillion, Parrolles, and the whole Armie.'—at l. 73.

82. *places* i.e. brothels, which have not been mentioned in the conversation between respectable women, but have been hinted at; cf. ll. 70–1. Theobald wished to alter to 'paces' (=iniquitous courses) and some edd. follow.

90. *curtsy* F. 'curteſie' v. G.

S.D. F. 'Exit.'

91–2. *bring you/Where* F. 'bring/you, Where'—carrying the 'you' on into the next line, because there is no room for it in l. 91 or even tucked up at the end of l. 90, where the 'Exit' stands in the way.

92. *enjoined penitents* v. G.

97. *for me;* F. 'for me.'

98. *of this virgin* The 'of' belongs to 'worthy the note.'

99. S.D. F. 'Exeunt.'

3.6.

S.D. F. 'Enter Count Roſſillion and the Frenchmen, as at firſt.' Cf. note 3. 2. 43 S.D. The speeches of 'the Frenchmen' are headed 'Cap.E.' and 'Cap.G.', v. *Characters in the Play*, pp. 116–17.

6. *Do you...in him?* F. prints this in two lines like verse.

8–9. *to speak...kinsman* i.e. as if he were my kinsman.

33. *his success* (Rowe) F. 'this ſucceſſe'

34. *lump of ore* (Theobald) F. 'lump of ours' The sp. of the copy was probably 'oare' or 'oure', *e* and final *s* being liable to confusion.

35. *John Drum's entertainment* i.e. a rough reception, cf. 5. 3. 320 and G. 'Drum.'

35–6. *your...removed* i.e. nothing can shake your partiality for the fellow.

inclining (F2) F. 'inelining'

36. S.D. F. 'Enter Parrolles.'

37. *O, for the love of laughter* Note the clumsy duplication of the phrase already used in l. 31. Cf. p. 111.

51. *condemn* Kellner (*Restoring Shakespeare*, p. 150) proposes 'commend' which would give better sense. Transposition of letters is a common accident of the press, and the compositor may have inadvertently set up 'condem' for 'comend' and then 'corrected' it to 'condemne'

58–9. *or 'hic jacet'* i.e. or you may write my epitaph (Lowes).

63. *magnanimous* (F2) F. 'magnanimious'

73. *mortal preparation* i.e. preparation in case of death, e.g. taking the sacrament.

79–80. *I know...Farewell* F. spaces this out in verse lines. N.B. it comes near the foot of p. 244; cf. note 3. 5. 1–15.

81. S.D. F. 'Exit.'

81–2. *I love not...water* A play upon the name 'Parolles'; cf. notes 2. 4. 26; 5. 2. 40.

98. *case* A term in venery; v. G. *smoked* A quibble, (*a*) smoked out like a fox from his hole, (*b*) smelt out, v. G. 'smoke.'

101. *twigs* i.e. limed twigs; cf. 3. 5. 24. Note how the scene suddenly breaks into verse here.

102. *Your brother* This is our first intimation that the 'two Frenchmen' are brothers; in 4. 3. we learn their name. Cf. pp. 116–17.

103. *As't please* etc. F. heads this speech 'Cap.G.' which has hitherto stood for '1. Lord.' Theobald made the obvious rectification. Likewise F. prints 'Cap.E.' as headings for ll. 105, 111, where it should have given 'Cap.G.' (i.e. 1. Lord).

S.D. F. gives no 'exit.'

111. S.D. F. 'Exeunt.'

3.7.

S.D. F. 'Enter Hellen, and Widdow.'

3. *But I shall lose* etc. i.e. without frustrating my whole object by revealing myself to Bertram.

8–12. *First give me trust...bestowing it.* Most edd. read 'give me trust' as a parenthesis, placing it between commas. We follow F. punctuation and make it the principal sentence—a reading which renders the context more intelligible.

19. *Resolved* (Collier) F. 'Refolue'—an *e* : *d* misreading.

25. *wore it:* F. 'wore it.'

26. *idle fire* i.e. in the delirium of lust. v. G. 'idle.'

28–9. *Now...purpose* F. prints in one line.

34. *after this* (F2) F. 'after'

41. *To her unworthiness* i.e. to her disgrace; it got her 'talked about.'

44–7. *which if it speed...fact* For this passage, which Warburton calls a 'jingling riddle,' v. pp. 108–109. The scene might well have ended with 'Let us assay our plot' (l. 44). The sense is obscure, but Malone explains thus: Bertram's 'meaning' is wicked, Helena's lawful; the 'fact' is sinful in Bertram, yet neither sin since they are a wedded couple.

48. S.D. F. gives no 'exeunt.'

4. 1.

S.D. F. 'Enter one of the Frenchmen, with fiue or fixe other fouldiers in ambufh.' The speeches of 'the Frenchman' are headed '1 Lord E.', 'Lor.E.', or 'L.E.' It is 'Lord E.' who goes off to set the trap for 'the fox' in 3. 6. 103, but the F '1' is an error here as he should be styled '2 Lord.'

16–19. *therefore...fancy; not...another, so we...purpose:* (Perring *apud* Clark & Wright) F. 'therefore... fancie, not...another: fo we...purpofe:' Most edd.

follow F., and are at a loss to explain the sense. Perring's pointing makes the passage straightforward; the emphatic word is, of course, 'seem.'

23. S.D. F. 'Enter Parrolles.'

40. *what's the instance?* i.e. what evidence can I furnish? Kellner (*Restoring Shakespeare*) conj. 'inference' for 'instance', i.e. what conclusion must I draw from all this?—which makes an easier reading.

42. *Bajazet's mate* F. 'Baiazeths Mule' Much debated. Hanmer reads 'Bajazet's mute', Thistleton 'Bajazet's mewl' (= caterwauling), and Addis even conj. 'Balaam's mule'. Our emendation assumes a simple *a* : *u* misprint of the kind very common in Shakespeare, while 'Bajazet's mate' = Zabina, wife of Bajazet, in Marlowe's *Tamburlaine* (pt. i.) and the greatest termagant in Elizabethan drama. The reading fits in with 'butter-women' who were notorious for scolding (cf. N.E.D. 'butter-quean,' 'butter-whore,' 'butter-woman'). Parolles' only chance of getting out of the scrape into which his tongue has led him is to scold or swagger himself out of it; but for this he will need Zabina's tongue at least—no butter-quean's hectoring will serve.

47. *afford you so* i.e. grant you that.

48. *the baring of my beard* Cf. *Meas.* 4. 2. 173–74 'the beard...to be so bared.' The expression is not found elsewhere in Shakespeare, and is so rare that it is not cited in N.E.D. It is moreover peculiar, since it is the chin and not the beard which is 'bared' in shaving. Cf. pp. 112–13.

60, 63. *the enemy's* (Malone) F. 'the enemies'

63. S.D. F. 'Alarum within.'

72–3. *I will...Florentine* (Malone) F. 'Ile...Florentine'—as one line.

73. *Boskos* etc. F. gives this to 'Inter.' (= interpreter), and thus designates '1 Soldier' for the rest of the scene. It may be a coincidence that from this point

onwards the dialogue breaks into verse, interspersed with prose.

88. *thou art* (F2) F. 'thou are'

S.D. F. 'Exit./A ſhort Alarum within.' No one seems to have asked the meaning of this 'short alarum'; I take it to be the drum once more giving a comic 'burden' to the whole episode.

93. *Inform 'em* (Rowe) F. 'Inform on' Rowe's emendation was accepted by all 18th cent. edd., and pronounced by Dyce as 'positively required' by the context.

94. S.D. F. 'Exit.'

4. 2.

S.D. F. 'Enter Bertram, and the Maide called Diana.'

The style and feeling of the dialogue in this scene very closely resemble those in the scenes of *Measure for Measure* between Isabella and Angelo which deal with a similar situation.

8. *now,* F. 'now:' *stern;* F. 'ſterne,'

21–31. *'Tis not the many...opinion.* A speech which has puzzled most edd. including Dr Johnson. I paraphrase thus: 'It is not the quantity but the quality of oaths that matters. We swear by God Himself when we take an oath, but the use of God's name does not make the oath more credible when it is palpably contrary to the facts. It is just as absurd to swear by God to perform something that He disapproves of. Your oaths are but words.'

25. *Jove's* 'The word "Jove's" has here probably been substituted for the original "God's" in obedience to the statute against profanity. Read "God's" and all is plain' (Clark & Wright).

28, 29. *Him* (Lowes) F. 'him' The use of this capital makes all the difference to the meaning of the passage.

30. *Are words...unsealed* Hitherto edd., following F. punctuation, have read 'Are words and poor conditions, but unseal'd', which is very awkward, since not only is the expression 'poor conditions' strange in itself, but the word 'poor' is so oddly followed by 'but unsealed' that for long I felt 'but' must be a misprint for 'yet'. Then I shifted the comma and daylight came!

36. *recover* (Rowe) F. 'recouers' The connexion between 'sick' and 'recover' shows that 'desires' must be the antecedent of 'who'

38. *make rope's in such a scarre* So F. One of the prime cruxes in the canon. Scores of proposals, both for 'rope's' and for 'scarre', most of them being like Malone's 'hopes...scene' difficult to justify on graphical grounds. The reading we suggest is *make rapes in such a scour* (scour = a sudden rush or onset, v. N.E.D.), explaining the F. 'rope's' and 'scarre' as misreadings of the regular type, due to *a* : *o* and *u* : *r* confusion (v. T.I. pp. xli–xlii; Ham. Sp. and Misp. pp. 41–4); 'rapes' was originally proposed for 'rope's' by Fleay. The reading gives good sense: 'I see', says Diana drily as she avoids the embrace, 'that men try to take us by storm, in the hope that we shall fall a prey to them in mere giddiness.'

50–1. *Brings in...assault* The metaphor is, of course, drawn from the tournament.

65. *though there...done* She means him to understand 'though my surrender be the end of my hopes of marriage,' while at the same time she hints at the accomplishment of her hope concerning Helena; v. G. 'done.'

67. S.D. F. gives no 'exit.'

73. *braid* 'Of doubtful meaning and origin' (N.E.D.); variously interpreted as (i) = braided, i.e. plaited, tortuous, deceitful, (ii) = brayed, or braided, i.e. damaged (goods). But is it not simply the Scotch for 'broad' = loose, a word used to please King James and rhyme with 'maid'?

76. S.D. F. 'Exit.'

4. 3.

S.D. F. 'Enter the two French Captaines, and ſome two or three Souldiours.' The speeches of the 'Captaines' are headed 'Cap.G.' and 'Cap.E.' but so carelessly are these two 'lords' or 'captains' distinguished in the F. text that though 1 Lord (= Cap.G.) was Bertram's accomplice in the matter of Diana at 3. 6. 104–11 while 2 Lord (= Cap.E.) goes off to deal with Parolles, we have here 2 Lord telling 1 Lord all about the Diana affair. No previous editor seems to have noticed this, but we have set the matter right by transposing the parts in ll. 1–71, after which all is well in F.

4. *changed...man* Brigstocke explains this as 'turned pale,' and quotes *Jew of Malta*, 4. 4. 67 'At the reading of the letter he looked like a man of another world.' It can hardly refer to a moral change in view of ll. 13–17 below.

16. *monumental* v. G.

17. *made* i.e. a made man. 'He thinks he has won a fortune with his unchaste bargain.'

18. *God lay* F. 'God delay' 'Delay' can hardly be right, seeing that, as Williams remarks, 'no advantage could arise from mere postponement.' Hanmer accordingly read 'allay'. But 'lay' (= exorcise, lay the spirit of) gives a much better sense and 'Godde lay' might by misdivision easily get printed as 'God delay.' For 'rebellion' the meaning of which seems to have escaped even N.E.D. v. G. and cf. 5. 3. 6.

18–19. *ourselves* i.e. unaided by God (Brigstocke).

22. *attain to their abhorred ends* not 'attain their evil purpose' but 'come to their dreadful death' i.e. to the block. If 1. 1. 122 be an allusion to the Gunpowder Plot, this passage about traitors may be another.

24. *in his proper...himself* i.e. betrays his own secrets in his own talk (Dr Johnson).

25. *Is it not...in us* i.e. isn't it a damnable notion of ours.

28–9. *dieted to his hour* i.e. restricted (or regulated) to his hour. Bertram had promised to remain an hour only (4. 2. 58). The passage has been generally misunderstood. 'Diet' had no necessary reference to food in Shakespeare's day; the word comes from 'dieta' (med. L.) = a plan of life or a day's work, and still retained its general meaning. Cf. note 5. 3. 220 and *Cor.* 5. 1. 57 'dieted to my request.'

31. *company* i.e. companion, v. G. Probably a misprint.

32. *judgement* (Pope) F. 'iudgements'

32–3. *so curiously...counterfeit* A metaphor from jewelry; i.e. so cunningly set this sham brilliant.

40. *travel higher* i.e. further into Tuscany; cf. note 2. 1. 12.

43–4. *Let it be forbid, sir...act* Is not this an odd style for one brother to use to another?

46. *house: her* F. 'houſe, her'

56. *come, was* F. 'come: was'

71. S.D. F. 'Enter a Meſſenger.' But the speech is headed 'Ser.'

79–82. *They cannot be too sweet* etc. F. gives this to *Ber.* in spite of the fact that Bertram's ensuing speech is also headed *Ber.* v. p. 103.

80. S.D. F. 'Enter Count Roſſillion.'—at l. 78.

84. *by an abstract of success* i.e. to give an abstract of my successes. His summary follows (Thistleton).

86. *nearest,* F. 'neereſt;'

87. *entertained my convoy* i.e. engaged my means of conveyance home.

88. *effected* (F2) F. 'affected'

95–6. *dialogue between the Fool and the Soldier* The F. capitals add point, and should be retained.

97–8. *a double-meaning prophesier* A reference to equivocal oracles or prognosticators of any kind.

99. S.D. F. gives no 'exit.'

113. S.D. F. 'Enter Parolles with his Interpreter.'

116. *Hush! hush!* F. gives these words to Bertram, but they clearly belong to 1 Lord who acts as master of the ceremonies, as Hanmer first perceived. Cf. note l. 136 and p. 103. Possibly 'Hush! hush! Hoodman comes!' should be taken together as the traditional cry when the 'hoodman' enters in the game of blind-man's buff.

125. *out of a note* i.e. according to a memorandum of questions.

134–35. *how and which way you will* Parolles is ignorant of the supposed nationality of his interlocutors; he therefore promises a protestant or catholic sacrament according to requirement.

136. *All's one to him* F. prints these words at the end of Parolles' speech in the previous line; cf. note l. 116 and p. 103.

140. *theoric of war* Cf. 'the bookish theoric' *Oth.* 1. 1. 24.

149. *in the nature* i.e. after the fashion in which. For 'con thanks' v. G.

157. *leave* (Staunton) F. 'liue' The F. makes Parolles say just the contrary of what he means. For 'leave' = die cf. *Ham.* 5. 2. 235 'what is't to leave betimes.' A confusion between 'leve' and 'lyve' would be easy; the reverse misprint is found in *Ham.* 3. 4. 158 (Q2). Hanmer proposed 'live but'

158–62. The names in this speech are remarkable: Corambus seems to derive from the old *Hamlet*, while Guiltian and Chitopher are curiosities of invention, unless they are misprints for Guilliam and Christopher. Gratii and Bentii are strange too.

161, 162–63. *two hundred and fifty* (Rowe) F. 'two hundred fiftie'

169. *condition,* F. 'condition:'

183–84. *the shrieve's fool* 'Shrieve' is a form of

'sheriff.' The sheriff had charge of idiots whose property was not of sufficient value to make them profitable wards for the Crown. *innocent* = idiot.

187. *forfeit to the next tile* i.e. a sudden death awaits such a liar.

193. *lordship* F. 'Lord'—probably 'L.' in the copy.

220. *When he swears* etc. F. heads this 'Int. Let.' i.e. Interpreter's Letter, which looks like the heading of a stage-paper, v. *M.V.* pp. 96–9.

221. *scores* v. G.

222. *Half won...make it* i.e. 'A match well made is half won; make your match, therefore, but make it well' (Mason).

225. *mell with* Steevens and Malone disputed whether this word possessed an indelicate meaning; N.E.D. 'mell' vb. 5 leaves no doubt.

but to kiss (Pope) F. 'not to kis'

226. *count of this* i.e. reckon on this.

236. *the general's* (F3) F. 'your Generals' Possibly 'ye' misread as 'yr'

245. *valour:* F. 'valour.'

246. *an egg out of a cloister* i.e. 'anything, however trifling, from any place, however holy' (Dr Johnson).

262–63. *led the drum...tragedians* i.e. beat the drum at the head of the procession of actors through the streets, an advertisement which commonly preceded the performance of a play (v. Chambers, *Eliz. Stage*, ii. 547, n. 2; iv. 199).

266. *Mile-end* The London militia or city trained bands exercised themselves at Mile-end Green. Most references in contemporary drama to the militia pour ridicule upon them: cf. 2 *Hen. IV*, 3. 2. 298–306, and the famous scene in *The Knight of the Burning Pestle*.

271. *a cat still* Bertram's 'damnable iteration' on the cat is contemptible beside the soaring invention of Parolles.

274. *cardecue* F. 'Cardceue'

274–76. *fee-simple...remainders* v. G.

275. *inheritance of it;* F. 'inheritance of it,'

286. *outruns any lackey* A lackey at this time was a 'running footman' (N.E.D.) for the dispatch of messages and errands.

296. *lascivious* F. 'lafciuious'

309. *So, look* etc. A line of verse in the midst of prose.

310. *Good morrow* etc. F. heads this 'Count.' though up to this all Bertram's speeches in the scene have been headed 'Ber.' Note also that we suddenly get 'Lo.E.' for 'Cap.E.' at ll. 311, 313. Have we come upon a different stratum of text?

318. S.D. F. 'Exeunt.'

326. S.D. F. 'Exit.'

330. *shall: simply* F. 'fhall. Simply'

331. *live. Who* F. 'liue: who'

337. S.D. F. 'Exit.'

4.4.

S.D. F. 'Enter Hellen, Widdow, and Diana.'

3. *'fore* (F2) F. 'for'

7. *Through flinty Tartar's bosom* Cf. *M.V.* 4. 1. 30–2:

> pluck commiseration of his state
> From brassy bosoms and rough hearts of flint,
> From stubborn Turks and Tartars.

9. *Marseillës* (Rowe) F. 'Marcellae' The metre requires three syllables; cf. *Shrew*, pp. 103–104.

11. *dead: the* F. 'dead, the'

16. *you, mistress* (F4) F. 'your Miftris'

19. *brought me up* We should now use the biblical phrase 'raised me up.'

21–4. *But, O strange men* etc. Malone aptly quotes *Meas.* 2. 4. 45–6:

> Their saucy sweetness, that do coin heaven's image
> In stamps that are forbid.

23. *saucy...thoughts* i.e. lust's readiness to accept delusions.

31. *the word, that time* F. 'the word the time' The emendation proposed assumes the kind of petty change that compositors are particularly prone to, and gives an easy and straightforward reading to a passage that has puzzled most edd. 'Yet suffer I pray you,' says Helena repeating her 'yet' of l. 27, 'but with my word, my promise, that time will turn the bitter into sweet.' The second half of this paraphrase is taken from a note of Brigstocke's which suggested the emendation.

34. *waggon* The word gives us a glimpse of the way in which ladies travelled at this period; cf. Sh. Eng. i. 203–204.

time revives us This, remarks Henley, 'seems to refer to the happy and speedy termination of their embarrassments.' Nevertheless, I suspect with Dr Johnson, that Shakespeare wrote 'time invites us'; cf. *Ham.* 1. 3. 83.

35. *All's well* etc. The introduction of the title of the play, a proverbial expression, into the dialogue is one of the many parallels between this play and *Measure for Measure* (5. 1. 407).

the fine's the crown Tilley quotes *Troil.* 4. 5. 224 'the end crowns all.'

36. S.D. F. 'Exeunt.'

4.5.

S.D. F. 'Enter Clowne, old Lady, and Lafew.' The order of entry is significant; it is unlikely that Shakespeare placed the Clown first.

2. *villanous saffron* Saffron was used at this time as a sudorific or cordial for promoting perspiration, as a colouring for pastry and as a fashionable starch. Probably Lafeu has all three meanings in mind.

3. *doughy* F. 'dowy'

6. *humble-bee* a profitless, buzzing creature—a good description of Parolles. For 'red-tailed' cf. note 1. 1. 113.

7. *I would I* Hanmer read 'I would he' which gives better sense.

9. *partaken* F. 'pertaken'

10. *dearest* F. 'deereſt' I retain the usual form, with some reluctance, since 'deerest' almost = 'direst' here; cf. N.E.D. 'dear, dere,' *Temp.* note 5. 1. 146–47, and G. 'dear.'

13. *salads* F. 'ſallets' 16. *salad* F. 'ſallet'

17. *knot-herbs* F. 'not hearbes' The F. reading has puzzled all, as it seems to contradict the second half of Lafeu's remark, and Rowe, followed by most 18th-cent. edd., read 'not salad-herbs' which gave the required sense, and marked the difference between what we should now call the vegetable-garden and the flower-garden. But a flower-bed in Shakespeare's day was known as a 'knot' (cf. N.E.D. which quotes 1577 B. Googe, *Heresbach's Husbandry* 'Basyell...is an hearbe that is used to be set in the middest of knottes...for the excellent savour that it hath'), while for the mute *k* which gave rise to the F. 'not' see Zacchrisson, *English Pronunciation at Shakespeare's Time*, 1927, p. 108, and cf. the pun on 'knight' and 'night' (1 *Hen. IV*, 1. 2. 27) and on 'nave' and 'knave' (2 *Hen. IV*, 2. 4. 281).

18. *nose-herbs* cf. nosegay.

20. *in grass* (Rowe) F. 'in grace' The Clown is punning of course upon 'grace,' cf. 'herb of grace.'

29. *bauble* v. G. and cf. *R. & J.* 2. 4. 97.

38. *name* (Rowe) F. 'maine'—a simple minim-misreading; cf. T.I. p. xli. The 'English name' is, of course, the Black Prince; the Elizabethans always thought of the Devil as black.

39. *fisnamy* F. 'fiſnomie' The Clown is clearly punning on 'name,' and the two spellings were interchangeable.

39. *more hotter* Warburton suggested 'more honour'd,' denouncing the F. reading as 'intolerable nonsense.' But Steevens pointed out that 'hotter fisnamy' is probably a reference to the so-called French disease. v. note ll. 94–7 below and G. 'French crown,' 'pile.'

44. *suggest* i.e. tempt, v. G.

52. *chill and tender* i.e. pampered and sensitive. The whole speech is a disquisition, from 'a shrewd knave and an unhappy,' on the text 'How hardly shall they that have riches enter into the kingdom of God.'

52–3. *the flowery way* Shakespeare was fond of this conception; cf. *Macb.* 2. 3. 23–4 'the primrose way to the everlasting bonfire,' and *Ham.* 1. 3. 50 'the primrose path of dalliance.'

58. *tricks* Cf. the description of the good ostler in *Knight of the Burning Pestle*, 2. 6. 50–2:

> Who will our palfreys slick with wisps of straw,
> And in the manger put them oats enough,
> And never grease their teeth with candle-stuff.

This greasing made it difficult to bite and so diminished the consumption of oats. For 'jades' tricks' v. G. and cf. *Ado*, 1. 1. 138.

61. S.D. F. 'exit'

62. *A shrewd knave and an unhappy.* Usually explained 'an evil and mischievous rascal'; but surely 'unhappy' means what it says—his pessimism is the very salt of the Clown's wit. Moreover, Lafeu approves of him—'I like him well, 'tis not amiss' (l. 67).

64. *him: by* F. 'him, by'

66. *has no pace* i.e. is not yet broken in. v. G. 'pace.'

67–8. *And I was about to tell you* This 'and' is odd. Is there textual patchwork here?

71. *in the minority of them both* Cf. note 1. 1. 5.

79. *Marseilles* (Pope) F. 'Marcellus' F2 'Marsellis' Cf. note 4. 4. 9.

83. *It rejoices* (F2) F. 'Ir reioyces'

87–90. *Madam, I was...honourable privilege* This has hitherto been passed over in silence; but it needs explanation. Lafeu has himself 'moved the king' in the matter of the marriage of his daughter with Bertram, why then should he now hesitate to meet him? And to what is the Countess referring?

92. S.D. F. 'Enter Clowne.'

94–7. *patch of velvet...worn bare* The same jest and very similar words are found in *Meas.* 1. 2. 32–5. It is a dreary joke upon the French disease, or syphilis, which when it affected the face was treated by the barber-surgeons of the time with incisions (cf. 'carbonadoed face') which were then covered with velvet plasters. For an account of the operation v. *Knight of the Burning Pestle*, 3. 4. 84–99. Cf. p. 110.

96. *a cheek of two pile* etc. Possibly a quibble upon 'check' (i.e. a fabric with a check-pattern) is intended here. v. G. 'pile.'

98–102. *A scar...soldier.* F. spaces these speeches out in short lengths so as to fill out the column and avoid printing the large heading 'Actus Quintus' at the foot of the page. Cf. note 3. 5. 1–15.

105. S.D. F. 'Exeunt.'

5. 1.

S.D. F. 'Enter Hellen, Widdow, and Diana, with two Attendants.'

5. *Be bold* i.e. be assured.

6. S.D. F. 'Enter a gentle Aſtringer.' An astringer (v. G.) is a kind of falconer, and his unexplained entry at this point has puzzled all commentators. Brigstocke suggests that 'the word "astringer" may have been added to the MS by the manager of the theatre merely to indicate the costume.' But why dress this gentleman as a falconer, unless the setting of the scene lent appropriateness to the costume, which it does not? Why not just 'Enter a Gentleman' as so often in Shakespeare and

as we find at his second entry 5. 3. 128, and leave it at that? There seem only two possible ways out of the difficulty: either (i) 'astringer' is a misprint for 'a stranger,' as the printer of F3 (following F2 'Enter a gentle Astranger') actually gives us, or (ii) this 'astringer' played a more conspicuous part in some earlier version of the play. [1929] Sir Edmund Chambers (*William Sh.* i. 450) plausibly suggests that Sh. wrote 'gentle(man) usher'. A spelling 'usscher' might be misread 'astriger'. [1952]

31. *Commend* F. 'Commend'

35. *Our means...means* It is natural to suspect corruption here. An anon. conj. would omit the second 'means' altogether.

38. S.D. F. gives no 'exeunt.'

5. 2.

S.D. F. 'Enter Clowne and Parrolles.'

1. *Master Lavache* (Tollet) F. 'Mr. Lavatch' It is a token of Parolles' fallen estate that he should address the Clown with such ceremony.

4. *muddied in fortune's mood* Theobald suggested 'moat' for 'mood' but, as Dyce points out, 'a quibble between "mood" and "mud" is intended here—the two words having been formerly pronounced nearly alike.' v. G. 'mood.'

18. S.D. F. 'Enter Lafew.'

19. *Here is a pur* etc. The Clown's speech is broken in two by the entry of Lafeu, and F. heads this second half with a fresh 'Clo.'

a pur of fortune's i.e. a knave of fortune's. A reference to the popular card-game of the time 'post and pair,' in which the knave was known as a 'pur'; v. N.E.D. 'pur' 2 and 'post' sb. 4 which quotes Bp. Jewel, 1565 'Hee commeth in onely with iolly brags and great vants, as if he were playing at Poste and should winne all by vying.' Parolles had indeed played 'post and pair,' and lost. Hitherto unexplained.

fortune's cat The proverbial jumping cat, I suppose, which men watch to see which way it leaps.

23. *ingenerous* (Brigstocke conj.) F. 'ingenious' The F. reading cannot be right and might easily have arisen from a hasty misreading of 'ingenerous' = mean-spirited, dastardly.

24. *similes* (Theobald) F. 'ſmiles' Steevens quotes an entry from the Stat. Reg. 1595 'A book of verie pythie similies, comfortable and profitable for all men to reade.'

25. S.D. F. gives no 'exit.'

32. *under her* (F2) F. 'vnder'

33. *the justices* i.e. the justices of the peace, who under the new Poor Law of 1601 were entrusted with the relief of the poor, and required to distinguish between able-bodied poor unwilling to labour who must be set to work and the impotent poor who werc to be relieved.

40. *more than one word* (F3) F. 'more then word' Cf. ll. 35–6 'hear me one single word.' Lafeu is playing upon the name Parolles.

43. *found me* Cf. note 2. 3. 210, p. 111 and G. 'find.'

44–5. *lost thee* i.e. took away your character. v. G. 'lose.'

47. *bring me out* Very much the same meaning as 'find me,' i.e. expose me.

51. S.D. F. gives none. Theobald added 'Trumpets sound.'

55. S.D. F. omits 'exeunt.'

5. 3.

S.D. F. 'Flouriſh. Enter King, old Lady, Lafew, the two French Lords, with attendants.'

1. *esteem* v. G.

3–4. *know her...home* i.e. appreciate her to the full. v. G. 'home.'

6. *blaze* (Theobald) F. 'blade' The F. reading,

which suggests the springtime of youth, has a certain plausibility, but the context ('oil and fire...burns on') makes 'blaze' necessary, and this word, if written with an oversized *e* might be misread as 'blayd,' a common 16th-cent. sp. of 'blade.' Tilley (234) quotes *Euphues* 'the tottering estate of lovers who think...with oil to quench fire.'

10. *high bent* i.e. aimed with all my might; cf. 'high-repented,' l. 36 below.

12. *pardon—* F. 'pardon:'

17. *richest eyes* Steevens explains 'eyes that have seen the greatest number of fair women' and quotes *A.Y.L.* 4. 1. 22–3 'to have seen much...is to have rich eyes.' *eyes,* F. 'eies:'

22. *All repetition* i.e. all raking-up of the past. Dr Johnson writes here, characteristically: 'Decency required that Bertram's double crime of cruelty and disobedience, joined likewise with some hypocrisy, should raise more resentment; and that though his mother might easily forgive him, his king should more pertinaciously vindicate his own authority and Helen's merit. Of all this Shakespeare could not be ignorant, but Shakespeare wanted to conclude his play.'

25. *Th'incensing relics* Cf. 1. 1. 100, and v. G. 'relics.'

27. S.D. F. gives no 'exit.'

28. F. prints 'What...daughter,/Haue you ſpoke?'—probably because the compositor could not find room for the whole line and the speech-heading 'Kin.' without over-running.

29. *hath reference* N.E.D. quotes Daniel, *Civil Wars*:

> We will ourselfe take time to heare
> Your cause at large: wherein we will you haue
> No other reference, but repaire to vs.

30–1. *Then...fame.* F. prints as prose probably because 'Then...sent' with the speech-heading 'Kin.'

occupies the whole of a line of type, and there is no room to tuck the word 'me' over the top, owing to the length of the line before.

31. *sets* 'Letters' is singular; cf. 4. 5. 84.

S.D. F. 'Enter Count Bertram.'

32. *a day of season* a seasonable day.

35. *Distracted clouds* i.e. the parting clouds.

39. *take...top:* Cf. *Ado*, 1. 2. 13 'take the present time by the top,' and v. G. 'top.' Tilley (468) quotes Pettie's *Petite Pallace*, ii. 185 'Let not occasion slip, for it is bald behind, it cannot be pulled back again by the hair.'

41–2. *Th'inaudible...Steals* Steevens quotes *Arcadia* 'The summons of Time had so creepingly stolne upon him, that hee had heard scarcely the noise of his feet.'

44. F. punctuates 'Admiringly my Liege, at firſt' which leaves it doubtful whether 'at first' begins a new sentence or not. We follow Rowe; Clark and Wright make 'admiringly' qualify 'I stuck my choice.'

48. *Contempt* This is the subject of the sentence. For 'perspective' v. G.

54. *loved,* F. 'lou'd;'

59. *turns a sour offence* As good food turns bad and smells when kept too long.

63–6. *Oft...afternoon.* v. p. 108. For 'shameful hate' *Globe* reads 'shame full late'

65. *done,* F. 'don,e'

69–72. *The main...cesse!* These couplets are not much superior to ll. 63–6. L. 72 is particularly awkward.

71–2. *Which better...cesse!* F. prints these lines as part of the King's speech. Theobald first restored them to the Countess.

74. *digested,* F. 'digeſted:'

76. S.D. F. gives none.

79. *The last that e'er* Though the sense is clear enough, there is obviously something wrong with the

text. The simplest emendation, suggested by more than one ed., would be to read 'the last time e'er,' i.e. the last time ever.

81. *see it;* F. 'ſee it.'

91. *life's* F. 'liues'—as often in Shakespeare.

96. *ungaged:* (Theobald) F. 'ingag'd.'—a minim-misreading; v. T.I. p. xli. Most edd. read 'ingag'd' and explain as = unengaged; but there is no other instance of such a word. 'Ungaged,' on the other hand, is the natural negative of 'gaged' (*M.V.* 1. 1. 130) and is found in Campian's *Fourth Booke of Ayres*, no. xiii (v. Fellowes, *English Madrigal Verse*) 'Shall my wounds onely weepe, and hee vngaged goe?'

96–7. *subscribed...fortune* i.e. made a statement of my affairs (namely that he was already a married man). Bertram is clever in the way he reminds the King of his 'clog.'

100. *satisfaction* i.e. my statement convinced her.

101–102. *Plutus...med'cine* (Rowe) F. 'Platus... med'cine' Plutus, the god of gold, the discoverer of hidden treasure, is here spoken of as 'the grand alchemist, who knows the tincture which confers the properties of gold upon base metals and the matter by which gold is multiplied' (Dr Johnson). 'Medicine' = the alchemist's elixir; cf. *A. & C.* 1. 5. 36–7 'that great medicine hath/ With his tinct gilded thee,' and v. G.

105. *if you know* i.e. as sure as you know.

111. *come—* F. 'come:'

113. *falsely,...honour;* (Rowe) F. 'falſely:... Honour,'

114. *conjectural* (F2) F. 'connecturall'—a minim-error.

116. *That thou* F. 'That rhou'

121–23. *My fore-past...little* i.e. the previous evidence ('fore-past proofs') is weighty enough to warrant more than my present fears, and hitherto my fears have been all too slight.

122. *tax* (F2) F. 'taze' i.e. blame, reprove.

127. S.D. F. gives no 'exit.'

128. S.D. F. 'Enter a Gentleman.'—at l. 127.

131. *removes* Dr Johnson explains this as 'post-stages'; but it is not exactly that. The word denotes the *departures* of the King upon each stage of his journey, and the gentleman conveys by it how Helena has four or five times just missed the King at his 'remove.'

139. *Upon his many* etc. F. heads this 'A letter' and supplies no speech-heading. Rowe assigned it to the King. Cf. *M.V.* pp. 96–9.

146. *Capulet* (Rowe) F. 'Capilet' Here, as often elsewhere, Shakespeare catches at a name, already used in another play, and employs it for a minor purpose.

147–48. *toll for this* i.e. pay toll to get rid of this one, v. G. 'toll.'

150, 151. S.D. F. gives no 'exit' either for the gentleman or for attendants.

153. S.D. F. 'Enter Bertram.'—at l. 151.

154. *sir, sith wives* (Dyce) F. 'ſir, ſir, wiues'

156. S.D. F. 'Enter Widdow, Diana, and Parrolles.' The appearance of Parolles is odd here, more especially as F. also gives him his right entry at l. 229. Is it a survival of some earlier state of the MS? Ll. 198–99 (v. note) would seem to suggest this.

158. *Capulet* (Rowe) F. 'Capilet' Cf. note l. 146 above.

163. *And both...remedy* i.e. both age and honour will perish unless you help us.

169. *mine;* F. 'mine,'

182. *them: fairer* (Hanmer) F. 'them fairer:'

194. *'tis it* (Capell) F. 'tis hit' Most edd. read 'it', of which 'hit' is a not uncommon 16th-cent. sp. Thistleton, taking 'hit' as a verb, interprets: 'the mark is hit, whereof the blush is the proof.' Rather, I think, the blush was the proof of the ring, which the Countess could not identify from where she stood.

198–99. *Methought...witness it* She has said nothing of the kind in the text as it stands. The words, together with the double entry for Parolles (cf. note l. 156 S.D.), strongly suggest textual adaptation.

203. S.D. F. gives no 'exit.'

What of him etc. F. heads this speech 'Roſ.' and likewise all Bertram's speeches, for the rest of the play; up to this point of the scene the heading has been 'Ber.' Probably a sign of revision; cf. notes ll. 156, 198–99.

204. *perfidious* F. 'pe fidious'

205–206. *deboshed;...sickens but...truth.* (Hanmer) F. 'deboſh'd,...ſickens: but...truth,'

211. *She knew her distance* i.e. she knew how to fence, v. G. 'distance.'

215. *infinite cunning* (Singer) F. 'inſuite comming'—a fine example of minim-confusion, 'conning' being a common sp. for 'cunning.'

modern grace i.e. commonplace charm. Bertram is subtle: he emphasises the cunning and depreciates the personal attractions of Diana.

219. *that turned* (Rowe) F. 'that haue turn'd'

220. *diet* Brigstocke pronounces this 'undoubtedly corrupt'; but cf. 4. 3. 28. I connect the expression with 'market-price' (l. 218) and 'turned off' = discharged from service (l. 219) and explain as 'pay off after a day's work.' The word derives from med. L. 'dieta' = a day's work, a day's wage, etc. (v. N.E.D. 'diet' sb. 2). 'You,' says Diana, 'who dismissed so noble a first wife, may properly enough send me packing after a day's work'—which is what he imagined he had done.

222. *return it home* i.e. return it you again.

224–25. *Sir, much...finger.* F. prints this in one line.

228–29. *The story...casement?* F. prints no query, but the King is evidently asking Diana a question.

229. S.D. F. 'Enter Parolles.' v. note l. 156 above.

234. *master*— F. 'maſter:'

236. *By him* etc. v. G. 'by.'

237–39. *So please your majesty* etc. Note this prose-section in the midst of a verse-scene, a section entirely concerned with the evidence of Parolles.

238. *gentleman:* F. 'Gentleman.'

242. *but how?* Malone suggested that this rightly belonged to the King, and it may well be so. For other examples of incorrect assignment of parts of speeches, v. notes 4. 3. 116, 136, and p. 103.

244. *gentleman* (F2) F. 'Gent.'

249. *companion* Contemptuous, as usual, in Shakespeare.

252. *drum* i.e. drummer. *naughty* i.e. worthless.

294. S.D. F. gives no 'exit.'

298. *quit* The meaning is deliberately left obscure, v. G.

303. S.D. F. 'Enter Hellen and Widdow.'

exorcist A term applicable both to the summoning and the expulsion of spirits. Cf. R. Scot, *Discovery of Witchcraft* (xv. xii. 412) 'I doo conjure and I doo exorcise you...that you do come to me.'

312. *And are* (Rowe) F. 'And is'

320. *Tom Drum* v. G. 'Drum.'

handkercher: F. 'handkercher.'

322. *curtsies* F. 'curtſies' v. G.

324. *even truth* i.e. the whole truth; cf. note 2. 1. 191. v. G. 'even.'

330. *Resolvedly* (F2) F. 'Reſolduedly'

332. S.D. F. 'Flouriſh.' The epilogue follows in italic type with no heading of any kind.

333. *The king's a beggar* Malone suggested a reference here to the ballad 'of the King and the Beggar' (*L.L.L.* 1. 2. 106–7) and quoted *R. II*, 5. 3. 79–80:

> Our scene is altered from a serious thing,
> And now changed to 'The Beggar and the King.'

336. *strife* (F2) F. 'ſtrift'

day exceeding day growing better and better every day.

337. *yours our parts* It is characteristic of this riddling style that the words can be interpreted as 'it is for you to take our parts' (Johnson) or as 'we have played our parts for you' (Brigstocke).

338. S.D. F. 'Exeunt omn.'

THE STAGE-HISTORY OF
ALL'S WELL THAT ENDS WELL

The stage-history of this comedy is brief and inglorious. There is no record of its performance (or of any performance of *Love's Labour's Won*) before the closing of the theatres; and although it appears in the list (of January, 1669) of plays allotted to Killigrew for the King's Company (Nicoll, *Restoration Drama*, 316), he seems to have made no use of it. The first known performance was at Goodman's Fields Theatre on March 7, 1741, seven months before 'a Gentleman (who never appeared on any Stage),' in other words David Garrick, made theatrical history by appearing on those same boards as King Richard III. The play was given for the benefit of Mrs Giffard, the manager's wife, who acted Helena, her husband taking Bertram, with Peterson as Parolles and Miss Hippisley as Diana. The novelty was evidently liked, for it was given four times more in as many weeks. Just about that time Shakespeare's long-neglected comedies were coming into public favour; and in January, 1742, *All's Well that Ends Well* made its first known appearance at the Theatre Royal, Drury Lane, with Mills as Bertram, Theophilus Cibber as Parolles, Mrs Woffington as Helena, Mrs Butler as the Countess and Macklin as the Clown. Mrs Woffington was taken ill and fainted on the stage. Milward, as the King, caught the cold of which he died not many days later. Theophilus Cibber had stolen the part of Parolles from Macklin, to whom it had been promised; and there was ill-feeling as well as illness in the company. But in spite of this untoward start the play had good success when it was tried again in February, and it reached ten performances that season. Cibber liked acting Parolles, and had brought the part into notice; but succeeding performances of the play seem to have been determined by the fancy taken for the part by Woodward, who, during nearly thirty years from 1746, acted Parolles in whichever of the two theatres he happened to be engaged at and also in his own management at Dublin. Mrs Pritchard, who began by being Helena, changed about 1756 to the Countess, and made it one of her best and best-liked impersonations. But at this period the comic elements in the play were given prominence over the romantic theme; and although Helena was acted by Miss Macklin, Mrs Palmer, Mrs Mattocks and Miss Farren, and Bertram by Palmer and Lewes, these parts were shorn of their poetry in order that more attention might be paid to Woodward as Parolles and to Yates, or Shuter, or Edwin as the Clown.

In or about 1794 John Philip Kemble took the play in hand and made a judicious version of it which brought it back pretty nearly to the original. At Drury Lane on December 12, 1794, he produced it, playing Bertram himself, with King for Parolles, John Bannister for the Clown, Mrs Powell for the Countess, and Mrs Jordan for Helena. Even with these players, the comedy cannot have been well received, for John Kemble did not try it again; and in 1811 Charles Kemble only got two performances out of it (May 24 and June 22) when he presented the same version at Covent Garden, with himself as Bertram, Fawcett as Parolles, Munden as 'Lefeu,' Blanchard as the Clown, Mrs H. Johnston as Helena (though from the printed acting edition it seems that that part had been intended for Sally Booth), and Mrs Weston as the Countess. We find Mrs Weston 'every thing that could be wished' in the same part at Bath in May, 1821, when the play had the good fortune to reach a third performance. But all readers of it will share the surprise of Professor Odell (*Shakespeare from Betterton to Irving*, ii. 146) at discovering that on October 12, 1832, *All's Well that Ends Well* was given at Covent Garden as an opera. Laporte had recently assumed the management of the theatre; and the playbill (which is in the collection of the Garrick Club) shows that he boldly gave the piece the sub-title, *Love's Labour Won*, got music for it from Rophino Lacy and scenery from the Grieves, cast Wilson for Bertram, Bartley for Lafeu, Jones for Parolles, Mrs Lovell for the Countess, Miss Shirreff for Diana (here surnamed Capulet) and Miss Inverarity for Helena, freely culled songs for the medley from other works by Shakespeare, and made a vaunted attraction of a masque of *Oberon and Robin Goodfellow*, more or less from *A Midsummer-Night's Dream*, with Miss Horton as Oberon and Miss Poole as Robin. Twenty years later, on September 1, 1852, the unhappy play, as found in the Folio, was given a trial by Samuel Phelps (who played Parolles) in his ninth season at Sadler's Wells; but more than half a century was to pass before anyone had the courage to try it again. In 1916 the Benson Company did the play at the Memorial Theatre, Stratford-upon-Avon. In May, 1920, the Elizabethan Stage Society, under Mr William Poel, gave two performances of it at the Ethical Church, Bayswater; and in 1922 the New Shakespeare Company made it the 'Birthday Play' at Stratford-upon-Avon. It is, of course, in the repertory of the Old Vic. I have found no record of its ever having been staged in the United States of America.

[1929] HAROLD CHILD

GLOSSARY

Note. Where a pun or quibble is intended, the meanings are distinguished as (*a*) and (*b*)

ABLE FOR (be), be a match for; 1. 1. 66

ACCORDINGLY, in proportion; 2. 5. 9

ACROSS. An expression from the tilt-yard, implying that the jest or sally has missed its mark, as the unskilful tilter breaks his lance across his opponent's body instead of goring him with its point (cf. *A.Y.L.* note 3. 4. 39–41); 2. 1. 67

ACT, activity, the life of action; 1. 2. 30

ADDITION, title, style of address; 2. 3. 130

ADMIRATION, wonder, marvel; 2. 1. 88

ADOPTIOUS, assumed, adopted (a coinage of Shakespeare's); 1. 1. 174

ADVERTISEMENT, warning, admonition; 4. 3. 210

ADVICE, prudence, forethought; 3. 4. 19

AMES-ACE, i.e. ambs-ace, double ace, the lowest possible throw at dice; 2. 3. 82

AMPLE, adv. completely (cf. *Tim.* 1. 2. 136 'how ample you're beloved'); 3. 5. 42

ANATOMIZE, lit. dissect (surg.), lay open minutely, expose; 4. 3. 31

APPEACH, turn informer, peach. 'Peach' and 'appeach' are originally the same word, but 'appeach' generally means (both in Sh. and elsewhere) to accuse or charge with a crime, without any implication of treachery on the part of the accuser; 1. 3. 188

APPLICATION, medical treatment; 1. 2. 74

APPOINTMENTS, engagements, business. Bertram may be referring to his equipment for the journey, 'appointment' being a common word for equipage; 2. 5. 69

APPREHENSIVE, quick to apprehend or receive impressions; 1. 2. 60

APPROOF, confirmed reputation, general recognition (cf. *approve*); 1. 2. 50; 2. 5. 3

APPROVE, test, confirm, prove; 1. 2. 10; 1. 3. 225; 3. 7. 13

ARAISE, raise from the dead. An archaic word chosen to suit 'King Pepin' (N.E.D. quotes no later example); 2. 1. 76

ARGUMENT, subject-matter of conversation; 2. 3. 7

ARMIPOTENT, mighty in arms (a conventional epithet, here ludicrous, usually applied to Mars; cf. Chaucer, *Kt's Tale*, 1982 and *L.L.L.* G.); 4. 3. 233

ARTIST, man of skill or learning, (here) physician; 2. 3. 10

ASTRINGER, i.e. austringer, falconer, keeper of goshawks; 5. 1. 6 S.D.

AUTHENTIC, legally qualified or authorised; 2. 3. 14

BAND, bond, promise (cf. *R. II*, 1. 1. 2 'thy oath and band'); 4. 2. 56

BARE, shave (v. note); 4. 1. 48

BARNES, bairns, children (? with a quibble upon 'barns'); 1. 3. 25

BATE, remit, except; 2. 1. 13; 2. 3. 226

BAUBLE, i.e. the fool's stick, ending in a fool's head. Here used in an equivocal sense (cf. *R. & J.* 2. 4. 97); 4. 5. 29

BEFORE ME, (*a*) in my presence, (*b*) upon my soul; 2. 4. 30

BESTOW, confer as a gift. Most edd. interpret 'put away' (cf. note); 1. 3. 222

BLOOD, i.e. passion (cf. *M.V.* 1. 2. 17); 1. 3. 128

BOARD, accost, make advances to (the orig. nautical meaning still felt in the word, conveying the sense of hostile attack); 5. 3. 210

BOGGLE, shy like a startled horse, take alarm; 5. 3. 231

BOLD (be), be assured (cf. *L.L.L.* 2. 1. 28 'Bold of your worthiness'); 5. 1. 5

BOTCHER, a tailor who does repairs; 4. 3. 182

BRAID. 'Of doubtful meaning and origin' (N.E.D.). Possibly Sc. for 'broad' = loose, lascivious (v. note); 4. 2. 73

BRAVELY, i.e. (i) with a light heart; 2. 1. 29; 2. 3. 303; (ii) at a high rate or value; 3. 5. 51

BRAVING, defiant; 1. 2. 3

BREAK, break up, disband; 4. 4. 11

BREATH, speech, utterance (cf. *Ado*, 5. 1. 256; *Meas.* 5. 1. 121); 2. 1. 148

BREATHE (one's self), take exercise; 2. 3. 259

BREATHING, exercise; 1. 2. 17

BRIEF, (i) legal document, contract; 2. 3. 182; (ii) a summary; 5. 3. 137

BROKE, to trade as a procurer. 'A broker in our author's time meant a bawd or pimp' Malone (cf. *Ham.* 1. 3. 127–30 'brokers ...like sanctified and pious bawds'); 3. 5. 70

BROKEN, i.e. gap-toothed; 2. 3. 63

BY, about, concerning; 5. 3. 236

CALENDAR, register; 1. 3. 5

CANARY, a lively Spanish dance; 2. 1. 74

CAPABLE, ready to learn (cf. Hooker, *Eccl. Pol.* v. lvii. 1 'infants which are not capable of instruction,' and *L.L.L.* 4. 2. 82); 1. 1. 97, 209

CAPRICCIO, It., caprice (the word 'caprice' did not enter the language before 1660); 2. 3. 297

CAPTIOUS, (*a*) fallacious, deceptive, (*b*) receptive (v. note); 1. 3. 199

CARBONADOED, slashed or scored (like a piece of meat for broiling); 4. 5. 100

CARDECUE, Fr. 'quart d'écu' (a silver coin = c. 1*s.* 6*d.*); 4. 3. 274; 5. 2. 32

CARP, (*a*) freshwater fish commonly bred in ponds, (*b*) talkative person (v. 'carp' vb. N.E.D.); 5. 2. 22

CASE, vb. skin, strip (a term in venery. Cf. Turbervile, *Booke of Hunting*, 1576, p. 241 'The Harte and all manner of Deare are flayne....The Hare is stryped and...the Bore also: the Foxe, Badgerd and all other vermine are cased'); 3. 6. 98

CASE, sb. cause, suit (? with a quibble upon 'case' = body; cf. *Tw. Nt.* 5. 1. 168); 1. 3. 23

CASSOCK, long loose cloak, cloak worn by musketeers and other soldiers in 16th–17th cent. (the ecclesiastical sense is app. unknown before 1660); 4. 3. 166

CATASTROPHE, lit. the dénouement of a play, conclusion of any kind, tail-end; 1. 2. 57

CAUSE, disease, sickness (v. N.E.D. 'cause' 12, and cf. *Cor.* 3. 1. 235 'Leave us to cure this cause'); 2. 1. 111

CESSE, an archaic form of 'cease' (cf. *Ham.* 3. 3. 15 (Q2) 'The cesse of majesty'); 5. 3. 72

CHALLENGE, lay claim to, demand as a right; 2. 3. 137

CHAPE, 'the metal plate or mounting of a scabbard or sheath; particularly that which covers the point' (N.E.D.); 4. 3. 141

CHECK, reproach, rebuke; 1. 1. 68

CHOICE, 'special value, estimation' (N.E.D., quoting this as its only instance of the meaning). Probably a coinage from 'choice' adj. which is frequent in Sh.; 3. 7. 26

CHOUGH, 'a bird of the crow family; formerly applied somewhat widely to all the smaller chattering species, but especially to the common jackdaw' (N.E.D.); 4. 1. 19

CHRISTENDOM, christian name. A favourite expression with Nashe (cf. McKerrow, iii. 161. 12 'the right christendome of it is Cerdicke sands'). N.E.D. overlooks this meaning; 1. 1. 174

CITE, witness. A legal term = lit. to call witnesses; 1. 3. 207

CLEW, ball of thread or yarn; 1. 3. 179

CLOSE-STOOL, commode, 'a chamber utensil enclosed in a stool or box' (N.E.D.); 5. 2. 17

COARSELY, meanly, slightingly; 3. 5. 56

COIL, 'keep a coil' = make a fuss; 2. 1. 27

COMFORTABLE, lending moral or spiritual support; 1. 1. 77

COMMONER, prostitute; 5. 3. 193

COMPANION, fellow (in a contemptuous sense); 5. 3. 249

COMPANY, i.e. companion; 4. 3. 31

COMPOSITION, (i) product, combination; 1. 1. 203; (ii) bargain; 4. 3. 17

COMPT, reckoning; 5. 3. 57

CON THANKS, offer thanks, acknowledge gratitude; 4. 3. 149

CONDITION, nature, way of going on; 4. 3. 169, 253

CONGEE WITH, take leave of (cf. Fr. 'congé'); 4. 3. 85

CONVOY, means of transport, conveyance; 4. 3. 87; 4. 4. 10

CORAGIO!, courage!; 2. 5. 94

CORANTO, a lively dance (v. *Sh. Eng.* ii. 448–49); 2. 3. 46

COUNT OF, reckon with, attend to; 4. 3. 226

COX MY PASSION! A variant of 'Cock's passion' (cf. *Shrew*, 4. 1. 108), which is a corruption of 'God's passion'; 5. 2. 40–1

COZEN, cheat; 4. 2. 76; 4. 4. 23

CREATION, 'the investing with a title, dignity or function' (N.E.D.); 2. 3. 172

CURIOUS, fastidious, difficult to please, minutely accurate; 1. 2. 20

CURIOUSLY, carefully, with cunning art; 4. 3. 32

CURTAL, a horse with its tail cut short—here used as a name; 2. 3. 62

CURTSY, bow, salute (not as now confined to the feminine bow); 3. 5. 90; 5. 3. 322

CURVET. Term of the manège = 'a leap of a horse in which the fore-legs are raised together and equally advanced, and the hind-legs raised with a spring before the fore-legs reach the ground' (N E.D.); 2. 3. 286

CUSTOMER, common woman, prostitute (cf. *Oth.* 4. 1. 123); 5. 3. 285

DEAR, severe, dire (cf. note); 4. 5. 10

DEBILE, weak; 2. 3. 37

DEBOSHED, old form of 'debauched'; 2. 3. 141; 5. 3. 205

DEFAULT (v. note); 2. 3. 233

DELIVERANCE, manner of speech, speech; 2. 1. 82; 2. 5. 4

DERIVE, (i) inherit (cf. *well-derived*); 1. 1. 45; (ii) bring down upon (cf. *Hen. VIII*, 2. 4. 32 'What friend of mine/That had to him derived your anger, did I/Continue in my liking?'); 5. 3. 263

DIAL. May mean (i) a watch, (ii) a pocket sun-dial, or (iii) a mariner's compass; the last seems intended here; 2. 5. 6

DIET, (i) regulate to a fixed programme (v. note); 4. 3. 28; (ii) pay off after a day's work (v. note); 5. 3. 220

DIGEST, assimilate, amalgamate (cf. *Lear*, 1. 1. 130 'With my two daughters' dowers digest this third'); 5. 3. 74

DILATED, extended (an affected expression); 2. 1. 57

DILEMMAS. Meaning doubtful = either 'alternative courses of action' or 'difficulties to be faced'; 3. 6. 72

DISCIPLE, vb. teach, train; 1. 2. 28

DISSOLVE, discharge (cf. *M.W.W.* 5. 5. 215); 1. 2. 66

DISTANCE. A term of fencing = the interval to be kept between the combatants (cf. *R. & J.* 2. 4. 22; *M.W.W.* 2. 1. 201; and *L. Comp.* 151 'With safest distance I mine honour shielded'); 5. 3. 211

DISTEMPERED, inclement (of the weather); 1. 3. 148

DISTRACTED, torn asunder, divided; 5. 3. 35

DOCTRINE, science, knowledge; 1. 3. 238

DOLE, 'a portion sparingly doled out' (N.E.D.); 2. 3. 172

DONE, (*a*) lost, ruined (cf. *Ham.* 3. 2. 172; *V.A.* 197), (*b*) accomplished; 4. 2. 65

DOWER, one who gives a dowry to the bride (N.E.D. does not record this meaning); 4. 4. 19

DRUM, i.e. drummer; 5. 3. 252

DRUM (John or Tom). 'Tom Drum's entertainment' = a rough reception. There are many references to it in Eliz. literature; probably all go back to some anecdote now lost; 3. 6. 35; 5. 3. 320

EAR, plough; 1. 3. 43

EMBOSS, 'to drive a hunted animal to extremity' (N.E.D.); 3. 6. 95

EMBOWEL, i.e. disembowel; 1. 3. 238

EMPIRIC, quack; 2. 1. 122

ENGROSS, buy up wholesale, monopolise; 3. 2. 64

ENJOINED, 'enjoined penitents' = persons upon whom penance has been imposed by their spiritual director (cf. N.E.D. 'enjoin' 2); 3. 5. 92

Ensconce, lit. 'shelter within or behind a fortification' (N.E.D.); 2. 3. 4

Enter (v. *well-entered*); 2. 1. 6

Entertain, engage, take into one's service; 4. 3. 87

Entertainment, service; 3. 6. 11–12; 4. 1. 15

Esteem, sb. (*a*) value of a property, (*b*) reputation of a man; 5. 3. 1

Even, vb., adj., adv. The word is a commercial one and refers to the balancing of accounts (v. N.E.D. 'even' vb. 10); thus (i) 'to even' = to accomplish; 1. 3. 4; (ii) 'to make even' = to accomplish or carry out; 2. 1. 191 (v. note); and (iii) 'even truth' = completed or full truth; 5. 3. 324

Examine, test, question closely; 3. 5. 62

Exception, disapproval (cf. mod. Eng. 'take exception'); 1. 2. 40

Exorcist. Strictly speaking one who expels spirits, but commonly used at this period as synonymous with 'conjurer' = one who conjures or summons spirits (v. note); 5. 3. 303

Expedient, expeditious, swiftly performed (v. note); 2. 3. 182

Facinerious (or 'facinorous'), infamous, abominably wicked (v. note); 2. 3. 32

Fact, crime; 3. 7. 47

Fall, decline, decadence; 2. 1. 13

Fancy, lit. fantasy, and so—a lover's fantasy, amorous inclination, love (in not a very serious sense); 5. 3. 213, 214

Fated, fateful, controlling the destinies of men; 1. 1. 216

Favour, good looks, face, feature; 1. 1. 85, 98; 5. 3. 49

Fee-simple, an estate belonging to the owner and his heirs for ever; 4. 3. 274

Figure, astrological term = 'a scheme or table showing the disposition of the heavens at a given time' (N.E.D. 'figure' 14); 3. 1. 12

File, (i) roll, list; 3. 3. 9; (ii) file for letters; 4. 3. 201; (iii) rank, line of soldiers; 4. 3. 266

Find, i.e. find out, unmask; 2. 3. 210; 2. 4. 32; 5. 2. 43

Fine, adj. subtle; 5. 3. 267

Fine, sb. end; 4. 4. 35; 5. 3. 214

Fisnamy (or 'fisnomy') = old form of 'physiognomy,' face (v. note); 4. 5. 39

Fistula, 'a long sinuous pipe-like ulcer with a narrow orifice' (N.E.D.); 1. 1. 35

Fit, to supply (e.g. with goods) 2. 1. 90

Flesh, to sate, gratify (lust); 4. 3. 15

Follow, attend upon, wait on; 2. 1. 99

Fore-past, already passed, previous (cf. Raleigh, *Discov. Guiana*, 21 'neither could any of the fore-passed vndertakers...discouer the country'); 5. 3. 121

Forsake, (i) decline, refuse; 2. 3. 59; (ii) abandon, desert; 4. 2. 39

Frank, (i) liberal, generous; 1. 2. 20; (ii) free; 2. 3. 58

French crown, (*a*) the coin paid to the 'taffeta punk,' (*b*) the 'French disease' or syphilis; 2. 2. 21

Friends, relations; 1. 3. 192

Furnish to, equip for; 2. 3. 294

Furniture, trappings; 2. 3. 62

GALEN, or Claudius Galenus (A.D. 131–? 200), the celebrated Greek physician, whose voluminous medical writings when translated into Latin in the 6th and 7th cents. acquired an authority which remained paramount in Europe for more than a thousand years. It was however challenged by Paracelsus (q.v.) in the 16th cent. and controversy followed which for a time split the medical profession into two schools, the Galenists and the Paracelsians; 2. 3. 12

GAMESTER, 'a lewd person, whether male or female' (N.E.D., cf. *Troil.* 4. 5. 63 'daughters of the game'); 5. 3. 187

GENERALLY, i.e. completely (cf. *Shrew*, 1. 2. 270 'generally beholding' = entirely beholden); 1. 1. 8

GO TO THE WORLD, get married (N.E.D. 'world' sb. 4c quotes from Calvin's *Sermons*, Eng. trans. 1579, 'This man is of the worlde, that is to say, he is maried: This man is of the Churche, that is to say, Spirituall'); 1. 3. 18

GO UNDER, i.e. go under the name of, appear to be; 3. 5. 20

GOSSIP, vb. to be gossip or sponsor to, to give a name to (a 'gossip' =lit. god-kin, i.e. godfather or godmother); 1. 1. 175

GROAT, a coin equal to four pence; 2. 2. 20

GROSS, obvious, palpable; 1. 3. 175

HAND (in any), in any case (cf. *Shrew*, 1. 2. 144 'at any hand'; *L.L.L.* 4. 3. 215 'of all hands'); 3. 6. 38–9

HAWKING, keen as a hawk's; 1. 1. 96

HEEL (on the), at the end; 1. 2. 57

HELP (sb. & vb.), cure (freq. in Shakespeare); 1. 3. 235–36; 2. 1. 124, 189, 190; 2. 3. 18

HEN, a chicken-hearted person; 2. 3. 217

HERALDRY, rank, precedence; 2. 3. 267

HERB OF GRACE, or herb-grace, the old name for rue ('supposed to have arisen like the synonym, Herb of repentance, out of the formal coincidence of the name Rue with rue =repentance' N.E.D.); 4. 5. 16

HILDING, good-for-nothing (lit. a vicious horse); 3. 6. 3

HOLD, i.e. uphold (v. note 1. 1. 9); 1. 1. 9, 79; 2. 3. 231; 3. 2. 89

HOLDING, consistency, coherence (cf. 1 *Hen. IV*, 1. 2. 34 'Thou sayest well, and it holds well too'); 4. 2. 27

HOME, adv. (i) completely, effectively; 5. 3. 4; (ii) back again to its right place; 5. 3. 222

HONESTY, chastity; *passim*

HOODMAN, the blind-man in 'hoodman-blind' or blind-man's-buff; 4. 3. 116

HOST, vb. lodge, put up; 3. 5. 92

IDLE, foolish, cracked, delirious; 2. 5. 51; 3. 7. 26

IMAGE, representative; 2. 1. 198

IMPORTANT, urgent, importunate, not to be withstood (cf. *Err.* 5. 1. 138; *Ado*, 2. 1. 63); 3. 7. 21

IMPORTING, important; 5. 3. 136

IMPOSITION, a task laid upon one; 4. 4. 29

IN, vb. gather in grain, harvest; 1. 3. 44

INCLINING, partiality, favouritism; 3. 6. 35–6
INDUCEMENT, instigation, influence; 3. 2. 87
INGENEROUS, dastardly; 5. 2. 23
INHIBITED, forbidden; 1. 1. 146–47
INNOCENT, imbecile; 4. 3. 184
INSTANCE, evidence; 4. 1. 40
INTEEMABLE, incapable of being emptied, inexhaustible (v. note); 1. 3. 199
INTER'GATORY. A legal expression ='a question formally put, or drawn up in writing to be put, to an accused person or witness' (N.E.D.); 4. 3. 180

JADE, a sorry nag; 2. 3. 288; 'jades' tricks' = mischievous tricks; 4. 5. 60
JOWL, vb. to dash or knock (two heads) together; 1. 3. 53
JUSTIFY, make good, confirm, prove; 4. 3. 52

KICKY-WICKY, 'a jocular or ludicrous term for a wife' (N.E.D., which suggests that it may be a humorous formation after the pattern of 'kicksey-winsey' = whim or erratic fancy); 2. 3. 284
KIND (in their), in their own way; 1. 3. 176
KNOWINGLY, i.e. with knowledge to justify one's opinion; 1. 3. 247

LAPSE, fall, ruin; 2. 3. 166
LATTICE (window of), 'a window of lattice-work (usually painted red), or a pattern on the shutter or wall imitating this, formerly a common mark of an ale-house or inn' (N.E.D.); 2. 3. 217
LAY, exorcise or calm (a disturbed spirit); 4. 3. 18
LEAGUER, camp; 3. 6. 24
LEAVE OFF, give up as incurable (cf. N.E.D. 'leave' 14 c (*b*)); 1. 3. 238
LEVEL, aim, the act of taking aim, the mark at which the weapon is aimed; 2. 1. 156
LIME, to catch with bird-lime (a glutinous substance smeared upon twigs to take small birds); 3. 5. 23
LING (old), salted ling (N.E.D. quotes a cookery book of 1747, 'old ling, which is the best sort of salt fish'), commonly eaten in Lent (v. note); 3. 2. 13, 14
LINSEY-WOOLSEY, lit. coarse material, part wool part flax. Hence—neither one thing nor another, a medley, nonsense; 4. 1. 11
LIST, lit. border, edge, strip. Hence—limit, boundary; 2. 1. 52
LIVELIHOOD, animation. The word is found once elsewhere in Sh. (i.e. *V.A.* 26); 1. 1. 52
'LONGING, belonging; 4. 2. 42
LOSE, orig. meaning = to ruin. Hence—to ruin in estimation (cf. N.E.D. 'lose' 2 b); 5. 2. 44
LOUSY, contemptible, of no importance (cf. fig. use of 'scurvy' and 2 *Hen. VI*, 4. 1. 50 (F) 'Obscure and lousy swain'); 4. 3. 191
LOVE-LINE, love-letter; 2. 1. 78
LUSTICK, an exclamation inviting joviality, well known in 17th-cent. England; 2. 3. 44

MADE, i.e. a made man (cf. *Oth.* 1. 2. 51 'he's made for ever'); 4. 3. 17
MAGNANIMOUS, very valiant; 3. 6. 63
MEASURE, dance; 2. 1. 56

Medicine, (i) a physician; 2. 1. 72, (ii) alchemical drugs, the elixir of life or philosopher's stone (cf. licence of 1456, quoted *Sh. Eng.* i. 465 'In former times wise and famous philosophers in their writings and books have left on record and taught under figures and coverings that from wine, precious stones, oils, vegetables, animals, metals, and minerals can be made many glorious and notable medicines, and chiefly that most precious medicine which some philosophers have called the mother and Empress of medicines, others the priceless glory, others the quintessence, others the Philosopher's Stone and Elixir of Life'); 5. 3. 102

Mell, vb. to have sexual intercourse; 4. 3. 225

Mere, absolute, plain; 3. 5. 54

Merely, absolutely, altogether; 4. 3. 20

Mettle, the stuff of life, the substance out of which man is made (cf. *Macb.* 1. 7. 73–4 'thy undaunted mettle should compose nothing but males,' and *Meas.* G.); 1. 1. 131

Misprise, despise, depreciate; 3. 2. 30

Misprision, (*a*) contempt—cf. *misprise*, (*b*) i.e. mis-prison, false imprisonment (cf. 'shackle up'); 2. 3. 155

Modern, commonplace; 2. 3. 2; 5. 3. 215

Module, pattern (lit. architect's plan). The word is of different origin from 'model' but the two forms are used indiscriminately in Sh.; 4. 3. 97

Moiety, share; 3. 2. 65

Monumental, (*a*) memorial—cf. 3. 7. 22–5, (*b*) serving to identify ('monument'=sign, token, cf. *Shrew*, 3. 2 93); 4. 3. 16

Mood, anger (cf. *Two Gent.* 4. 1 51 'Whom, in my mood, I stabbed unto the heart'); 5. 2. 4

Motion, (i) speed; 2. 3. 238; (ii) action (v. note); 3. 1. 13; (iii) suggestion, proposal; 5. 3. 262

Motive, something or somebody that causes another thing or person to move; 4. 4. 20; 5. 3. 214

Muse, wonder; 2. 5. 67

Musk-cat, or musk-deer, the animal from which musk is procured; 5. 2. 20

Muster-file, muster-roll; 4. 3. 163

Mystery, skill, art; 3. 6. 61

Naturalize, familiarise; 1. 1. 208

Nature, character, disposition, (here perhaps) rank (cf. Jonson, *E. Man in H.* 5. 3. 138, Herford & Simpson, *Works*, iii. 279 'vncase & appeare in mine owne proper nature, seruant to this gentleman'); 3. 1. 17

Naughty, worthless; 5. 3. 252

Ne, and not (an archaic form not found elsewhere in Sh. except *Per.* 2. prol. 36); 2. 1. 173

Nessus, the Centaur who ravished Deianira, bride of Hercules; 4. 3. 247

Next, nearest; 1. 3. 58

Note, distinction; 1. 3. 154

Office (ob.), act as a servant, 'run' a house (cf. *Wint.* 1. 2. 172); 3. 2. 125

Or, before (cf. *Ham.* 5, 2, 30 (Q2) 'Or I could make a prologue'); 1. 3. 85

Ordinary, 'a public meal regularly

provided at a fixed price in an eating-house or tavern' (N.E.D.); 2. 3. 205

OUTWARD, without inside knowledge; 3. 1. 11

OWE, own; 2. 1. 9; 2. 5. 81; 3. 2. 118

PACE, the short walking steps of a horse when trained (N.B. the contrast with '*runs* where he will'); 4. 5. 66

PALMER, pilgrim. The 'palmer' was strictly speaking a special kind of pilgrim, but no special significance seems intended here; 3. 5. 34

PARACELSUS (c. 1493–1541), the famous Swiss alchemist and physician, who applied his chemical knowledge to the traditional pharmacy and therapeutics, and attacked orthodox medical opinion which derived from Galen (q.v.); 2. 3. 12

PARCEL, small party (cf. *M.V.* 1. 2. 103); 2. 3. 55

PASS, reputation; 2. 5. 55

PASSAGE, (*a*) phrase, expression, (*b*) passing-away; 1. 1. 19

PASSPORT, an official document issued by town corporations or J.P.s giving beggars permission to ask alms and specifying the route they were allowed to take from one town to another; 3. 2. 55

PERSPECTIVE, lit. any kind of optical instrument for viewing objects, but 'in early use applied to various optical devices, as arrangements of mirrors etc. for producing some special or fantastic effect, e.g. by distortion of images' (N.E.D.). Cf. *Sh. Eng.* ii. 10 for the portrait of Edward VI painted in perspective; 5. 3. 48

PHŒNIX, paragon, unique person; 1. 1. 168

PILE, (*a*) the downy nap on velvet or other fabrics. Velvets were cut in three heights; 'two pile and a half' therefore = something a little less than the best velvet; (*b*) ? quibble upon 'piled' = pilled or peeled, i.e. hairless as a result of the 'French disease' (cf. *Meas.* G.); 4. 5. 96

PILOT'S GLASS. Some have supposed that Shakespeare erred in making the nautical glass an hour and not a half-hour glass; but v. *Sh. Eng.* i. 164, and cf. *Temp.* G.; 2. 1. 165

PIN-BUTTOCK, narrow or pointed buttock; 2. 2. 17

PLACE (take), take effect, succeed, find acceptance; 1. 1. 105

PLAUSIVE, plausible; 4. 1. 26

PLUCK, draw (in cards). Cf. Fletcher, *Custom of the Country*, 1. 1 'Would any man stand plucking for the ace of hearts, with one pack of cards, all days on's life?' (v. N.E.D. 'pluck' vb. 2 d); 1. 3. 87

PLUTUS, the god of gold, and therefore the god of alchemists (v. note); 5. 3. 101

POLL, the number of soldiers in the muster (cf. *Cor.* 3. 1. 134); 4. 3. 164

PORT, gate; 3. 5. 35

PREDOMINANT. A predominant star was one in the ascendant, i.e. in that degree of the Zodiac which at any given moment (esp. at child-birth) is just rising above the horizon (v. N.E.D. 'ascendant' B. i. 1); 1. 1. 197

PRETENCE, design, intention; 4. 3. 46
PRIME, youth; 2. 1. 182
PROFESSION, i.e. what one professes; 2. 1. 83
PROPER, own; 4. 2. 49
PROPERTY, particular quality; 2. 1. 187
PUDDING, sausage; 2. 2. 26
PUNK. harlot; 2. 2. 21
PUR, the name of the knave in the card-game 'post and pair' (v. note); 5. 2. 19
PUT OFF, (*a*) brush aside, (*b*) palm off (lit. 'dispose of fraudulently,' v. N.E.D. 'put' 45 k); 2. 2. 6, 9

QUALITY, rank, social position; 1. 3. 111
QUATCH-BUTTOCK. The only recorded instance of 'quatch': probably = quat, i.e. fat; 2. 2. 17
QUESTANT. A Shakespearian coinage from 'quest' = (of hunting dogs) 'to search for game' N.E.D. Cf. *Meas.* 4. 1. 61 'Run with these false and most contrarious quests,' where 'quests' = the cry of hounds upon the trail; 2. 1. 16
QUIRKS, ups and downs. The orig. meaning of 'quirk' seems to have been 'a flourish or sudden twist or turn in writing or drawing' (v. N.E.D.); 3. 2. 48
QUIT, (*a*) absolve, acquit, cf. *Hen. V*, 2. 2. 166 'God quit you in his mercy,' (*b*) pay him back; 5. 3. 298
QUOTED, well-known, notorious; 5. 3. 204

REAVE, rob by force; 5. 3. 86
REBELLION, irresistible desire, outbreak of lust. This meaning, not recorded in N.E.D., is common in Shakespeare (cf. *Meas.* 3. 2. 112; 2 *Hen. IV*, 2. 4. 380; *M.V.* 3. 1. 33 'Out upon it, old carrion, rebels it at these years?'); 4. 3. 18; 5. 3. 6
RECTOR, ruler, governor (cf. *Cor.* 2. 3. 213); 4. 3. 56
RELICS, mementoes, souvenirs (cf. *Jul. Caes.* 2. 2. 89 'Great men shall press for tinctures, stains, relics and cognizance'); 1. 1. 100; 5. 3. 25
REMAINDER, interest in an estate coming into effect upon the death of a legatee; 4. 3. 276
REMOVE, departure from one place to another; 5. 3. 131
RENDER, represent, describe, report (cf. *A.Y.L.* 4. 3. 122); 1. 3. 227
REPEAL, recall from exile (cf. *R. II*, 2. 2. 49 'The banished Bolingbroke repeals himself'); 2. 3. 52
RESIDENCE, continuance in a course of action (v. N.E.D. 'residence' 3); 2. 5. 41
RESOLVEDLY, i.e. until everything is explained; 5. 3. 330
RESPECTS, reasons; 2. 5. 68
REST, 'set up one's rest,' i.e. to be determined, resolved. The expression, derived from the card-game primero, in which the 'rest' was the name for the reserved stakes, originally meant 'to hazard one's all'; 2. 1. 135
RETROGRADE. 'A retrograde star was one apparently moving in a direction contrary to the order of the signs of the Zodiac, or from east to west' N.E.D., quoting Culpepper 'If a planet retrograde...he denotes much discord and contradiction in the business'; 1. 1. 198

RIDDLE-LIKE, mysteriously; 1. 3. 214

RING-CARRIER, go-between; 3. 5. 90

RUFF, or ruffle, 'the loose turned-over portion or flap of a top-boot' (N.E.D. 'ruffle'). It is possible that 'ruff' is a misp. for 'ruffle' (v. note), but it is also possible that 'ruff' and 'ruffle' were used interchangeably; 3. 2. 7

RUTTISH, lecherous; 4. 3. 212

SADNESS, seriousness; 4. 3. 200

SAUCY, (i) insolent, impertinent; 2. 3. 265; (ii) wanton, lascivious; 4. 4. 23

SCIENCE, profound knowledge; 5. 3. 103

SCORE, to obtain drink, goods, etc. on credit (N.E.D. 'score' 11, quoting Heywood, *Fair Maid of West*, 1. 12 'It is the commonest thing that can bee for these Captaines to score and to score, but when the scores are to be paid, Non est inventus'); 4. 3. 221

SEASON, 'to preserve by salting' (Malone); 1. 1. 49

SENSE, (i) perception, apprehension; 1. 3. 169; (ii) reason; 2. 1. 124

SET DOWN, lay siege (cf. *Cor.* 4. 7. 28 'All places yield to him ere he sets down'); 1. 1. 120

SHREWD, (i) 'a shrewd turn' = a nasty trick; 3. 5. 67, (ii) keen-witted (cf. *Troil.* 1. 2. 206); 4. 5. 62

SHREWDLY, grievously; 3. 5. 87

SHRIEVE, old form of 'sheriff'; 4. 3. 184

SMOKE, smell out, suspect; 3. 6. 98 (v. note for quibble); 4. 1. 27

SNIPT-TAFFETA, slashed silk. Taffeta = thin silken stuff of lustrous appearance; masks and vizards were commonly made from it, which perhaps accounts for its frequent use in expressions denoting at once dressiness and lack of substance (cf. *L.L.L.* 5. 2. 406 'Taffeta phrases, silken terms precise'); 4. 5. 1–2

SNUFF, (*a*) a wick on the point of extinction; a feeble old man, (*b*) something offensive to the nose (cf. 'take it in snuff' = take offence, 1 *Hen. IV*, 1. 3. 41); 1. 2. 59

SOLEMN, ceremonial; 2. 3. 273

SQUARE, to frame or adjust something according to some standard or principle. A metaphor from stone- or wood-work; 2. 1. 150

STAGGERS, giddiness, 2. 3. 166

STAIN, a dash or touch; 1. 1. 113

STALL, keep. A metaphor from the stable not found elsewhere in Shakespeare; 1. 3. 123

STAND FOR, stand up for, fight for; 1. 1. 135

START, alarm, startle; 5. 3. 231

STICK, fix, pin (like an ornament); 5. 3. 45

SUBSCRIBE FOR, undertake on behalf of; 4. 5. 31

SUCCEEDING, i.e. consequences; 2. 3. 194

SUGGEST, tempt (as often in Shakespeare); 4. 5. 44

SUGGESTION, temptation; 3. 5. 17

SUITED, clothed, apparelled; 1. 1. 158

TABLE, lit. 'a board or flat surface on which a picture was painted; hence, the picture itself' (N.E.D.); 1. 1. 97

TAFFETY, i.e. dressed in silk or taffeta (v. *snipt-taffeta*); 2. 2. 21

TAKE OFF, relieve one of; 2. 1. 89

TAKE PLACE (v. *place*); 1. 1. 105

TAKE UP, (*a*) pick up, (*b*) enlist; v. note; 2. 3. 211

TAX, blame, reprove; 1. 1. 69; 2. 1. 170; 5. 3. 122, 205

THICK!, i.e. quick!; 2. 2. 43

TIME (in happy), i.e. Fortune favours us!; 5. 1. 6

TITLE, i.e. what one is worth, lit. that to which one has a title; 2. 4. 26

TOLL, to get rid of, lit. to enter for sale on the toll-book of a market (cf. Bacon, *Use Com. Law*, 'If hee bee a horse hee must be ridden two houres in the market or faire...and tolled for in the toll-book'); 5. 3. 147

TOP (forward), forelock. The orig. meaning of 'top' (v. N.E.D.). 'To take by the top' = to seize by the hair, lay hold of by main force; 5. 3. 39

TOUCH, feeling, emotion of a subtle kind (cf. *Temp.* 5. 1. 21; *Two Gent.* 2. 7. 18); 1. 3. 115

TRICK, 'a characteristic expression (of the face or voice), a peculiar feature, a distinguishing trait' N.E.D. (cf. *John*, 1. 1. 85 'He hath a trick of Cœur-de-lion's face,' and *Lear*, 4. 6. 108 'The trick of that voice I do well remember'); 1. 1. 98

TRIPLE, one of three, third (cf. *A. & C.* 1. 1. 12 'The triple pillar of the world'); 2. 1. 108

TWIGS, covered with lime (q.v.) to catch birds; 3. 6. 101

VALIDITY, worth; 5. 3. 191

VENT, 'make vent of' = talk of (cf. *V. A.* 334 'Free vent of words love's fire doth assuage'); 2. 3. 206

WEAR, sb. fashion; 1. 1. 205

WEAR, vb. to be in the fashion; 1. 1. 159; 2. 1. 53

WEIGH, rate, estimate; 3. 4. 32

WELL-DERIVED, i.e. of a good stock (cf. *derive*); 3. 2. 86

WELL-ENTERED, thoroughly initiated, well trained (N.E.D. quotes Udall, 1548, 'Sounde meate for such as are wel entred'); 2. 1. 6

WELL-FOUND, 'of tried merit' (N.E.D.); 2. 1. 102

WILL, lust; 4. 3. 15

WIND (have i'th'), have scent of; 3. 6. 108

WOODCOCK, gull, dupe, fool (in allusion to the ease with which the woodcock could be snared); 4. 1. 90

WORLD (go to the), v. *Go to the world*; 1. 3. 18

WRACK, old form of 'wreck'; 3. 5. 22

WRITE, to attain to, (i) 'to write man' = to reach man's estate; 2. 3. 201; (ii) 'writ as little beard' = attained to as little beard (in allusion to the stock phrase 'to write man'); 2. 3. 64